The Strategic Use of Stories in Organizational Communication and Learning

The Strategic Use of Stories in Organizational Communication and Learning

Terrence L. Gargiulo

M.E.Sharpe
Armonk, New York
London, England

Library of Congress Cataloging-in-Publication Data

Gargiulo, Terrence L., 1968–
The strategic use of stories in organizational communication and learning / by Terrence L.
Gargiulo.
p. cm.
Includes bibliographical references and index.
ISBN 0-7656-1412-X (hardcover : alk. paper)
1. Organizational communication. 2. Organizational learning. 3. Storytelling—Social
aspects. 4. Storytelling—Psychological aspects. 5. Executives—United States—Interviews.
I. Title.

HD30.3.G365 2005
658.3—dc22   2004019153

MIC

Printed in the United States of America

The paper used in this publication meets the minimum requirements of
American National Standard for Information Sciences
Permanence of Paper for Printed Library Materials,
ANSI Z 39.48-1984.

BM (c)   10   9   8   7   6   5   4   3   2   1

For my mother, Gloria, whose life has been a constant example
for me and everyone she encounters.
Thank you for showing me the arts of communication and learning.

Contents

List of Tables and Figures   ix
List of Exercises   xi
Acknowledgments   xiii

Part I. Frameworks

1. Introduction   3
2. A Working Model of Stories   7
3. Organizational Communication: Broadcasting Signals   24
4. Case Study: Dreyer's Ice Cream   42
5. Organizational Learning: Building Bridges   55
6. Case Studies: DTE Energy and Jeff Bukantz   65

Part II. Interviews

7. Introduction to the Interviews   77
8. Interview with Bernice Moore, CTB/McGraw-Hill   86
9. Interview with Robert Kraska, DTE Energy   103
10. Interview with Sherrie Cornett, Dreyer's Ice Cream   118
11. Interview with Marty Fischer, Starbucks Coffee   136
12. Interview with Father Marus, Woodside Priory School   151

Part III. The Competency Map

13. Introduction to the Competency Map   161
14. The Core   171
15. The Process Ring   196
16. The Interaction Ring   211
17. Summary   225

Appendix: Folktale Illustrating Principles of Active Listening   233
Suggested Reading   237
Index   243
About the Author   253

List of Tables and Figures

Tables

6.1	Breakdown of Classes at DTE Energy	68
7.1	Individuals and Companies That Participated in Interviews	79
7.2	Responses to Survey—Part I	81
7.3	Responses to Survey—Part II	82
13.1	Summary of the Competency Map	166
13.2	The Relationship Between Themes from Interviews and the Competency Map	168
14.1	Exercise 2d. Building Self-Awareness—Strengths and Weaknesses	179
14.2	Exercise 3a. Sensitivity—Room Awareness	180
14.3	Exercise 3b. Sensitivity—Sore Spots and Hot Buttons	181
14.4	Three Levels of the Eliciting Competency	191
15.1	Exercise 8a. Indexing—Personal History (Part I)	199
15.2	Exercise 10a. Synthesizing—Childhood Stories and Me	207
16.1	Decision Matrix for Selecting What Type of Story to Tell	213
17.1	The Relationship Between Themes from Interviews and the Competency Map	229

Figures

2.1	The Nine Functions of Stories and Their Unique Effects	9
3.1	Conceptualizing Communication: The Communications Matrix	25
3.2	Key Targets and Channels	28
3.3	Untapped Areas of the Communications Matrix	29
3.4	Personal/Internal Communication	31
3.5	Push-to-Pull-to-Push	33
3.6	Personal/External and Personal/Partner Communication	34
3.7	Formal/Nonspecific Communication	35

3.8	Social/Nonspecific Communication	36
3.9	Personal/Nonspecific Communication	38
3.10	The Relationship Between Story Functions and the Communications Matrix	40
5.1	The Relationship Among Communication, Learning, and Collective Experience	61
5.2	The Flow of Learning	62
7.1	The Relationship Between Story Functions and the Communications Matrix	78
7.2	Survey Used in Interviews	80
13.1	The Relationship Among Communication, Learning, and Collective Experience	162
13.2	Untapped Matrix Combinations	162
13.3	The Relationship Between Story Functions and the Communications Matrix	163
13.4	The Competency Map	164
14.1	Competency Map—The Core	173
14.2	The Relationship Between Care and Intention	175
15.1	Competency Map—The Process Ring	197
15.2	Exercise 8a. Indexing—Personal History (Part II)	199
15.3	The Crystal Ball of Synthesis	206
16.1	Competency Map—The Interaction Ring	212
17.1	Visual Summary of the Book	226
17.2	The Relationship Between Story Functions and the Communications Matrix	227

List of Exercises

THE CORE—CHAPTER 14

Observing

General Exercise: Simple Observation   172
1a.   Care/Intention—Self-Assessment   174
1b.   Care/Intention—Fostering Positive Intentions   175
1c.   Care/Intention—Name Badges   175
2a.   Building Self-Awareness—Survey of Habits   176
2b.   Building Self-Awareness—The Power of Breath   177
2c.   Building Self-Awareness—Journaling   177
2d.   Building Self-Awareness—Strengths and Weaknesses   178
3a.   Sensitivity—Room Awareness   180
3b.   Sensitivity—Sore Spots and Hot Buttons   181
4a.   External Focus—Recall   182
4b.   External Focus—Locking Eyes   182
4c.   External Focus—Conversation Tracking   183
5a.   Process Dialogue—Conversation Recorder   184
5b.   Process Dialogue—New People/New Situations   184
5c.   Process Dialogue—Group Discussion   185

Listening

6a.   Listening—Life Story   186
6b.   Listening—Music   186
6c.   Listening—Paraphrase and Validate   187
6d.   Listening—Clarification and Follow-up Questions   188
6e.   Listening—Following Directions   188
6f.   Listening—Editorial Interpretation   189
6g.   Listening—Tape-recorded Conversation   189
6h.   Listening—Frame of Reference   190

Eliciting
    7a.   Eliciting—Job Interview Questions   193
    7b.   Eliciting—Words and Feelings   193
    7c.   Eliciting—Statement–Story—Story   194

THE PROCESS RING—CHAPTER 15

Indexing
    8a.   Indexing—Personal History   198

Reflecting
    9a.   Reflecting—Historical Visualization   203
    9b.   Reflecting—Personal History   203
    9c.   Reflecting—Daily Rewind   204

Synthesizing
    10a. Synthesizing—Childhood Stories and Me   206
    10b. Synthesizing—Mind Map of Experiences   208

THE INTERACTION RING—CHAPTER 16

Selecting
    11.   Selecting Competency—Communication Plan   215

Telling
    12a. Telling Competency—Movie in Five   216
    12b. Telling Competency—Stories in Conversation   217
    12c. Telling Competency—Listener Involvement   218

Modeling
    13a. Modeling Competency—Memorable Actions   219
    13b. Modeling Competency—Creating Stories Through Actions   219
    13c. Modeling Competency—Answering the Key Questions   221
    13d. Modeling Competency—Presentations   221

Acknowledgments

Every book is a creative endeavor that exceeds its writer. I feel like I am just a conduit. If it has been my charter to bring these ideas to fruition, none of them would be possible without all the blessings and rich experiences my life has afforded me. These ideas are the sum total of all the people who have touched my life and shared their stories with me. Professor Luis Ygelessias of Brandeis University opened my eyes to the magic of stories and has been a wonderful mentor and friend throughout the years. I am very grateful for my editor, Eric Valentine. He has been incredibly patient and instrumental in helping me transform my ideas into this book. Lynn Taylor and her team at M.E. Sharpe have been consummate professionals in helping me navigate the publishing process. Bill Zornes has one of the sharpest minds I have ever encountered. Conversations with him made me stop and look at my ideas from a fresh perspective. I am indebted to the sensitive and insightful treatment David Bemelmans contributed in helping me to polish the raw transcripts of the interviews I conducted in Part II of the book. Watching my father's parallel creative process, evidenced by the recent completion of our opera *Tryillias*, was an incredible inspiration to me. My sister, Franca, encouraged me every step of the way. My beautiful wife, Cindy, and my precious son, Gabriel, were always present, sustaining me with their tireless love. Last of all I wish to thank you, the reader, for your curiosity about stories I want to share with you.

The Strategic Use of Stories in Organizational Communication and Learning

Part I

Frameworks

1
Introduction

The universe is made of stories not atoms.
—Muriel Rukeyser, *The Speed of Darkness*

Effective organizational communication and learning depends upon stories. Stories are used as a way of understanding the underlying principles of communication and learning. As we move through this book, we will begin with a theoretical examination based on analyses of two new frameworks. The first framework demonstrates the functions of stories and the impact of their unique effects. The second framework will uncover areas of organizational communication that go unnoticed and require strategic attention. Building upon these two frameworks, we use both of them to look at organizational learning. We continue with interviews conducted with organizational leaders, and conclude with a collection of personal and organizational activities based on a behaviorally derived Competency Map.

I must begin with a word of caution. Over the years there has been a fair amount written about stories. For a list of books and articles, be sure to review the Suggested Readings at the end of this book. Much has been said and much has been claimed about the nature of stories. We will be taking a novel approach. I am not working with stories in the manner with which many of you may be familiar. We will probe beyond the obvious benefits of stories, such as persuasion and entertainment. Telling stories and crafting stories is only the beginning. As we explore the power of stories to shed new light on organizational communication and its links to organizational learning, we will focus on the necessity of eliciting stories rather than telling them, and how listening to them is critical for the success of the organization. It is a nuance that can be lost. This book offers a unique twist on the phenomenon of stories that is often misunderstood or overlooked.

There is a rich tradition of narrative in the social sciences. Without the hard work of these scholars, we would not have developed many of the psychological and therapeutic understandings we have today. A large number of these conclusions have found their way into other disciplines such as comparative literary theory and organizational behavior. However, to claim that everything can be reduced to narrative or story moves in a direction counter to where we are heading in this book. I am not interested in understanding how we craft meaning. This is a topic that is best left to others more qualified than myself. This is first and foremost a business book, and I plan to examine how understanding the mechanisms of stories enables us to gain new insights into better ways of communicating and actualizing the promises of creating a continuously learning organization. We are interested in identifying specific ways that communication and learning can be used strategically by organizations to gain competitive advantage.

Structure of the Book

The book is divided into three parts. Each part is written in a style appropriate to the goals and materials of that section. Chapter 2 develops a working model of stories and employs a conversational style to whet your appetite. If we are to use stories as metaphors, we must first understand how they function. Nine functions of stories are discussed. These are:

1. Stories empower a speaker.
2. Stories create an environment.
3. Stories bind and bond individuals.
4. Stories require active listening.
5. Stories negotiate differences.
6. Stories encode information.
7. Stories act as tools for thinking.
8. Stories can be used as weapons.
9. Stories are medicine for healing.

Each function includes at least one example. The examples are taken from a variety of disciplines including literature, psychology, and business. My intention is that through a variety of examples I will succeed in engaging your imaginations. Some of the examples may speak more to you than others. This is by design. One of the examples I use to illustrate the function of "Stories Require Active Listening" is a folktale that is longer in its telling than the other examples. It serves an important purpose and is the only story of its kind in the book.

The tone of Chapter 3 shifts from conversational to theoretical. The chapter introduces a framework called the Communications Matrix to analyze organizational communication. The framework identifies major gaps in organizational communication structures and points out how these gaps can be turned into new opportunities that can be seized by a simple strategy that I call *push-to-pull-to-push*. The strategy is derived from the functions of stories and the impact of their unique effects. Chapter 4 uses the case study of Dreyer's Ice Cream to see how things discussed in Chapter 3 fit together.

Chapter 5 builds upon the principles of communication identified in Chapter 3 to understand organizational learning. Communication is demonstrated to be the cornerstone of learning and knowledge, which in this book we will refer to as *collective experience*. Chapter 6 provides the case studies of DTE Energy and Jeff Bukantz to illustrate the points discussed on learning and knowledge.

Part II of the book leaves the rigor of theoretical treatments and offers a series of five interviews with organizational leaders. Here the style returns to conversational. Chapter 7 provides a background on the interviews, description of the methodologies used to conduct them, and a summary of the key themes found in the interviews. Chapters 8–12 contain the interviews. These are presented as dialogues. They are to be read as conversations and serve three purposes: They examine to what degree people are aware of stories in communication and learning; they model how to elicit stories and use them in informal modes of communication; and they uncover communication and learning competencies individuals need to develop.

Each interview is preceded by a short introduction and summary of its major themes. I encourage you to resist the temptation to read the summaries and skim the actual interviews. The style of communication modeled in the interviews is as, if not more, important than the major themes and findings that emerge from them.

Part III ties everything together. Written in an informal style, it presents a map of competencies composed of three areas termed rings. Each of the rings consists of three competencies: making a total of nine competencies in the map. Rather than focus on organizational initiatives aimed at improving communication and learning, Part III focuses on how to develop the competencies in employees. The Competency Map dissects the specific "story," behaviors, and skills required to be a successful communicator and learner. An extensive list of exercises for developing each competency is offered in every chapter. Chapter 13 synthesizes the first two parts of the book and presents the Competency Map.

Chapter 14 explores the first ring of the map, called the Core, which describes how we open ourselves to be aware and sensitive to stories. The three competencies in the Core are Observing, Listening, and Eliciting. Practicing mindfulness to become aware of the stories implicit in others' words and actions is the Observing competency. Absorbing stories and invoking the imagination to enter them in a fundamental and deep way is the Listening competency. And asking questions and finding ways to pull stories from others is the Eliciting competency.

The second area of the Competency Map, called the Process Ring, is the subject of Chapter 15. The three competencies in the Process Ring are Reflecting, Synthesizing, and Indexing. Reviewing experiences with circumspection and extracting knowledge from them is the Reflecting competency. Finding patterns in new experiences and creating connections between them and old ones is the Synthesizing competency. And developing a flexible, vast, mental schema for retrieval of experiences and knowledge is the Indexing competency.

Chapter 16 works through the last ring of the Competency Map, the Interaction Ring. The three competencies in the Interaction Ring are Selecting, Telling, and Modeling. Picking a story that is appropriate to the situation at hand and that clearly communicates concepts, ideas, or feelings is the Selecting competency. Relaying a story with authenticity that paints a vivid, engaging picture for listeners is the Telling competency. And being aware of one's actions, using them to create lasting impressions in the eyes of others and employing a variety of analogical techniques to bring an idea or concept alive is the Modeling competency. Chapter 17 is a summary of the book. Two figures are used to show how all the chapters tie together and recapitulate the book's major points.

2
A Working Model of Stories

Stories provide us with a way of understanding the underlying operating principles behind organizational communication and learning. In this chapter we will lay the groundwork for the rest of the book by showing how stories work. Stories are fundamental to the way we communicate, learn, and think. They are the most efficient way of storing, retrieving, and conveying information. Since story hearing requires active participation on the part of the listener, stories are the most profoundly social form of human interaction, communication, and learning. Throughout this book we will concern ourselves with the subtle aspects of stories. Telling stories for any organizational purpose only scratches the surface. We are interested in using stories as powerful vehicles for eliciting each other's experiences and knowledge, listening to each other and ourselves in deeper ways, and providing our imaginations with a canvas for reflection and learning.

We will examine a new theoretical framework of stories that includes nine functions. These functions are responsible for producing unique effects that are central to communication. The nine functions of stories and their unique effects provide us with a way of peering into the black box of effective communication. In Chapter 3 we will use this framework to see how organizations can seize opportunities for improving their communications. Once we have established the connection between stories and communication, in Chapter 5 we will show how communication is the cornerstone of learning. This tripartite inextricable link between stories, communication, and learning is the heart of this book's groundbreaking contribution to the field of organizational behavior.

Stories surround us. Everywhere we turn there is a story vying for our attention. This is not just the stories in newspapers or television programs either. Do you ever find yourself in the uncomfortable position of having nothing to say in the middle of a conversation? Suddenly the memory of a past experience you can share rushes in to fill an otherwise awkward void. Or, when you are listening to someone else, do you notice the change in the quality of your attention and level of interest when the person begins to vividly recount a past experience and ceases speaking in abstractions? The most meaningful conversations are full of memorable stories.

There are many labels you might choose for this unique form of communication. Take a moment and jot down any words or descriptions that come to mind. Here are some potential candidates:

- anecdote
- conversation
- experience
- "Once upon a time . . ."
- memory
- tale
- recollection
- image
- myth
- parable
- metaphor
- fib
- analogy
- illustration
- cliché
- allegory
- word picture
- narrative
- joke
- snapshot
- picture

For the purposes of this book, let's gather all such ways of conversing under the umbrella of "storytelling." That way we can draw upon the rich and varied understanding you already likely have, at some level, about what constitutes a story. The functions of stories and their unique effects offer us insights into the nature and dynamics of communication and learning. There is no reason for us to restrict what we accept as stories or to try and reduce them down to a single definition. Unlike many trend-setting management theorists, I am not trying to manufacture something new. I am acting as an observer of and as a guide to a communication paradigm that is already so much a part of how we communicate and learn that we have lost sight of it. I am seeking to invigorate an innate capacity and promote its conscious usage and cultivation in business and in all else that we do.

Figure 2.1 **The Nine Functions of Stories and Their Unique Effects**

Functions of Stories:	Unique Effects of Stories:
• Empower a speaker	To entertain
• Create an environment	To create trust and openness between yourself and others
• Bind and bond individuals	To elicit stories from others

• Require active listening	To listen actively in order to:
	   Understand context and perspective
	   Find the critical point in a system
	   Uncover resistance and hidden agendas

• Negotiate differences	To help us shift perspectives in order to:
	   See each other
	   Experience empathy
	   Enter new frames of reference
	
	To hold diverse points of view
	
	To create awareness of operating biases and values

• Encode information • Act as tools for thinking • Act as weapons • Act as medicine for healing	To create a working metaphor to illuminate an opinion, rationale, vision, or decision To establish connections between different ideas and concepts to support an opinion or decision To encourage thinking outside the box, generating creative solutions and breakthroughs

While we should be wary of too narrowly defining stories and storytelling, it is useful to set forth a framework for our inquiries and some ground rules that we will follow. In Figure 2.1 you will find a description of how stories function and their unique effects.

Stories Empower a Speaker

Effective speakers grab our attention with stories. Without them, our minds tend to wander. Why should this be? Why are we more prone to daydream than to pay close attention to the speaker? Is it simply a lack of will power or of the ability to focus, or are our minds wired for imagination—for something more than just being passive receivers of words?

I'll never forget watching my sister, Franca, in a speech contest. I was about nine years old at the time. In the finals, contestants were each given a random topic they were expected to talk about extemporaneously. Naturally, my attention was heightened when it came to be my sister's turn, but when she spun around to face the audience and the judges after her thirty seconds of prep time, exclaiming "Smile, you're on Candid Camera!" my level of involvement spiked. I had watched the television show she was referring to on numerous occasions, and my mind immediately conjured up a rich array of images. Franca had me hooked. In just this way, a speaker is empowered by empowering his audience. Give listeners a way to "dock themselves" to whatever it is you're talking about, and your ideas will find a more receptive audience.

A speaker may have no other goal than to entertain or persuade, and that's fine; however, a speaker empowered with a story can invite listeners to consider new possibilities and perspectives. Motivational speakers and religious leaders, for example, often use a central story to anchor their message, a story to which they frequently return in order to reiterate and provide context for the points they've made. Once again I want to stress that a story can be as short as a phrase. Consider President Bush's use of the phrase "axis of evil" after the September 11 attacks on the World Trade Center. This phrase played a critical part in the speeches the president made to the American people; it empowered both the speaker and his administration's agenda. Each new detail or picture regarding that tragedy was associated with this "axis of evil." And with every picture a new flood of stories rose to the surface. It is precisely this associative nature of stories that empowers speakers. So, to paraphrase a cliché, if a picture is worth a thousand words, a story is worth a thousand pictures. See, that's a story.

Stories Create an Environment

What do you do before dinner guests arrive? Do you find yourself tidying up your house, arranging flowers in vases, and setting the table with care? During my bachelor days, when preparing for an important date, I did all I could to create a romantic setting. These are examples of how we meticulously arrange our physical world and space to reflect our mood and sensibilities. We can do the same with words. The stories we tell have as much to do with creating the environment we want as selecting the right piece of music for an occasion.

Through stories we can create a broad spectrum of environments. Humor is a perfect example. If we need to loosen up a group, an amusing anecdote is just the thing to provide the necessary levity. Likewise, if our goal is to help members of a group to be vulnerable with one another, we might find that sharing a personal story is appropriate.

Our understanding of how stories empower a speaker is deepened by the way in which stories create an environment. A speaker empowered with a story usually has a specific message in mind; but a communicator using stories to create an environment may not always know what story to tell. It is not uncommon for me to give a talk, especially to a very large group, and not have a clear idea beforehand about what stories I will use to create the environment that best facilitates transmittal of my message. I will try, of course, to gauge the group by speaking to as many attendees as possible ahead of time; and I can always pose a few rhetorical questions at the beginning of my talk to see how they react. However, sometimes I simply depend on intuition to guide me in selecting what story is appropriate for the moment. This is a theme we will explore in greater detail later. Regardless of how we select a story, it is important to realize that stories can be used to create different environments. Establishing the right environment enables us to reach our audience and communicate more effectively.

Stories Bind and Bond Individuals

In 1967 the sociologist Stanley Milgram introduced the notion of the "small world phenomenon," according to which everyone in the world can be reached through a short chain of social acquaintances. John Gaure adopted this notion for his play *Six Degrees of Separation*, the title becoming a part of common parlance. Whether the notion is true or not is inconsequential. What is fascinating is how easily and quickly we find things in common with other people. To borrow a truism, "no man is an island." Indeed, the world becomes smaller and more interconnected every day. To see this, we need look no further than the ongoing advances of computers and the role networks play in communication. But there is a difference between these superhighways of digital bits and bytes and social networks: personal relationship. Here, stories offer us some important insights into the nature of communication.

The quickest path between yourself and another person is a story. Successful sales people learned this long ago. Facing a total stranger, sales people employ stories in a variety of ways to create a bond with a prospective customer. It may be a personal story, or maybe a joke, or perhaps a testimonial of how the product or service helped another customer. If you happen upon the right story, two people with no prior knowledge of one another can quickly find a flood of common experiences. You see this sort of thing happen on planes all the time, when passengers strike up conversations with one another. And the conversations that last the longest are the ones in which mutual storytelling occurs.

Sharing a story, especially a personal one, strikes a chord of trust in others, and people are usually quick to reciprocate. I will state this theme several times throughout the book: The appropriate response to a story is another story. More probably, if I share enough stories from my own personal life, I will eventually hit on one that resonates with the other person. Of course, these techniques can be abused by those looking to instill a sense of trust in another person, a trust they might later take advantage of. Or they can be used by trained interrogators in taking someone's statement in the law enforcement setting. The point is that, similar to our example of the empowered speaker, stories can facilitate connections between people because our minds work in terms of associations, and I would argue with few exceptions that we are wired to be social and we desire to feel a connection to others. Stories are the perfect tool for the job.

Stories Require Active Listening

Can you recall a time when, pulling together the requirements for a project, you discovered you were not exactly clear about what was wanted or needed? How about conversations with partners? Have you ever found yourself responding to what you think your partner said, only to realize that you were completely off base? It is clear that effective listening goes beyond what we hear with our ears, what we want to hear, or what we expect to hear. Unlike gathering requirements for a project or conversations with partners, stories demand that we engage in active listening.

If we do not actively listen to stories, the value we derive from them is sure to be minimal or superficial. Take our examination above of how stories allow individuals to bind and bond with one another. The quality and depth of the bond is directly related to the degree to which active listening takes place. Recall the travelers on the plane: If the mutual storytelling is nothing more than a temporary relief from travelers' ennui, any bond that is formed is likely to be weak. However, if the travelers listen actively to the stories the other has to tell, they may find themselves responding in surprising ways. It is possible that they may begin to understand their own experiences in a new light. By doing so, two bonds are strengthened, the bond with another person and the bond with one's self.

Stories require and evoke from the listener active listening. This is the most central and subtle of all the functions of storytelling that we will explore. Here are three examples.

Example 1

While a little long in the telling, here is one of my favorite stories that offers some insights into the nature of active listening.

Once upon a time there was an orphaned girl who lived with her cruel stepmother and stepsister. The poor girl slaved every day under the harsh and relentless scrutiny of her stepmother and incessant ridicule of her stepsister. One day the girl was down at the river washing silverware. One of the spoons slipped from her fingers and quickly sank to the depths far beyond her reach. As she fought back her tears she noticed an old woman sunning herself on the rocks. The old woman called out to her, "What's the problem, sweetie?"

"I have lost one of mother's best silver spoons. She will never forgive me and beat me for sure," the girl cried.

"Perhaps I can help you," responded the old woman. "But first, will you come over here and scratch my back?"

The girl composed herself and began to climb across the rocks to reach the old woman. As she scratched the old woman's back her hands were cut and torn by the woman's rough skin. Despite the discomfort the girl continued to scratch her back. The old woman turned to look at the girl and noticed how her hands were scraped. She quickly healed them by releasing a long slow exhale, breathing directly on the girl's hands. Then the old woman said to the girl, "Before I help you recover your spoon, please come to my home for a meal."

The girl agreed, and the two set off to the old woman's home. She took a huge pot and handed it to the girl saying, "Let's make a scrumptious soup. Fill the pot with water, place this single bean in the water along with this bone and a grain of rice, and we will have a feast."

The girl looked incredulously at the old woman, but she could sense her earnest conviction. Pushing aside her doubts, the girl did as the old woman had instructed. When the soup was done, the two sat down to a splendid meal. It was the most wonderful soup the girl had ever tasted. When the meal was over, the old woman turned to the girl and said, "I need to go out for a little bit; stay here, and when I return, we will recover your spoon. While I am out, if a black cat comes by, you mustn't feed him no matter how much he meows. Beat him with this broom." The girl nodded and the old woman left.

After a little while a black cat wandered into the house and began meowing loudly. The girl glanced at the cat and at first tried to ignore him, but before too long she took some leftovers from lunch and fed the cat. When the old woman returned, she was noticeably happy and said to the girl, "You are so kind and helpful, why don't you stay with me a little while?"

Although tempted by the offer, the girl responded, "I would love to, but I must get back to my stepmother and stepsister. Would you please tell me how I can recover the spoon I lost?"

"As you walk home," started the old woman, "you will come to a crossroads. You will see a pile of eggs. There will be large ones shouting out to you: 'Take me, take me!' Among the eggs there will be some tiny ones saying nothing. Take one of the tiny eggs and break it open when you reach the next crossroad."

The girl hugged the old woman, thanked her for her hospitality, and set out. Just as the old woman had described, when the girl got to the first crossroad, she saw a pile of eggs. Unperturbed by the large eggs' incessant cries of "Take me, take me," the girl searched for the tiniest egg she could find. When she got to the next crossroad, per the old woman's instructions, she took the egg and cracked it open. To her utter surprise, a magnificent golden chest grew in front of her eyes and inside were hundreds of spoons, knives, and forks made of the finest silver. When she returned home with her treasure, the girl's stepmother and stepsister were seized with jealousy. They insisted that she reveal to them how she acquired such a treasure.

The next day, the girl's stepmother sent her own daughter to the river to wash some silverware. When the girl got to the river, she threw in a spoon. Without much of an effort to recover it, the girl began to cry in a loud voice. Once again there was an old woman sunning herself on the rocks. The old woman called out to her, "What's the problem, sweetie?"

"I have lost one of mother's best silver spoons. She will never forgive me and beat me for sure," the girl cried.

"Perhaps I can help you," responded the woman. "But first, will you come over here and scratch my back?"

The girl climbed across the rocks to reach the old woman and began to scratch her back. Suddenly the girl shrieked. "What's the matter?" asked the old woman.

"Your back is disgusting, and it is cutting my hands and making them bleed!"

The old woman healed the girl's hand by releasing a long slow exhale and directing it on the girl's hands. Then the old woman said to her, "Before I help you recover your spoon, please come to my home for a meal."

The girl agreed, and the two set off to the old woman's home. She took a huge pot and handed it to the girl saying, "Let's make a scrumptious soup. Fill the pot with water, place this single bean in the water along with this bone and a grain of rice, and we will have a feast."

"You have to be kidding. This will make a vile soup," said the girl.

"Mind your tongue and do as I have asked," responded the old woman.

Shortly later a delectable stew brimming with rice and beans was ready and the two ate their meal in silence. When the meal was over, the old woman turned to the girl and said, "I need to go out for a little bit; stay here, and when I return, we will recover your spoon. While I am out, if a black cat comes by, you mustn't feed him no matter how much he meows. Beat him with this broom." The girl nodded and the old woman left.

After a little while a black cat wandered into the house and began meowing loudly. Immediately the girl picked up the broom and beat the cat senseless until she broke one of its legs. The cat managed to hobble away. Later that evening the old woman came home leaning on a cane because one of her legs was broken. She instructed the girl to leave her house.

The girl reminded the old woman that she would not go home without her silver spoon. "As you walk home," started the old woman, "you will come to a crossroad. You will see a pile of eggs. There will be large ones shouting out to you: 'Take me, take me!' Among the eggs there will be some tiny ones saying nothing. Take one of the tiny eggs and break it open when you reach the next crossroad."

Without a word of thanks, the girl ran out of the house. When she got to the first crossroad, she saw a pile of eggs. The large ones all yelled, "Take me, take me!"

"I am not naïve," the girl thought to herself. "I will listen to what these eggs are telling me." She picked out the biggest egg and broke it right where she was standing. Instantly, a horde of dragons, demons, and devils appeared and ate the girl up.

What a marvelous story; it is one of my favorite folktales. On the surface it may seem like the story is more about trust and following instructions than active listening. However, these are essential components of active listening. In the last section of the book we will look at how to cultivate a variety of listening competencies. For now, there are two questions we can ask to dive deeper into this story. First, how do the girls react differently to the old woman's instructions? And second, what guides each girl's actions in the story? The first girl trusts her own sense of things to decide when to follow the woman's instructions. Her listening involves reflection. She is not blindly obedient. Each instruction given to her by the woman is processed individually. She listens as much to herself as to the woman. The second girl, on the other hand, is blinded by greed. Her internal dialogue is dominated by a single preoccupation of acquiring the treasure discovered by the first girl. She is incapable of listening actively.

Stories require active listening because they are encrypted. Each listening demands our full and undivided imagination. Stories are most effective when we use their multilayered nature. For example, I have offered a few thoughts on why the story above is an example of active listening. These thoughts are just a starting point. Stories encourage us to seek meaning and generate personal associations with them. Stories are not meant to be left in isolation. Meaning arises through a series of relationships: each story is somehow tethered to another, and it is through this sea of associations that we generate meaning and behavior.

Example 2

Compassion is an implicit outcome of active listening. There is a powerful scene between Akhilleus and Priam toward the end of Homer's *Iliad*. These two characters are diametrically opposed to one another. Akhilleus has been engaged in destroying and warring against the city of Troy while Priam, who is king of Troy, is doing everything he can to defend it. In the scene, Akhilleus has just lost his best friend, Patroklos, and Priam has lost his son Hektor at the hands of Akhilleus. Homer vividly describes the moment the two encounter each other. Despite being enemies, they feel the unity of their suffering. Akhilleus and Priam listen actively to one another to realize their common ground.

> *Akhilleus,*
> *be reverent toward the great gods! And take*
> *pity on me, remember your own father.*
> *Think me more pitiful by far, since I*
> *have brought myself to do what no man else*
> *has done before—to lift to my lips the hand*
> *of one who killed my son.*
>
> *Now in Akhilleus*
> *the evocation of his father stirred*
> *new longing, and an ache of grief. He lifted*
> *the old man's hand and gently put him by.*
> *Then both were overborne as they remembered:*
> *the old king huddled at Akhilleus' feet*
> *wept, and wept for Hektor, killer of men,*
> *while great Akhilleus wept for his own father*
> *as for Patroklos once again; and sobbing*
> *filled the room.*

The phrase, "then both were overborne as they remembered," is the key to understanding this passage. Akhillius and Priam see themselves in each other. What a powerful moment of compassion when warriors put themselves in the shoes of the enemy. Their memories are stories joined by a common thread: the pathos and sadness of loss.

The Appendix on page 233 contains a wonderful story that speaks of the relationship of empathy and stories. We cannot fully understand the feelings and emotions of another without invoking the rich knowledge and experience captured in our own reservoir of stories. To be summoned by a story and its buried treasures we must suspend all preconceptions we may have. Curiosity and wonder serve as our guides.

I am lingering in our discussion of how stories require active listening because, as I said above, it is the most important and subtle of all the ways stories function. In fact, if the model of story functions presented in Figure 2.1 had to be reduced to one guiding principle or one all-encompassing explanation, active listening would best be chosen. The greatest amount of confusion and misuse of stories derives from the seductive assumption that most people make about the nature of stories—that stories can be crafted or told to achieve specific results. Forget it. Stories are for the listening. Even telling a story becomes valuable only when we do so in response to what someone said.

Example 3

In his essays on analytical psychology, Karl Jung recounts a case that holds some fascinating insights for us on the nature of stories and active listening. His patient was a young, sentimental man caught in the throes of infatuation. Completely drawn into his own fantasy, when the young man finally approaches the object of his desires, his affections are unrequited. Despondent, the young man goes to a river to throw himself in and commit suicide. When he gets to the river and sees the stars of night reflected there, he becomes distracted. He sees the stars as pairs of lovers destined for one another. He also feels like the stars are speaking to him. His despair begins to subside, and he forgets the woman of his desires. The young man becomes convinced that the stars must hold a special treasure for him. He decides to take action and goes to the nearby observatory to dig under it to find his promised treasure, and instead of finding a treasure ends up landing in jail for his actions.

In this example we see the relationship between stories and thinking. The young man is caught in a story he has built and fabricated with no external validation. When he seeks the reciprocity of feelings by the woman he desires, but is denied it, he is faced with the fantasy of the story he has spent so much energy concocting and sustaining. Unable to see a way out of the drama he has created, he seeks relief in the form of suicide. However, his unconscious has yet another surprise for him. While he gazes into the water, the reflection of the stars piques his poetic sensibility. His imagination saves him with an epiphany. His story mind envisions the stars as pairs of lovers destined for one another. Not cured of his delusional tendencies, his story mind turns his poetic vision into a literal one. The young man becomes convinced that the stars are telling him he will find a special treasure that they have hidden just for him. His rational mind surmises that the best place to find this treasure bequeathed by the stars is at an observatory.

In the context of stories and the active listening they require, the problem with this young man is that he is incapable of listening actively to the stories that guide his feelings and behaviors. Given his penchant for intensifying whatever story is guiding him at the moment, he decides to dig for the stars' treasure.

I am afraid we are all guilty of doing much the same at times. We treat our experiences and interactions with others with very little circumspection, and are content with interpreting them in whatever way is easiest. These interpretations become the stories that guide our communications with others. To enlist the power of stories we must be vigilant about always trying to listen actively. If we do, we are assured of ongoing insights, authenticity, and effectiveness as a communicator and learner.

Stories Negotiate Differences

Do you ever feel a chasm between yourself and another person? Perhaps his point of view is so different from your own that you find it unthinkable to even entertain it. Like many of you, I'm sure, I have sat through quite a few meetings in which the ostensible subject is diversity among employees. Instead, however, most of the meeting is given over to celebrating similarities rather than recognizing the uniqueness of every individual—a uniqueness that goes beyond race, ethnicity, gender, or creed. Differentiation is the key to survival. Millions of species would not be alive today were it not for Nature's careful attention to differences. The question is, how can we account for both similarity and difference? Stories can save the day.

Stories enable us to encompass multiple points of view simultaneously. Imagine a visitor from another country who is limited to traveling to only one or two locales. What sort of impression will he form of our country as a whole? Is it likely that he will have an accurate picture? He hasn't been to enough places to have a good idea. Yet, whatever impressions he forms will be the basis for communicating his experiences and ideas to others. In a case like this, the visitor is likely to realize the limitation of his experience and how it may affect his perception. He will probably be open to different perspectives since he realizes the limitations of his own. When a native of our country or a visitor with a different set of experiences shares with our traveler their stories, he is likely to expand the narrowness of his initial impressions and add the experiences recounted by others. The gap between the visitor's experiences and someone else's is bridged by stories.

If only it were always this easy. Our view of the world is crafted from lots of experiences we store in our minds as stories. These in turn help us form the values, beliefs, assumptions, and biases that guide our behavior. Listening to stories encourages us to reflect on our similarities, appreciate other perspectives, and negotiate our differences. It is amazing to watch how quickly conflicts can disappear when we take the time to hear and validate someone else's side of the story. Consequently, a new story can often be created that incorporates parts of different stories to produce a new interpretive framework and a new understanding of available possibilities.

Stories Encode Information

We can put only so much information in our brains. As a result, stories are a little like freeze-dried food that is reconstituted later. Putting the point in the language of computers, we do not store all bits of information. There is a finite space for 0's and 1's in our computer brain. Stories act as wonderful storage vessels that succinctly archive our data and compress it into more manageable units. But the storyteller does not store in his brain the story, word for word. He does not memorize the story as such. The long epic poems and stories told by roaming minstrels were remembered by reliving the tales as they were told. Here again, look at the word *remember*. We remember by putting something back together, that is, by taking its parts and rejoining them as members to the whole. This process can result in new treasures of meaning not previously possible.

There are deliberate ways in which we use stories to encode information. What about all those allegories, parables, and fairy tales? Although multitextured in nature, these story forms are vehicles for wrapping specific messages in the guise of narrative. Every culture, creed, and philosophical system has a rich tradition of using stories deliberately to store, transmit, and retrieve critical norms and values espoused by their respective groups. Much confusion about the nature of stories such as these can be summed up in the overused question, "So what's the moral of the story?" But stories potentially are much more dynamic, because it is not possible to know what impact a story will have on every listener. This latent capacity of a story is due to its associative nature.

That is, stories work by triggering the listener's own indices of experiences, all of which may be reformulated creatively in a novel way.

Stories Act as Tools for Thinking

Take a moment and think about some of your favorite movies or novels. Do you find yourself revisiting these stories and gaining new insights? Do you relate these stories and characters to any of your own experiences? We engage in this type of imagination more than we realize, as we constantly relate one area of knowledge or set of experiences with others. Consider this humorous example by an anonymous author:

Things We Can Learn from Dogs

1. *Never pass up the opportunity to go for a joy ride.*
2. *Allow the experience of fresh air and the wind in your face to be pure ecstasy.*
3. *When loved ones come home, always run to greet them.*
4. *When it's in your best interest, practice obedience.*
5. *Let others know when they've invaded your territory.*
6. *Take naps and stretch before rising.*
7. *Run, romp, and play daily.*
8. *Eat with gusto and enthusiasm.*
9. *Be loyal.*
10. *If what you want lies buried, dig until you find it.*
11. *When someone is having a bad day, be silent. Sit close by and nuzzle them gently.*
12. *Thrive on attention and let people touch you.*
13. *Avoid biting when a simple growl will do.*
14. *When you're happy, dance around and wag your entire body.*
15. *No matter how often you're scolded, don't buy into the guilt thing and pout . . . run right back and make friends.*
16. *Delight in the simple joys of a long walk.*

This illustrates what we are talking about: We have a set of impressions about dogs that, by applying certain "story images," we can use to unearth some fun insights that benefit our lives. Dogs, or anything else we might choose, become a rich metaphor for guiding our thinking. Any of us could undoubtedly add to the above list with just a little bit of imagination. Later in the book we will go through similar exercises for the purposes of developing our story mind.

This principle of reflective thinking through stories can be applied in a much deeper way than humor or clever twists of words. Stories are mirrors we can use to bounce the light of our thoughts into totally new directions. Working within the framework of stories, we can manipulate new and abstract ideas in a concrete fashion. Let's illustrate this point in another way. Stories are like models. We use models to understand and manipulate otherwise unwieldy forces. When I build a miniature model of a building, I can visualize, analyze, and scrutinize its design. The same could be said for building computer and mathematical models. Stories turn out to be great for modeling ideas, acquiring new knowledge, understanding complex emotions, and analyzing situations; best of all, stories are wonderful for managing ambiguity and paradoxes.

Dreams are a perfect example of how stories can be used as a tool for thinking. Dream analysis involves pulling back the layers of images and sensations to find meaning. Ordinary objects and symbols give form to immaterial dynamics of the unconscious mind. Dreams generate paradoxical situations that feel perfectly normal in the dream. We can play with our dreams. We toss and turn them over and over in our heads to find new meanings. Like dreams, stories may contain paradoxes that seem perfectly normal. In other words, our conscious thoughts are guided by logic, whereas stories have an expansive quality to them, unfettered by the limitations of what is logical. This can lead to insights otherwise impossible to experience.

Another example of stories being used as tools for thinking is the case method of inquiry. The case method of teaching dates much earlier than from its adoption by business and professional schools. Plato used something of the sort in his allegory of the cave, by which he sought to explore human nature. When we use stories as tools for thinking, we can approximate behaviors and anticipate outcomes. This is, of course, what strategic planners do when they use scenario planning as a tool. I am reminded of a wonderful science fiction story I read once in which a commander examines the art and stories of the world he will be attacking to predict how its people will react. Stories are a rich medium. Where else could we quickly wander through a dense mesh of possibilities? I opted to use the word *where* in the previous sentence because when we use stories for thinking, we are constructing elaborate warehouses in our imaginations to turn over complex ideas. Along the way we are bound to break old patterns and discover a wealth of new ones. Bypassing tired, habituated pathways in our minds and opting for new connections through story thinking is a powerful way to learn.

Stories Can Be Used as Weapons

Recall your childhood. Did you ever get in trouble for something you did not do? Was your assumed guilt influenced by someone else's fib? Now try imagining your favorite courtroom scene from a book, television program, or movie. How did the prosecuting attorney use stories to sway the jury?

Whether we are right, wrong, or indifferent, we interpret the world around us and spin a story to communicate our sense of the way things are. It is bad enough when we misrepresent an event with an innocent but erroneous story. How about those times when a story is consciously crafted for purposes of deception or self-gain? Con artists and pathological liars are brilliant at creating compelling stories that rope us into their schemes. It is always disappointing to watch a political campaign mired in mudslinging. Stories from the past are dredged to cast a candidate in a bad light. Earnest apologies are made after the fact, and the campaigners vow to clean up their acts, but the damage has already been done.

Stories are powerful. However, the force that can be generated by them is value neutral. Stories can be used for positive or negative purposes. When we are required to argue a point, the most influential tool we can select is a story. Facts and figures rarely move listeners. If anything, they provide an opportunity for others to poke a hole in our presentation. Bring out a story to make your point and you are much more convincing. Likewise, it is more difficult for any dissenter to easily refute your assertions. Consider how some pieces of legislation come into being. Lawmakers are presented with an occurrence. Committee members listen to testimonials given by parties impacted by the proposed law. Since decisions are largely guided by irrational dynamics, stories are very persuasive.

Stories can have deceptive intentions and outcomes without exposing the teller as a liar. Marketers have been known to abuse the power of stories in this way. The association of products with sex appeal, healthiness, success, celebrities, or any other such scheme demonstrates our gullibility as consumers. It is not a function of our lack of discernment. This massive popular exercise of autosuggestions hints at the inner workings of our minds' black boxes. It is much more difficult to pry out a story guiding behavior than a set of erroneous facts that can be challenged or validated. If we recognize the more insidious uses of stories, I am hopeful that we will employ the same principles for loftier goals.

Stories Are Medicine for Healing

Have you ever thought about how most therapeutic disciplines work? There is almost always some narrative involved. Stories from a patient's past are examined in terms of the present and future. Relationships are understood by revisiting experiences that are retold, discussed, and analyzed in the form of stories. There is a wonderful book by Erica Helm Meade entitled *Tell It by*

Heart: Woman and the Healing Power of Story. In it, Meade recounts some of her work as a therapist. In each of the case histories, she describes how a story became the focal point for a patient's growing self-realization and self-knowledge.

Have you ever spent an hour two listening to the stories of an older relative? My father is a conductor, and I can spend hours listening to his tales of conducting around the world and working with a host of eccentric characters. It is as beneficial to me as it is for him. In the great Greek epic poems, all the heroes long to be remembered in song and story. A moment passes quickly. It is a stand-alone point in time with no value of its own. Stories give our lives meaning and continuity. At wakes and funerals, humorous stories provide relief and joy to the mourning. A collage of memories relived through storytelling gives us an opportunity to honor the dead and make them an ongoing part of our lives.

These effects of healing are not relegated to therapy, the elderly, or the dead. Telling and hearing each other's stories is profoundly healing in any context. We are naked without stories. Do you remember the children's story called "Stone Soup"? A single rock is set in a cauldron filled with water. Allured by its mystique, it is not long before townspeople are adding all sorts of delicious ingredients to it. Nothing is metamorphosed into something. We are like the empty cauldron filled with water and a stone. Through our relationships and by engaging our imaginations and the imaginations of others via stories, we are healed and made whole. To limit the use of such powerful and essential mechanisms to a therapist's office robs us of vital opportunities to be more fully alive. So in business or in our personal lives, why should we not invoke the power of stories?

Summary

We have explored a model of how stories function. In any given circumstances, a story will not be functioning in all of the ways we've described. Throughout the rest of the book we will use stories as a metaphor for understanding communication and learning in an organization. This model will serve as a set of guiding principles for realizing different ways we can put the power of stories to work in organizations.

3

Organizational Communication: Broadcasting Signals

If we spend less time concentrating our efforts on broadcasting signals and more energy tuning in to all the frequencies around us, we will be capable of delivering more messages with fewer broadcasts, smaller bandwidth, less information, and more impact.

Identifying Forms of Communication

What are the various forms of communication in organizations, and how do we understand and work with them? In this section we will develop a framework for conceptualizing communication. Organizational communications involve a target, a channel, and tools, and by understanding the relationships among them we can understand the uses and values of stories.

By target we mean the audience we want to communicate with. There are four of them:

1. internal
2. external
3. partner
4. nonspecific

By channel we mean the way in which information is delivered. There are three channels:

1. formal
2. social
3. personal

Figure 3.1 **Conceptualizing Communication: The Communications Matrix**

Conceptualizing Communication		Target			
		Internal	External	Partner	Nonspecific
C h a n n e l	**Formal**	Memos Policy manuals Intranet Newsletters Posters	Television Radio Advertisement Annual report Billboards Website	B2B Portal SLA Contracts Project debrief Conference	Focus group Survey
	Social	Trainings Meeting Briefings	News and media Job fair User groups	Trade shows Magazines	Books Philanthropy
	Personal	E-mail Telephone One-on-one meetings	E-mail Telephone Ad-hoc interactions	Meetings Telephone E-mail	Speaker bureaus Networking

Tools are the concrete objects we use to carry our information, such as memos, other written communications, and phone calls. Certain tools are better suited for some targets and channels than others, but there is a lot of overlap. It is easy to become preoccupied with tools, but they are not the most significant ingredients in our conceptualization of organizational communication. Figure 3.1 lists a sample of tools and relates them to targets and channels.

By examining how targets, channels, and tools interact with one another we can discover flaws in the communication practices and strategies used by most organizations and ways to correct them.

Internal Targets

Employees are the targets of internal communications. These are all the initiatives and processes used to keep employees informed. The breadth and extent of these communications will vary according to their purpose, importance, timing requirements, and the number of employees they affect. When leaders of organizations are queried, they usually rank good internal communications near or at the top of the ingredients responsible for success. Like our bodies, which need a strong heart, organizations require a hefty pump to transport all of the vital communicative nutrients to their metaphorical organs and cells to ensure a healthy, balanced whole.

External Target

External communications are targeted to customers and to media such as newspapers, magazines, radio, or TV, which carry key messages about a company's products, services, policies, or current status. Some examples include marketing promotions, advertising campaigns, press releases, investor relations, public relations, and community affairs. These ensure good lines of communication with constituents outside of the organization. Organizations allocate large amounts of money on tools, staff, and processes to reach external targets. As organizations grow, the number of external targets increases exponential. Multinational organizations are challenged to reach further and further.

Partner Targets

Partner communications are directed at anyone that is a part of an organization's value chain. Partners help organizations develop, distribute, support, or maintain the organization's products and services. These could include strategic partners, vendors, alliances, outsourcers, resellers, contractors, or collaborators because a certain degree of trust and disclosure between the organization and partner is necessary. These communications are unique; they are neither completely internal nor external. Organizations with outsourcing arrangements, such as for their information technology functions, are finding these communications to be a critical and strategic part of their growth and competitiveness. As organizations become increasingly dependent upon groups and chains of partners to produce their products, reach their customers, and provide a full range of services, communicating well with partners will be among some of the biggest challenges.

Nonspecific Targets

Informal messages and communications can be spread without an organization's knowledge and with no specific target. They simply happen. Think of it as "word of mouth." These messages can travel like a forest fire burning out of control. I remember a great scene from the movie *Contact*. In the movie, scientists are scanning the skies for radio frequencies from intelligent life in the cosmos. When a signal is discovered, it turns out to be a TV broadcast of Adolph Hitler at the 1940 Olympic games. Admittedly, this is not the most stellar broadcast, but once a broadcast has been made, it keeps traveling. We can't avoid it—all our targeted and nontargeted broadcasts are out there. The nature of organizational broadcasts is not so different from what happened in the movie. We have no idea which way communications will bounce back to us or in what form. Consequently, we do not expend any strategic time or energy on determining how to use them, since they are outside our scope of aim. Ironically, it is this background noise found in nonspecific targets, which are artifacts of our purposeful communications with all the other targets, that impacts the public perception of our organization more so than any other deliberate efforts.

Formal Channels

Formal channels are "official" pathways through which we communicate. People expect to receive information through such tools as companywide policy and procedure manuals. The tool itself is not significant. These are the metaphorical telephone booths in an organization. People know they can receive or deliver communications through these channels. They are visible and there is little confusion about how to use them. Like the telephone companies who deploy and maintain a massive infrastructure of wires and poles, organizations have taken the time and effort to erect formal channels for people to broadcast messages.

Social Channels

Social channels carry beliefs, attitudes, and values. An organization communicates its culture through social channels. Mission statements, vision statements, guiding principles, or strategies are good examples. Some of these communications also go through formal channels, but by traveling through social channels that utilize interconnection points among people inside an organization as well as outside, they become amplified and are continuously rebroadcast.

Personal Channels

Personal channels carry the largest and most dynamic load of all. These are the people-to-people connections. Whatever may have been purposefully broadcast through formal or social channels morphs and takes on a communicative life of its own in personal channels. People will digest and assimilate messages from the other two channels, but they will spin out their own interpretations of the same information through their informal interactions with others. Frequently there will be an incongruency between information broadcast through a formal channel and information found in a personal channel. For example, a policy or procedure may be formally stated one way but, because of personal preference, practiced another way. For example, a policy manual and employee orientation training communicate that all purchase orders over the amount of $500 need to be approved by a director. However, in practice it turns out that most department directors do not require managers to get their signature.

Figure 3.2 **Key Targets and Channels**

Key Targets and Channels		Target			
		Internal	External	Partner	Nonspecific
C h a n n e l	Formal				
	Social				
	Personal				

Information found in personal channels almost always overrides any other. Similar to nonspecific targets, communications occurring in a personal channel are difficult to tap into and even more difficult to manage, and yet they are the most critical. Taken together, nonspecific targets and personal channels are the two most important forms of communication organizations need to address (see Figure 3.2). In just a moment we will explore some ideas on how to do this.

Broadcasting Versus Frequency Tuning

The metaphor of organizational communication as broadcast breaks down when we try to devise strategies for reaching nonspecific targets and moving our messages through personal channels. Our propensity for always being active doers in control prevents us from entertaining a more powerful metaphor. Instead of pushing messages, what if we were to think of how to pull messages from nonspecific targets and tap into personal channels? What if we then catalyzed all of these mini-broadcasts? Each small message would then act as a snippet connected to other snippets forming a fabric of mass general consensus. We would keep our finger on the pulse of which messages are propagating and which ones are failing in our organization by eliciting stories from this fabric. Our communication experts must act more like anthropological ethnographers and less like radio disc jockeys.

Think of how language works. We use a word, and despite individual experiences and whatever other personal connotations that may come into play, the word strikes a familiar enough chord that others are able to understand us. Precision is achieved through a certain degree of imprecision. I would be unable to write a single sentence with any hope of your understanding it if this were not the case. We can tolerate several degrees of freedom while maintaining a high degree of confidence that we are successful in

Figure 3.3   **Untapped Areas of the Communications Matrix**

Untapped Areas of the Communications Matrix		Target			
		Internal	External	Partner	Nonspecific
C h a n n e l	Formal	1	2	3	10
	Social	4	5	6	11
	Personal	7	8	9	12

Key: Organizations can use stories to reach untapped areas 7–12.

expressing our thoughts. This same principle works if we apply it to the seemingly amorphous realm of nonspecific targets and personal channels.

If we were to build a matrix of our targets and channels, we could end up with a two-dimensional array of twelve areas (see Figure 3.3). The largest percentage of our efforts is focused on areas one through six. These are clearly identified channels and targets that utilize standard tools and processes that have been in use by organizations for some time. This leaves 50 percent of our communication potential untapped and unmanaged. We pretty much ignore anything that is nonspecific or personal.

Some might argue that focus groups and customer surveys are good ways to reach nonspecific targets and personal channels. I do not consider occasional surveys to constitute a significant strategic or sincere effort when you consider the amount of energy we spend on all the other targets and channels. The restrictive and self-serving nature of these survey tools seldom yields any meaningful exchange. Here's a perfect example: I remember having to call the customer service department of an unnamed telecommunications company. After a fruitless call that demonstrated a total lack of flexibility and poor business processes, I was asked to rate the quality of customer service I received on a scale of one to seven. The customer service representative was excellent. She was a good listener, patient, and very competent. Yet despite her qualities I felt compelled to refuse to participate in the survey. I thanked her for her excellent interpersonal skills but shared with her my frustration. I was totally nonplussed by the company's business processes. I told her I appreciated her as a person but that I was not happy with the company's lack of care or concern with my needs. I did not want her to get a bad rating, but I was not willing to reward the company for its bad practices. Furthermore, the customer service representative was given no mechanism to communicate back to management with my feedback. In other words, these folks were content to sit in a boardroom once a month and gloat over meaningless numbers and pat themselves on the back for listening to their customers. This was all about demonstrating good form and had little to do with real communication.

We might instead find ways of inciting others to share their experiences. People are always more engaged when they are sharing than when they are just listening. And when we place people in a listening mode it should be to excite their imaginations. Activating people's imaginations increases the likelihood of stimulating their reflective capacity. Self-reflection stirs up personal experiences in the form of insights, new linkages, and associations. If our communication efforts are effective, people should be bursting with thoughts and ideas they want to share. We can activate this raw energy and use it to carry messages that describe and define our organization. I liken it to a swarm of bees gathering the pollen of flowers and transforming it into honey. The messages we want to broadcast are assimilated into people's minds, and they then feel compelled to share them—and for proof they speak in stories. An organization that implements a centralized communication strategy and does not invest energy in reaching nonspecific targets and activating personal channels will never produce the quantity or quality of honey made by a swarm of bees.

Discussion of Untapped Matrix Combinations and the Role of Stories

Let's walk through each area of the matrix that is not tapped and determine what we can do to incorporate them into our organization's communication strategy. Throughout this discussion stories will play an important role. Remember two key things about stories:

1. Stories are not just for broadcasting messages.
2. Stories are an excellent way of eliciting others' thoughts, beliefs, perceptions, attitudes, and experiences.

Area 7: Personal/Internal Communication

Of all the areas on the communication matrix, the personal/internal is the easiest one to pay attention to (see Figure 3.4). We have plenty of opportunities to intercept these messages. Perhaps we need to be as attentive to how people act as much as we are to what they are saying. Actions do speak louder than words, and carefully crafted words are never as telling as a narrative selected and relived by a teller. We need to look at what stories a person chooses to

Figure 3.4   **Personal/Internal Communication**

Personal/ Internal		Target			
		Internal	External	Partner	Nonspecific
C h a n n e l	Formal	1	2	3	10
	Social	4	5	6	11
	Personal	7	8	9	12

tell us. Much about that person's motivation and intentions can be deduced from the stories told and the way they are told.

There is a powerful reciprocal climate of trust engendered by the dynamics of sharing personal stories. Once set in motion we do not need to go out of our way to fabricate opportunities for people to share personal stories. People within the organization will willingly and randomly share their experiences and insights in the form of stories. An organization's culture must foster a receptive environment that encourages people to freely share these things. How many times have you attended a weekly meeting where there is some sort of standing agenda item for people to discuss their experiences? Short of being a gripe session, this rote standard practice yields little information and receives even less respect from the individuals involved. Although these meeting rituals are well intentioned, they fall short of achieving any significant success. People do not share stories, insights are missed, and everyone feels like they are taking part in a charade.

Informal communications can be saturated with stories of the day and with incessant probing. Pushing out "key stories of the day" results in very short shelf lives for these communiqués. Using intranets and daily news or other such tools to broadcast stories aligned with key business objectives has value, but the range of these broadcasts is weak and shallow. What we want to be able to do is uncover stories while walking the beat and incite others to share them. The puller of stories helps the teller to realize that his story is an invaluable nugget that has a relationship to the efforts of other people in the organization and the business imperatives of the day. The teller becomes a "signal repeater." Suddenly realizing the value of his message, the teller takes his story and without any prompting, repeats and rebroadcasts his message throughout the organization. That's not even the real value. When there are lots of mini-broadcasts, the number of total broadcasts increases. In other words, when a story is shared, it is more than likely to trigger someone else's recollection and result in a fresh story. Now each repeater carries not only the original story but also a story of their own. Even if the signal of the first story drops somewhere along the way, the new story carries its own kinetic energy. Here is an image to clarify this concept: Imagine throwing rocks into water. Toss one rock in a glassy body of water and watch the concentric circles move away from the source. As the circles get larger and begin to weaken, imagine throwing in another rock slightly removed from the first source. Now you have multiple waves of concentric circles. The new waves are stronger and will cancel out the weakening waves before them to carry the information further. If the waves coincide exactly with one another, the force of the wave will be reinforced. Either scenario leads to a strengthened signal.

In this analogy our first communication functions as the initiating force. All of the other rocks tossed into the water that create new waves of circles are represented by employees rebroadcasting the message through their personal recapitulation. There is far less effort involved, a great deal more reflective insight, but it is a much richer way of economically transmitting information. The economy stems from the fact that we do not need to build the perfect communication and then clog our overfilled official channels with another piece of information. This strategy of pushing a message for the purpose of pulling out new perceptions and information in the form of stories, and then pushing these communications deeper inside the organization is what I will refer to from here on as *"push-to-pull-to-push"* (see Figure 3.5). It is organic and sets in motion a kind of Huck Finn–Tom Sawyer effect, except instead of getting others to whitewash fences for us, we are exciting them to broadcast messages.

Leaders and managers of an organization need to spend less time writing memos and e-mails and more time developing quality relationships with their employees. Stories are one of the best ways to develop relationships. In the previous chapter we discovered how important stories are to binding and bonding individuals, active listening, and negotiating differences. Knowing what questions to ask is important for two reasons. It requires a leader or manager to focus on the communications that will move people closer to achieving the organization's objectives. By doing so, the manager is continually directing and redirecting his or her attention to look for gaps in people's understanding. When there is confusion, people get stuck and lose their momentum, which creates negative energy in the organization. A high degree of mindfulness mixed with a sharp analytical mind serves leaders and managers the best. Not every instance of misperception floating around the organization can be reframed, however; the ones capable of inflicting the most damage can be effectively addressed in quick order. Knowing what questions to ask is also important because it involves the interaction between the potential storyteller and the elicitor. Pacing, thinking quickly, changing tack, entering different frames of reference, sharing personal experiences,

Figure 3.5 **Push-to-Pull-to-Push**

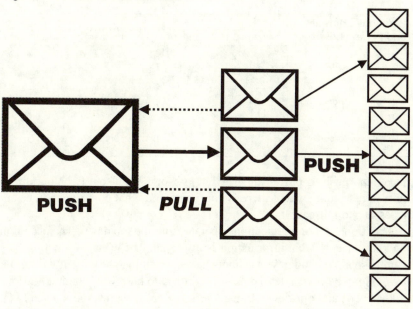

and using evocative language are some of the skills required to be a success-ful elicitor. Discovering a story is only half of the challenge. Next, the elici-tor must guide the storyteller to recognize the importance of her story and inspire her to retell it. We will revisit these issues in greater detail in the third section of the book.

Areas 8 and 9: Personal/External and Personal/Partner Communication

The personal/external and personal/partner areas of the communication ma-trix operate under the same principles as the area of personal/internal we discussed above (see Figure 3.6). Although the targets differ, we can fol-low the same strategy of "push-to-pull-to-push." As we move further from the organization, it becomes increasingly important to cultivate strong al-lies who interface with us in a diplomatic fashion. Depending on our busi-ness, it can be more difficult to communicate with external, partner, or nonspecific targets described in our communication matrix. We lack the direct contact with them. We need to rely on others to be our eyes and ears. From inside the organization we act as coaches. Once we identify the right people to act as our diplomats, and this is something we should revisit on a regular basis, we model and mold the story elicitor behaviors we require to

Figure 3.6 **Personal/External and Personal/Partner Communication**

Personal/External and Personal/Partner		Internal	External	Partner	Nonspecific
C h a n n e l	Formal	1	2	3	10
	Social	4	5	6	11
	Personal	7	⭐ 8	⭐ 9	12

make our "push-to-pull-to-push" strategy work. We also rely on our diplomats to determine where there is confusion and what communications are necessary to mitigate it.

Traditionally, communications operate from the top down. The people in the know decide what information is important and what information they want to share. Although you cannot share everything, and even if you could, it would not be advisable to do so, it is critical to base your communications on the needs and priorities of the targets you are reaching and not solely on the vague impressions of a few people. Use your "push-to-pull-to-push" strategy, stories, and your diplomats to start communications from the bottom up. By doing so, all the mini-broadcasts initiated by your diplomats will stand a good chance of addressing most of your targets' communication needs. I like the image of our immune system with its army of white blood cells. Lots of little healers go to work reaching all the infected parts of the body. The body's success lies in its immune memory and decentralized plan of attack. We can put the same strategy to work with our communications.

Area 10: Formal/Nonspecific Communication

Surveys and focus groups are the principal ways in which organizations reach the formal/nonspecific areas of our communication matrix (see Figure 3.7). The tools and strategies employed in this endeavor tend to be very limiting in nature. We need to move past numerical rating systems and other forms of constrained feedback. Have you ever sat in a focus group and felt like the questions being asked weren't the right ones in the first place? Sometimes the questions are self-serving. Or they may be worded in such a way that they do not elicit genuine feedback. Focus groups can be guilty of measuring what we want to measure or of biasing the people we are querying to obtain the answers we desire.

How do we get organizations to accept qualitative as well as quantitative

Figure 3.7 **Formal/Nonspecific Communication**

Formal/ Nonspecific		Target			
		Internal	External	Partner	Nonspecific
C h a n n e l	Formal	1	2	3	☆ 10
	Social	4	5	6	11
	Personal	7	8	9	12

data? Furthermore, how do we process qualitative information? We do not want to overreact to outliers. We have a tendency to assume that single qualitative data points such as stories can be abused. We do not want to create new policies or practices based on such limited information. At least statistics can be validated. Stories can make us uncomfortable. What if they are not true?

Consider the number of different customer interactions that can be used as opportunities to ask people to share stories in the form of personal narratives. Today, technology gives us a number of new touch points with customers such as websites, e-mail, and instant messaging. We are quick to include flowery testimonials in marketing brochures, but most of these come to us in the form of random communications pushed to us by customers or that we ourselves have solicited. We need to "pull" these forms of communication. What if we trained all employees, especially customer service representatives, to elicit and collect stories from our customers? We would need to provide mechanisms for them to share the stories they gather, and we would need to become organizationally adept at garnering insights from them. Some of this qualitative data would come in the form of observations. Reflective employees would be keyed into becoming more aware of stories happening around them, not just stories told them. These stories would be presented in management meetings where, typically, numbers and canned reports occupy the largest percentage of time.

Decision makers would also need to be trained in how to work with stories. Qualitative trend analysis, pattern recognition, and clear identification of decision-making objectives coupled with a high degree of self-awareness and honesty on the part of anyone working with this qualitative information will yield amazing results. For example, through stories I have helped groups work through difficult decisions, discover the root cause of problems, engage in creative problem solving, and reach a consensus in a fraction of the time it normally takes. Right now you may be questioning the relevancy of stories and the likelihood of finding enough employees you trust who either

Figure 3.8 **Social/Nonspecific Communication**

Social/Nonspecific		Target			
		Internal	External	Partner	Nonspecific
C h a n n e l	Formal	1	2	3	10
	Social	4	5	6	11
	Personal	7	8	9	12

have these story competencies or whom you believe can develop them, but I have been surprised by the innate capacities of people in these areas. Shifting the communication paradigm from broadcasting to tuning and exercising the unused reflective story muscle reinvigorates dormant capacities. In order for this to be achieved there are a number of competencies that would need to be developed in employees and managers. A model of these competencies and concrete practices for developing them are the subject of the last part of the book.

Area 11: Social/Nonspecific Communication

This area of the communications matrix deals with collective experience (see Figure 3.8). When two or more people randomly discuss an organization in conversation, what do they say? What are their experiences? How is their collective experience different from their individual ones? How are they influenced by each other's stories? We are trying to understand the combinations resulting from the mixing of people's perceptions. This is the rumor mill. When we tap into this area of the communication matrix, we are not as concerned with the validity of people's perceptions as we are with how our organization is represented in their social interactions. If our organization were mentioned in the same conversation as a competitor, how would we stack up?

Sony was involved in an interesting marketing campaign that is a perfect example of a company tapping into nonspecific targets and social channels. Actors were paid to go to a beach, use a Sony product, and engage people in conversation about the product they were using. We may find the strategy manipulative in a negative way, but it is a brilliant example of how to involve people in a story. Unknowingly, people on the beach were being given a story that they were likely to *socialize*. In other words, they would share their positive perceptions of the product with others. I frequently hear organizations use the verb *socialize* to describe how an idea becomes introduced to an organization's members and becomes an accepted part of its culture.

"What-if" scenarios turn out to be an effective way of predicting how people will socialize their perceptions of our organizations. A "what-if" scenario involves presenting people with a situation and asking them to imagine how they would respond or react. A well-designed focus group utilizing story methodologies can capture this information. Think of story methodologies as techniques for eliciting people's stories. In the last part of the book we will examine the underlying competencies that need to be developed in order to be effective at eliciting stories. The same story methodologies employed in a focus group can be used by anyone interacting with someone who has knowledge of or history with the organization. These "what-if" scenarios also leave people with the impression that you want to hear them and that you care about how they feel. People love to think about alternatives. Furthermore, people like to be asked to be advisors. It gives them a sense of importance. Employees need to be trained how to extemporaneously construct "what-if" scenarios and how to analyze the information they collect.

Depending on the organization, it is also possible to train employees to develop keen powers of observation. For example, watching customers' behavior and interactions with one another in a store, or while they wait in a line for customer service, can be fruitful. The danger lies in overreacting to a situation. Employees need to discover how to see things in relationship to one another and not as solitary events. One upset customer complaining to another may not be a sign of some larger looming problem. In all likelihood it simply reflects one customer's experience. In social situations, such as customer service, a well-timed and sincerely executed interaction becomes a golden opportunity to shift negative perceptions and leave people with a powerful story. We all have exceptional customer service stories to tell about the times when someone really went the extra mile to help us. These stories result in at least short-term and often long-term customer loyalty. A careful audit of an organization's business processes that includes isolating the ones that involve key customer interactions will yield a whole host of new places where we can direct our communication attention to improving how we tune in to people's perceptions and how we can reframe or guide them in the directions we desire.

Area 12: Personal/Nonspecific Communication

As one story leads to the next, the stories
themselves tell us who we are.
—Erica Lann-Clark

The personal/nonspecific area of the communication matrix deals with personal representations (see Figure 3.9). People are like ripe fruit, ready to burst open and communicate the moment they become connected to the social fabric. Individuals are members of social constructs. Once they plug into

Figure 3.9 **Personal/Nonspecific Communication**

Personal/ Nonspecific		Target			
		Internal	External	Partner	Nonspecific
C **h** **a** **n** **n** **e** **l**	Formal	1	2	3	10
	Social	4	5	6	11
	Personal	7	8	9	☆ 12

a social network, they bring their stories and perceptions. Do you remember playing with batteries and light bulbs in science class? When you connect lights in series, each bulb gets progressively dimmer. When you connect lights in parallel, they are much brighter. We have to find a way to prevent our communications from becoming diluted as people move further and further from the original sources of information. This is equivalent to light bulbs connected in series. People carry dimmer and dimmer perceptions of our organization. We need lots of different people operating in the personal channel carrying our communications to nonspecific targets. As other people encounter our messengers, they become like light bulbs connected in parallel because they are closer to the source of information.

This area of the communication matrix is the hardest to visualize. It is also extremely difficult to picture how we reach these solitary points of perception that lie so far away and have large distances between them. How would I ever justify an ongoing effort to reach them when I am virtually guaranteed there is no way of ever measuring my efforts? This requires a leap of faith. A company must be committed to an ongoing effort that will be difficult to measure. Consider the effects of corporate goodwill. We know it is important, and we acknowledge that there are other intangibles that play a part in determining our organization's success, yet we would be hard-pressed to measure them. I am considering more than the obvious gestures of corporate goodwill such as philanthropic cash donations. What about individuals who, with the support of their organizations, donate their time to community service? People on the outside observing the good works of these employees are likely to associate the good works with the employees' organization, thereby resulting in a positive perception of the organization. I cannot stick a meaningful price tag on that even if I account for the time absent from the office as an indirect expense.

So how do we create organizational communications initiatives that tap into the personal channels and aim for nonspecific targets? Here our efforts require discipline, attitude, and routine. These are ingrained behaviors of employee-vitalized organizations. Our efforts must be indirect. Instead of devising elaborate strategies and tools for reaching all the distant points of our organization, we need to spend time and money to create a culture of inspired, dedicated, and story-enabled employees. The rest will happen on its own.

A Note on Written Versus Oral Communication

Thus far our discussion on how to leverage underutilized areas of the communication matrix has been focused on oral communication. However, our principle strategy of "push-to-pull-to-push" works in the same manner with written communication. Written communication is asynchronous in nature and lacking in the same feedback loops as oral. While feedback is helpful, it is not necessary. Our written communications in organizations are usually very focused. We want to be as clear and concise as we possibly can. There is a time and place for this form of writing, but it will not be the best tack when we are trying to push a message for purposes of pulling information back and engaging the receivers of our message in acting as our broadcasters. I fear I will have to trust a paradox to make my point. Written communications need to be richer in ambiguity, provocative, and evocative in order to be more precise. Think of something as simple as sharing company results in an informational memo. Which are you more likely to remember—a column of bullets, or one or two short stories highlighting key areas of success? Now take it one step further: What if you were to use language that resulted in readers realizing and recounting contributions from their organizational areas that contributed to overall cooperate objectives? Those are stories that are sure to be rebroadcast around a water cooler and even farther. They are stories that will be owned by people and assume a myriad of forms appropriate for all the different audiences.

Summary

We started the chapter with the following assumption: If we spend less time concentrating our efforts on broadcasting signals and more energy tuning in to all the frequencies around us, we will be capable of delivering more messages with fewer broadcasts, smaller bandwidth, less information, and more impact.

We used a framework comprised of targets, channels, and tools to identify gaps in our organizational communications. This model uncovered opportunities for us to improve the effectiveness of our communications, reducing the number of broadcasts by tuning into frequencies in nonspecific targets

Figure 3.10 **The Relationship Between Story Functions and the Communications Matrix**

STORY FUNCTIONS	The Relationship Between Story Functions and the Communications Matrix	UNIQUE EFFECTS of STORIES
Empower a speaker		Entertaining
Create an environment	The functions of stories enable us to reach untapped areas 7–12 of the Communications Matrix....	Creating trust and openness between yourself and others
Bind and bond individuals		Elicit stories from others

Untapped Areas of the Communications Matrix

Communications Matrix	Target			
	Internal	External	Partner	Nonspecific
Channel — Formal	1	2	3	10
Channel — Social	4	5	6	11
Channel — Personal	7	8	9	12

STORY FUNCTIONS		UNIQUE EFFECTS of STORIES
Require active listening		Listen actively in order to: *Understand context and perspective* *Find the critical point in a system* *Uncover resistance and hidden agendas*
Negotiate differences		Shift perspectives in order to: *See each other* *Experience empathy* *Enter new frames of reference*
Encode information		Hold diverse points of view Become aware of operating biases and values Creating a working metaphor to illuminate an opinion, rational, vision, or decision
Tools for Thinking	Stories are effective at reaching areas 7–12 of the matrix because of their unique effects	Establish connections between different ideas and concepts to support an opinion or decision
Weapons		
Healing		Think outside the box to generate creative solutions and breakthroughs

and tapping into the personal channel. Some initial ideas were offered on how to move toward a decentralized communication strategy. Stories were shown to be an active metaphor for putting these dynamics to work. The functions of stories and their unique effects enable us to reach the untapped areas of our Communications Matrix (see Figure 3.10). Part III of this book lays out concrete activities that can be practiced and implemented to realize the benefits of this approach to communication.

4
Case Study: Dreyer's Ice Cream

Dreyer's Ice Cream of Oakland, CA, is a fascinating organization. In Part II we will learn more about the company in the interview with Sherrie Cornett. For now we will examine its cultural values, known as the Grooves. Let me preface our discussion by saying these values are more than touchy-feely ideals printed on pretty posters. People really believe these at Dreyer's Ice Cream and practice them.

This case study is in three parts. The first part spells out the Grooves philosophy as expressed in the company's employee manual. Next we identify the relationship between the Grooves and stories. Here we see how the nine functions of stories and their unique effects discussed in Chapter 2 help us achieve the communication and organizational behavior goal of actualizing the Grooves' cultural values. The push-to-pull-to-push principle discussed in Chapter 3 is an essential aspect of how the Grooves can be brought alive through stories in the personal channel (Area 7) of the Communications Matrix (see Figure 3.4). In the third and last part of the case study we see a very simple but effective communication intervention performed with stories to promote one of the Grooves by tapping into the personal channel of the Communications Matrix. First let's walk through what the Grooves are, as articulated by Dreyer's Ice Cream. The following text is taken from the company's employee manual.

Part I. Dreyer's Case Study—The Grooves

"Grooves," The Dreyer's Philosophy—I Can Make a Difference

At Dreyer's Ice Cream, we believe in the individual. We know that most people today relish their own uniqueness and want to be respected for their distinct characteristics, skills, strengths, weaknesses, and idiosyncrasies.

We believe that if we hire good people and respect them as individuals, they will commit both their unique perspectives and their enthusiastic involvement to the goals we are striving to achieve together here at Dreyer's. We seek individuals who want to enter into a **relationship** with our company, not just take a job. In return for committing their energy and enthusiasm to their jobs and identifying personally with the company's goals and challenges, we understand that employees expect that company to value and respect their hearts and souls as well as their minds and bodies.

We also know that people today want to be trusted. Trivial rules, procedures, or policies that imply individuals cannot be trusted to do the right thing on their own used to be standard in the workplace. Today most employees consider them an insult. People want their company to assume that they will come to work on time, work hard, and contribute to the cause each day without needing stopwatches, regulations, forms, or rigid policies and procedures to ensure this behavior. The days when employees were blindly willing to do what they were told and follow their bosses' instructions and their company's policies without question are gone forever. Today, most people want a voice in how their work environment functions, and want to contribute to as many decisions affecting their life on the job as possible.

At Dreyer's Ice Cream, we have always acknowledged and encouraged individual initiative and decision making to the maximum extent practicable. We believe that only by truly empowering our people can we sustain their enthusiasm and personal satisfaction over time.

This set of beliefs underlies our "I Can Make A Difference" philosophy and are [sic] at the core of everything we do here.

We express our "I Can Make A Difference" philosophy in ten tenets or "Grooves" by which we all try to live in our daily interactions with one another. Our grooves are our corporate culture, our values, and "the way we do things around here." We believe that if people understand this basic philosophy and "get in the Grooves," we don't need many policies, rules, or procedures manuals. Empowered individuals can simply use their own good judgment to arrive at appropriate decisions on their own. In other words, our Grooves create a work environment where each individual is empowered, involved, and encouraged (indeed expected) to truly "make a difference" in our success as a company.

Groove #1—Management Is People

We believe that people are the most important resource at Dreyer's. Therefore, people issues are the **primary** responsibility of our managers, supervisors, and self-managed teams. We expect them to hire, train, inspire, develop, coach, and discipline each person in [their] department, as well as foster an environment that encourages behavior consistent with the Grooves. Unlike many companies, we don't relegate these responsibilities to a centralized human resources or legal department. Our managers know their employees and situations best, they make the people-related decisions in their departments, and they live with the consequences. Our People Support and Legal Team exist to support employees and managers by providing information, resources, training, and guidance to assist in their decision-making but not to dilute the local responsibility.

Groove #2—Hire Smart

The most important thing we do in this company is deciding who should be on our team. If we hire smart, we will have well-qualified, highly motivated people who are a good fit for both our business challenges and our culture. In this case, we can simply get out of their way and let them succeed! Conversely, if we don't hire smart, we will spend interminable hours dealing with the consequences. (We call this "managing tough," and it's no fun.) Accordingly, we invest a great deal of time and care in the selection process to ensure we hire only the very best people possible. Everyone invited to join Dreyer's Ice Cream in any position should be in the top twenty percent of all qualified candidates for that position—including candidates from both inside and outside the company. Being a "top twenty percenter" is a high standard to maintain, and all Dreyer's employees are held accountable for continuing performance at that level. Hire Smart also means that when someone fails to maintain the standard, we need to be tough-minded in dealing with the situation. The way that we "eliminate mediocrity" is first through coaching and development aimed at eliminating the problem. If our best efforts to get an employee back to the level of a "top twenty percenter" in all areas of performance are unsuccessful, then we must make the decision to terminate the relationship. Obviously we always try to accomplish this in a sensitive, respectful, and appropriate manner.

Groove #3—Respect for the Individual

Respect for the Individual is the underlying philosophy running through every single Groove. If we consistently hire smart and are tough-minded about eliminating mediocrity, we will have responsible, competent, energetic, self-motivated people working for us throughout our company. People like this don't need to be motivated, they need to be **liberated**. Therefore, we respect our people's ideas, perspectives, and abilities by trusting them to do their jobs their way and without unnecessary rules, structure, or controls. Our job is to hire good people, inculcate our values, provide appropriate training, and then "let them do their thing."

Experience has shown that people will generally validate whatever their employer expects of them. If we assume people are honest and want to do a good job, they usually will. Conversely, if we do what most companies do, which is to assume people are not trustworthy, can't make decisions, and will cut corners at every opportunity, then that is the behavior that will result. Although this is a very powerful concept, it doesn't work 100% of the time. A few people will invariably abuse this trusting, open approach, but the vast majority will respect it for what it is and thrive under it. Our approach is to say, "we trust you" to **all** of the people who work here and to use the concept of weeding out mediocrity to deal with the few who abuse that trust. We have found the benefits of this approach vastly overweigh the risks. If we give people the freedom to do their jobs their way, they will develop ownership and pride and make the greatest contribution they possibly can. Our approach is to create the vision, engender enthusiasm for the task at hand, and then trust our people to do the right thing.

Groove #4—People Involvement

People Involvement means just that—allowing people to get involved in our business in a broader way than just doing their specific job or function. As a fast-growing company in a rapidly changing industry, we face a myriad of new challenges, problems, and opportunities every day. Our chances of successfully responding to all of this change are increased if we can harness the thinking, ideas, and energy of a wide cross section of people. Furthermore, if we allow people at all levels to participate and get involved in new aspects of our business, then they will grow as individuals and feel better about the contribution they are making. When this happens, they will inevitably experience greater levels of productivity and satisfaction.

There are many ways to involve people in this Groove. Examples include cross training, task forces, cross-functional project teams, involving peers in recruiting and interviewing prospective employees, and community support efforts on behalf of the company. Many of our departments or teams are organized in a team management system designed to increase involvement, responsibility, and accountability for their own work and development. One prerequisite condition for People Involvement is an open atmosphere of trust and respect. For people to truly feel involved, they must know that their input and ideas are valued as making a difference. People Involvement also means being aware of who is impacted by one's actions and decisions and finding ways to involve and communicate with those people effectively.

Groove #5—Ownership

Each of us only goes around the track once in life, so we owe it to ourselves to enjoy the journey.

We think the best way for people to enjoy the part of their journey that involves working here at Dreyer's is to derive satisfaction by being the best we can be at what we do. Taking ownership means taking pride in being the best at something. If you become "the best" at some aspect of your job, and are recognized as such by your co-workers, then you "own" it. If you go home with a smile on your face because you are recognized by your co-workers as being really expert at some aspect of your job, then you have achieved Ownership. And Ownership is lots of fun! We **expect** everyone here at Dreyer's to "own" some aspect of his or her job. This is truly the essence of our "I Can Make A Difference" philosophy. It is important to understand that achieving Ownership is each employee's responsibility. Ownership is like respect in that it can't be given or demanded; it has to be earned. While each individual is responsible for achieving Ownership, it is essential that we all provide an environment where it can flourish.

Groove #6—Hoopla

Hoopla is the celebration of ownership. Hoopla is simply acknowledging individual or team accomplishments of all kinds. Hoopla is one of our core values because we believe people deserve to be celebrated for their contributions. Praise and recognition are the most powerful motivators. People love to be told they are doing a good job or that they are "the best" at something. Nothing reinforces success or enhances performance more than recognition from one's peers or manager. Our people think they are great and there is no reason to disagree with them. We look for any opportunity to tell our people they did a good job—for both small and large accomplishments. People will always respond to honest, positive feedback with a desire to contribute even more. Hoopla is best when it is spontaneous, unpredictable, and intermittent. It's the care and personal recognition that counts in Hoopla, not the size of the plaque. While picnics and parties are a lot of fun, they are not Hoopla unless individuals or groups are being recognized for specific accomplishments.

Groove #7—Learn, Learn, Learn

If we have hired smart and, therefore, have highly qualified, motivated, and experienced people throughout the company, our only other prerequisite for success is ensuring these people get the information and learn the skills needed to be effective in their jobs. Learning is an everyday, never-ending process for all of us. Much like ownership, learning is not an optional activity. While it is the responsibility of the company to create an environment conducive to learning and development, each individual must seek ways within that environment to continually improve and update his or her capabilities. Learning opportunities are all around us and take many more shapes and forms than just traditional classroom training.

When people first join Dreyer's Ice Cream, they need to learn our

Grooves, they need to understand our history and our traditions, and they need to know how we operate, what will be expected of them, and what they can expect from us. Beyond this fundamental orientation, they obviously need to learn the specifics of their particular job. Over a period of time, they then need to develop to greater and greater depths so that they can become experts and "own" their job. Having achieved that, good people will inevitably want to learn additional skills and new functions so that they can grow as individuals, become more broadly involved with the business, and progress in their career. The need for learning never ends for anyone.

Groove #8—Face-to-Face Communication

One of the most effective ways we learn and grow is by getting feedback on what we're doing well and what we need to improve. Good people want feedback. We believe that everyone at Dreyer's needs and deserves honest feedback on a regular basis. Furthermore, managers need to carefully listen and learn from what their people have to say or suggest on an ongoing basis. We want our people to care about our company and our business, and to become personally involved in it. Face-to-Face Communication helps give them the information they need to do just that. Face-to-Face Communication should be an open dialogue—a respectful two-way exchange of ideas and information. It demands more of each of us than many traditional hierarchical approaches. Each individual at Dreyer's needs to know that he or she is expected to come forward with suggestions, ideas, questions, and concerns. It is equally important that we all have the skills and ability to handle conflict and receive feedback openly, as well. This kind of honest communication is often the catalyst for our greater learning.

At Dreyer's we want to maintain an environment where anyone can talk to anyone else at any time about any subject without fear of political implications or reprisals. Although people have an obligation to keep their supervisor, manager, or team informed of their activities and opinions, we encourage them to also communicate honestly and openly with anyone else they wish at any level of the organization. Because this practice is often frowned upon in other companies, we have to constantly work to insure that, here at Dreyer's, open and honest communication is both an expectation and a right of every employee.

Groove #9—Upside Down Organization

Organization charts, including our own, are invariably drawn upside down. We all need to recognize that the people who are in the best position to impact the business on a day-to-day basis are the people on the "front lines" of the organization. Front liners include those who actually make our products, move them through the distribution system, and do the necessary accounting. The rest of us are here to make their jobs easier and to help them be more effective. The manager's or supervisor's job is really that of a coach—creating the vision, aligning, energizing, and developing while allowing each individual the flexibility and autonomy to make his or her own decisions about the best way to get the job done. Oakland and management staffs exist to support our people in the field, not to control them. We believe that the person closest to an issue usually has the best perspective on it and can, therefore, usually make the best decision. Accordingly, we try to minimize the number of decisions made centrally to maximize the opportunity for our people to make decisions on the firing line in the way they think best. For this same reason, we try to minimize the number of policies we have here at Dreyer's. We think in terms of having proven practices as opposed to policies. Although we try to decentralize decision-making, there is no reason to constantly reinvent the wheel, and we should all seek to benefit from the collective wisdom of our past experience as reflected in these proven practices. Our proven practices are usually quite sound, but our managers can always choose to operate differently if they have good reason to do so.

Groove #10—Ready, Fire, Aim

One of our primary competitive advantages has always been that we are more flexible and can make decisions more quickly than most of our competitors. Here at Dreyer's, "we love change" because it usually works to our advantage.

As part of this philosophy, we want to encourage our people to learn by constantly trying new things and testing their ideas to see what actually works in practice. We call these tests "small starts." People will only experiment with small starts if they know it is okay to fail. We need to encourage "failing forward" by recognizing people for trying new things and pushing the envelope, even if they don't pan out. We have to remember that, like learning to ski, we aren't getting any better unless we are falling down from time to time.

Good ideas don't need to be perfect before we begin implementation. Whether a new product, a new manufacturing process, or a change in distribution or sales technique, often we can learn most effectively by "readying" ourselves with appropriate planning, "firing" by trying out the new idea on a small scale or test basis, and then "aiming" as we learn from our experience. Ready, Fire, Aim may sound somewhat risky, and does require that we are willing to take "intelligent risks." But we believe it is a far better strategy than the "analysis paralysis" that so many companies suffer from today. As we continue to grow, we must maintain our bias for action, our agility, and our ability to use change as our ally.

This is truly a powerful and admirable set of tenets for an organization. Even the way in which Dreyer's inculcates the Grooves is unique. They take a completely decentralized approach in how they communicate the Grooves and measure their impact on the organization. The Grooves are the meta-objectives that enable Dreyer's to succeed at its business objectives.

Part II. Dreyer's Case Study—The Grooves and Stories

The Oakland Grooves Task Force Team, composed of individuals from all different parts of the Dreyer's organization, asked me to analyze the Grooves and share with them some of the ways stories could be put to use. Below is a summary of the presentation I gave them. For each Groove, I discuss the role of stories and potential benefits.

Respect for the Individual

Tolerance is not respect. We pay a lot of lip service to giving each other respect; however, this has come about more as a result of political correctness than any real shift in consciousness or behavior. Real respect comes from active listening. When we listen actively to each other's stories, experiences, and ideas, we are able to enter someone else's point of view. This is the essence of compassion. We do not artificially lose our perspective, but we become simultaneously aware of another one. Stories enable us to imagine multiple perspectives and to compassionately stand in someone else's shoes. Entering new frames of reference requires a leap of creative imagination possible only through the agency of vehicles like stories.

Potential Benefits

- Diverse, well-integrated teams are possible.
- Synergized teams composed of individuals from different functional areas and personal backgrounds can act on corporate directives more quickly and with greater chances of success than homogeneous teams.

Management Is People

People are a priority. People are not effectively managed or motivated when they are links in a long chain of command. What tools do managers use to be responsive and fully present with people? Are best practices always the most effective tools? Managers need to hear employees' stories. Roger Schank at Northwestern University's Institute of Learning has demonstrated that intelligence can be measured in terms of how well we index our experiences and stories.[1] In order to manage people, we must be managers of stories. Managers need to be aware of their employees' stories, develop techniques for eliciting these stories, and learn how to think on their feet to respond with appropriate stories.

Potential Benefits

- Employees become invigorated, personally connected contributors.
- Work becomes a creative and personal outlet, not just a job.

Hire Smart

A hiring manager must be able to look beyond the dictates of a job description and the one-dimensional details of a resume. Each candidate is a story waiting to unfold. Hiring smart requires managers to look for relationships between candidates' experiences, personal competencies, and the requirements of the job. A standard set of questions will not reveal the valuable information needed to individually assess each candidate. Crafting a customized line of questions based upon the flow of conversation is a skill that can be learned. These questions will elicit stories from the candidate. The hiring manager must then examine these stories in relation to one another and in relation to statements made by the candidate. Are there any obvious incongruencies?

Hiring managers also need to use stories as a powerful means of painting a picture of the job. This enables the candidate to envision how he or she will make a difference, and motivates the candidate to join the organization.

Potential Benefits

- Low turnover.
- Motivated employees.
- Clear sense of purpose.
- Rapid, effective, task accomplishment.
- Understand and see how individual contributions benefit the organization and its objectives.

Ownership

We need to provide a forum and opportunity for people to share their success stories. Others need to hear our stories of how we have succeeded, and of how we have been able to make a difference in the organization. This also becomes a venue for employees to share stories of the times when perhaps they have not excelled. Such stories are also very important. One person's success may be another person's failure. We learn from each other's successes and failures. Story sessions are a great vehicle for owning our successes and raising the bar.

Potential Benefits

- Facilitates knowledge transfer.
- Enhances customer and product intelligence.

Learn, Learn, Learn

Stories used in training improve communication and accelerate learning. Any training we design should include stories as a core part of its method. Approached in this way, training becomes unpredictable but extremely powerful. Relegate informational or didactic training to self-paced delivery mechanisms. Eliciting participants' experiences in the form of stories during a training session allows an exchange of knowledge and experience.

Potential Benefits

- Employee retention.
- Career paths.

Upside Down Organization

Managers are challenged to be story collectors. Managers will not magically benefit from the experiences and ideas of those closest to the job unless they are skilled at getting employees to share their stories.

Potential Benefits

- Product, customer, and job intelligence enhanced.
- Reduction in overhead necessary to support processes and best practices.

People Involvement

Involve people in story making. Stories encourage people to see possibilities and to work with new ideas. Given a scenario, people can create situations and roles in order to envision bold ideas and realize latent possibilities. Stories offer the tools of images, analogies, metaphors, and visual cues for imagining new personal and organizational realities.

Potential Benefits

- Fewer management layers.
- Inefficient processes are reduced or eliminated.

Ready, Fire, Aim

Business moves quickly. An agile organizational structure requires employees to develop agile minds. Stories build flexible and dynamic minds. Ideas can take form and be morphed as necessary. Stories fuel our ability to quickly adapt to the ebb and flow of a dynamic market. They enable us to envision our plan even as it unfolds. In the end, we remember our experience in the form of a story, extract lessons learned, and share our knowledge with others in the form of stories.

Potential Benefits

- Fosters agile culture.
- Encourages entrepreneurial behavior.

Hoopla

We are sometimes guilty of believing we have no stories to tell. While each person has a different communication style, we all have a wealth of great stories to share. Regardless of the style or personality of the teller, we all have a wonderful capacity to amaze each other with our tales of success. Story sessions get the juices going and yield a treasure chest full of riches.

Potential Benefits

- Motivated employees.
- Attractive place to work = visible company and desirable product.

Face-to-Face Communication

Face-to-face communication is intimate. It requires trust and vulnerability. Stories need to be shared in both directions. Through stories we are able to create an environment of trust, and bind and bond with one another in ways not possible otherwise.

Potential Benefit

- Quick resolution of issues.

Part III. Dreyer's Case Study—Communication Intervention in the Personal Channel

The task force decided it wanted to do some work with Hoopla. Of all the Grooves, Hoopla was ranked the lowest on a recent survey in terms of people's perception of its use and adoption. We decided to put together a pizza and Hoopla stories session to get people's energy flowing. The hour-and-a-half session was very simple. People were naturally grouped around tables. Over 100 people attended. After some brief discussion on my part to give people an idea of what we were doing, and some background information on how stories work, people started sharing their Hoopla stories at the tables. Below is a copy of what we gave people to help them get started:

Stories and Hoopla

In order to inculcate Hoopla we need to Hoopla our Hoopla. In other words, let's celebrate the ways in which Hoopla has made a difference at Dreyer's. One of the best ways we can do this is by becoming aware of all the ways and times Hoopla has been present. Then if we share our experiences with one another, we will be fueling our commitment to creating a culture of praise and recognition.

Objectives

- Use stories to learn about areas of ownership and accomplishment.
- Use stories to gauge and chronicle Hoopla's presence and impact on our culture.
- Use stories to discover and understand how our actions small and large, individual and team, create a culture that facilitates the achievement and ongoing revisioning of organizational objectives.

Some Starters for Getting the Story Juices Going

Think of examples of things you have done that reflect your sense of ownership and care. Try rewinding your "mental video tape" of a typical day on the job as a way of getting started. Here are the questions to use to trigger stories from one another:

1. Recall times when others recognized your efforts.
2. What are some examples of small things you do that may easily go unnoticed?
3. What are small things that others have done that you have noticed but may not have acknowledged?

At the end we reconvened as a large group and went around the room while each table shared some of the stories they had heard. People had lots of examples to share. They were surprised to realize all of the different ways and times the Hoopla groove was at work. Listening to each other's stories brought forth a flood of stories and personal revelations. People left feeling more engaged with some concrete ideas of how to cultivate the values of the Groove, being more aware of how it operates, and with some memorable stories to share with co-workers who were not at the session.

This is a simple but powerful example of how stories were used to tune in to frequencies. Dreyer's did not try to broadcast a message or story to reinforce its cultural values; instead, they ignited a dialogue of reflective stories. Working in the personal channel we were able to push stories about the Hoopla groove in order to pull additional stories from people's untapped experiences and inspire them to leave the session equipped to push stories further into the organization. In addition, the experience of the session has become a triggering "story," acting as a reminder of all the Grooves at Dreyer's, especially Hoopla.

Note

1. According to Roger Schank, "Stories are everywhere, but not all stories look like stories. If you consider a story to be a previously prepared gist of something to say, something that you have said before or heard another say, then a great deal of conversation is simply mutual storytelling. Moreover, if the majority of what we say is in our memories in the form of previously prepared stories, the way we look at the nature of understanding and what it means to be intelligent must change. Is being very intelligent just having a great many stories to tell? Is it adopting superficially irrelevant stories into relevant ones, i.e., finding a story in one domain and applying it by analogy to another? Maybe it means combining stories and making generalizations from them, or, perhaps intelligence is embodied in the initial process of collecting stories to tell in the first place." (Roger Schank, *Tell Me A Story: A New Look at Real and Artificial Memory*, pp. 26–27).

5
Organizational Learning: Building Bridges

In this chapter we will examine how communication is the cornerstone of learning. Communication will be shown to be the key to building bridges between learning and collective experience. Organizational learning is a function of communication. Learning is fluid. It would be nice if learning could be tightly wrapped up into neat bundles of sustainable objectives, but that is rarely the case. Discrete skills that form a part of an organization's ongoing technical competencies can be rolled into repeatable training programs; however, these represent just a fraction of an organization's learning needs.

There have been some excellent efforts to revitalize learning in organizations. Most organizations have come to realize that training is not necessarily learning. As always, theory lags behind practice. Corporate universities offer a smorgasbord of courses that have little relation to the real-time needs of employees. And while we pay lip service to the importance of linking learning with business objectives, there are few success stories.

We can explore the meaning of learning by noticing that the word *learn* has the word *earn* within it. Learning does not happen in a passive manner. We have to work at it. Whatever we learn has been earned through effort. As students, we undoubtedly were reminded by our teachers and parents to "apply ourselves" and "put our minds to it." Stashing facts away in memory doesn't go very far, and it doesn't take long before we run out of room. Information left in memory quickly loses its relevance. Memorizing facts might have gotten us through exams, but it is unlikely to fundamentally change our understanding of ourselves or the world around us. Learning occurs as the result of building constructs.

Observe a baby in action, and you see a human sponge soaking up everything around him. Each new experience becomes a data point that has to be related to previous ones. In the beginning there are few known data points. Eventually, there comes a time when there is a critical mass of information.

Suddenly, enough is known to start connecting the data points. The brain's pattern recognition capacities take over. Shades of meaning become possible because they are related to known constructs. This understanding of learning as an act of building one construct from another leads us to the analogy of organizational learning as building bridges. If bridges enable us to safely cross over bodies of water or land, learning enables people in our organizations to close gaps in their skills and share experiences in order to succeed in achieving organizational objectives. Communication is the vehicle through which all of this happens.

Here are some underlying assumptions to guide our discussion:

1. Learning cannot occur without communication.

I think we get confused in organizations when we try to make learning an isolated activity. Learning happens all the time. Without it an organization would be unable to function. We can measure learning more easily when it is event driven. Training is a perfect case in point. We define a need, develop an intervention, and execute an event. Along the way we try to evaluate what we are doing and its impact on the organization. What if we were to see learning as a function of communication? When we start a new job, we attend various trainings and orientation sessions, but our greatest source of learning comes from conversations. As we strive to understand our job, people are our greatest source of information. The quality of the conversations we have will directly impact how quickly we get up to speed.

Conversations change in real time. Depending on the flow of ideas, a conversation has the potential to move in different directions. There is a similarity between the fluid nature of conversations and the learning needs of an organization. Learning is a moving target. We cannot pin down the learning requirements for an organization. We can develop competency models. We can perform gap analyses. We can articulate learning objectives. These are all valid pursuits; however, they will not help us build an agile company. Business objectives need to be adjusted. As our business objectives change, so do our learning requirements. There is not enough time to ramp up a whole new training agenda. Just-in-time information is required. Communication does not have the same overhead as instructor-led courses, job aids, or e-learning. We do not need a learning management system to track employees or a chief learning officer to institute corporate learning scorecards. What we need are communication fabrics that support reflective behavior and encourage sharing. Although this may sound idealistic, it can be more easily achieved than one might imagine. The problem is that these simple principles, which are capable of creating complex, rich behaviors, fly in the face of what we assume possible. This is more a function of arrogance than anything else. Arrogance is dangerous. It has a tendency to maximize our self-importance and minimize the potential of others.

If we understand the principles of effective communication, we can design continuously learning organizations. We need organizations composed of self-aware individuals in perpetual learning motion along with a culture that promotes sharing. Learning is not a trophy that is won by an individual. Learning increases the collective intelligence of the whole. We can accelerate learning by optimizing the social interconnections of people. In Chapter 3 we identified three channels of communication (formalized, socialized, and personalized). The greatest potential for learning lies in the personalized channel. While it may appear trite on the surface, everyone is a learner, everyone is a teacher, and anyone can pursue the learning required to succeed. These are themes we will spend considerable time addressing in the last part of the book, where we will focus predominantly on how to develop the communication and learning capacities of individuals in order to achieve greater organizational effectiveness. It turns out that top-down efforts to build a learning organization are unlikely to succeed and, if they do, even harder to sustain. Our hope lies in developing people.

2. There is a difference between learning and training.

The training function in an organization seems to be meeting the fate of Human Resources (HR). HR departments are rapidly losing their relevance. Lost in the minutia of legalese, they are trying desperately to reinvent themselves by outsourcing benefits administration, using enterprise resource planning tools to automate functions, putting in place self-service transactional portals for employees, focusing on human performance, embracing organizational development, developing knowledge management systems, and throwing around lingo like *human capital*. Despite these efforts, most HR departments fall short of being a true strategic tool for organizations. It is too cookie-cutter an approach, and while cookie cutters create pretty cookies to eat, they waste a lot of dough and require tedious amounts of attention. No one would disagree that people are an organization's greatest asset; we just don't match the talk with the walk.

In lean times the first thing a company cuts is training. It is viewed as expendable, and it is hard for companies to justify time away from a job to pursue learning objectives that in many instances only vaguely relate to the job, let alone the organization's objectives. Driven by the imperative to save money but salvage training, instructor-led programs are replaced with a myriad of self-paced modalities like computer-based training, web-based training, or distance learning. These are delivery tools and as such do not constitute any significant difference from their instructor-led counterparts. Oftentimes the quality of many of these products is so poor that they end up eroding the importance of training and the appeal of learning.

As companies look to reduce costs, we can expect a number of trends in the learning arena. To begin with, companies will spend less money on training and depend more on e-learning solutions. It is beyond the scope of our discussion here, but it is very difficult to design good e-learning courses. Many products fail to leverage the nonlinear, self-paced characteristics of e-learning. Companies spend less money on inferior products, with a growing dissatisfaction on the part of learners and frustration on the part of organizations when they realize that the learning interventions they are implementing are not having a significant, measurable impact on employees' performance.

Another trend we can expect in the learning arena is outsourcing. Learning is not perceived as a unique strategic advantage. Even if it is recognized as being important, it is ancillary. Given this mindset, learning plays a supporting role and is not accepted as a competitive advantage. Of course there are times when it makes sense to utilize the expertise of an outside partner. However, I think it is naïve to assume that even the best collaborative partners will be able to track shifting business objectives and link them back to real-time learning objectives. Any training business has to create repeatable processes and stock products that can be tweaked from one customer to the next. Companies that follow this trend will throw away a built-in competitive advantage. How a company communicates and how a company learns should be considered trade secrets. The companies that succeed in these arenas will be the most agile and successful.

3. Learning needs to be dynamically linked to business objectives.

We do an excellent job identifying what resources we need to bring a product or service to market. We have detailed processes for managing projects and creating work breakdown structures. However, when it comes to intangibles like learning and experience, we fail to adequately plan for what we will need in order to succeed. Business objectives involve a whole host of these intangible factors. Learning fits into that category. We confuse learning with training. The templates we use to create our project plans have an area called training. Someone throws a couple of bullets on a page, assigns a dollar amount, puts a date on a schedule, and in the end something that mimics a learning process is rolled out behind schedule and usually underfunded. It's a grim picture, but one that many of us see time and time again.

So how do we align learning objectives with our business objectives? If our business objectives are changing, how do we adapt our learning strategies to ensure they are supporting our objectives? We have to rely on employees. We need to inculcate reflective behavior. Imagine if employees constantly asked themselves, "What can I do that is within my scope of responsibility to help the business achieve its objectives?" "How do the business's objectives relate to my job?" and "What do I need to learn in order to succeed?" These questions should be in the back of every employee's mind. Managers and peers operate as coaches, cheerleaders, teachers, informants, and mirrors for the reflective employee.

Individual Learning Plans or Professional Development Plans are a step in the right direction but fail to achieve the type of dynamism I am driving at here. They tend to be focused on the employee. We have a habit of inadvertently playing a game of white lies with employees. We want employees to believe the organization cares about their personal and professional growth. This is truly admirable, and there is always an ounce of truth in a white lie, but the fact of the matter is that an organization is not a soft and fuzzy caring animal. Neither is it cold and calculating. It simply is. An organization is an entity without any other purpose than to survive and succeed. The mission of an organization persists with or without its same core group of people. Let's put a different spin on this. Here are three basic assumptions that give us something more honest to sink our teeth into:

1. Learning ensures the success of an organization.
2. Learning is fun.
3. Continually learning and stretching our knowledge in new directions and seeking unique experiences is a fundamentally exhilarating and desirable human endeavor.

If you are scrutinizing these assumptions because they are value laden, keep on scrutinizing. Of course they are value laden, but who can fault these lofty values? Too many employees are bored. Repetitive administrative tasks occupy a greater percentage of people's time than they should. Give people a chance to stretch into new responsibilities. Allow them to develop new skills and everyone will benefit in the process. This does not mean that everyone will succeed. There will be times when a delegated task that requires an employee to learn something new will fall through the cracks or be done less than satisfactorily. These are the risks. In my opinion these are also the exceptions and not the rule, so the benefits far outweigh the risks.

4. Communication ties together learning and collective experience.

We have established that learning cannot occur without communication. New information comes to us externally through various forms of communication, and we work with them through a series of internal communication processes in order to transform them into learning. Figure 5.1 shows how communication binds learning and collective knowledge together. It becomes much easier to design learning interventions if we think of them as communication and not discrete entities. Collective experience fits into this picture by showing how experiences shared through ongoing communication facilitate learning.

We need to picture an organization as a huge mass of learning potential. Every person has a wealth of experience. Whether it has been gained from life experiences, a previous organization, or the current one, people are constantly adding to their base of knowledge. True, there are many different types of knowledge, but the way we acquire and work with them is more or less the same. Expert information is an obvious example. When an individual possesses specialized experience in a particular area, we refer to this as expert information. It is easy to see a relationship between an individual's expert knowledge and its value to the organization. However, there are also more subtle forms of knowledge, such as wisdom, that can have a profound effect on others if we find a way to tap into them. We will explore this aspect of knowledge in Part III of the book. Suffice it to say, we want people to apply learning from one area into another.

5. Organizational learning needs to enhance employees' experiences to achieve business objectives.

Figure 5.2 illustrates the flow of learning and its relationship to different objectives. The box labeled "the world" represents all of our past, present, and future experiences. Fortunately, our lives are not confined to an organization. People move in and out of organizations. How much of what we experience in the world do we synthesize into learning? This is what the valve in the picture depicts. We have many opportunities to acquire new learning. Every experience becomes a story waiting to offer us learning. For the learning we do acquire, how much do we bring back into the organization? Some of that is dependent upon how much our organization promotes sharing of learning. Organizations with an open style of communication that treats the personalized channel of communication as a

Figure 5.1 **The Relationship Among Communication, Learning, and Collective Experience**

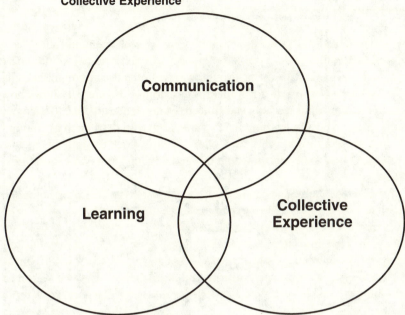

strategic tool succeeds in maximizing employees' learning experiences. These become accessible to others and an invaluable part of the potential collective experience of the organization. The arrows in the boxes labeled "self" and "organization" show the movement of learning within each domain and the relationship of these domains to business objectives, learning objectives, and personal objectives. Three separate objectives are used to signify the diversity of goals and the challenge of aligning these with one another.

The box at the bottom of Figure 5.2 narrates the process of learning. The process begins when we encounter any new construct. I am using the word *construct* loosely to refer to any entity that does not already fit into our set of known data points. Each new construct is brought into awareness by our experience of it. Even if this is strictly a mental phenomenon we must merge the abstract recognition with real-time awareness. By doing so, we win some level of understanding. Learning becomes actualized when we can apply it to achieve objectives.

Translating high-level business objectives into learning objectives is an iterative, reflective process. If the business objectives are too big, we need to break them down into smaller chunks and relate them to our responsibilities. For example, take the following objective:

Figure 5.2 The Flow of Learning

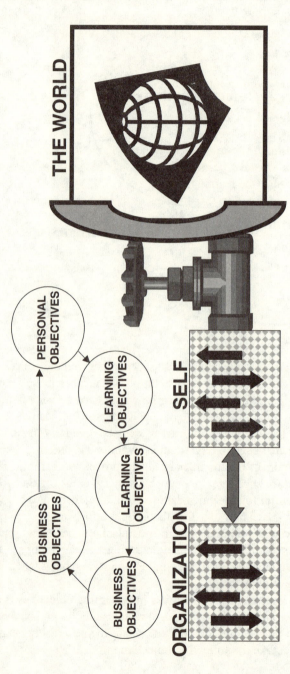

THE WORLD

PERSONAL
OBJECTIVES

BUSINESS
OBJECTIVES

LEARNING
OBJECTIVES

LEARNING
OBJECTIVES

BUSINESS
OBJECTIVES

SELF

ORGANIZATION

The Learning Process

- We *encounter* new CONSTRUCTS
- We *discover* them through EXPERIENCES
- We *gain* UNDERSTANDING so that by our BEHAVIORS we can *achieve* objectives

Increase revenues by 15 percent by developing distribution agreements with new partners in untapped markets. Here are some questions to guide the process of turning the business objective into a learning objective:

1. What parts of my current responsibilities or new responsibilities, if I take initiative to assume optional ones, can contribute to the success of this objective?
2. Is there anything I need to do differently to help the organization achieve this business objective?
3. Do I have the requisite experience and knowledge to take action?
4. What do I need to learn to be effective in tackling these responsibilities?
5. How can I acquire the learning I need?
6. Can I use any of my other experiences or the experiences of others to achieve my learning objectives?
7. How will I share the learning I acquire? Who else might benefit from it?
8. Did the successful completion of my learning objective help me contribute to the business objective in the manner I had hoped?
9. Do I need to modify my strategy? If I do, will I need to determine new learning objectives?
10. Has the business objective changed?

This is not a formula. What it amounts to is reflection in motion turned into learning. We determine the prize, keep our eye on it, and use it is a guide to help us determine how to win it. Learning will always be a fundamental aspect of winning the prize. Next, we capture the knowledge gained and bundle it into lessons learned. Then, in order to complete the cycle we look for opportunities to share the experience gained. When we share our experiences, it becomes part of the organization's collective experience.

6. Experiences are communicated through stories.

Throughout this book stories act as a central metaphor for understanding effective communication and learning. The best way to relate an experience is through a story. It is natural. Stories give the teller a container to package and move his information while simultaneously providing the listeners a handle on its context in order to understand what they are receiving. In essence, stories act as a communication delivery mechanism. Regardless of right- and left-brain differences, or a person's dominant thinking style, imagination plays a vital role in learning. The imagination is the medium through which connections are made, and stories are the richest way to stimulate the imagination.

Summary

We have shown how communication is the cornerstone of learning. To support this view of learning, we adopted six key assumptions:

1. Learning cannot occur without communication.
2. There is a difference between learning and training.
3. Learning needs to be dynamically linked to business objectives.
4. Communication ties learning and collective experience together.
5. Organizational learning needs to utilize employees' experiences to achieve its business objectives.
6. Experiences are communicated through stories.

These assumptions establish the relationship between communication, learning, and collective knowledge. The functions of stories and their unique effects were demonstrated to be a central aspect of how the relationship between these three works. The last section of the book will identify the competencies required to be an effective communicator and learner and show you how to develop them.

6

Case Studies: DTE Energy and Jeff Bukantz

The two case studies in this chapter illustrate the interrelationship between communication and learning. In the first, we see how DTE Energy overcomes change-management challenges brought about by a merger with another company. During the process, a technical training intervention becomes an opportunity for employees to share stories. This case study demonstrates the importance of the personal channel of the Communications Matrix we discussed in Chapter 2 and shows how one company succeeds in tapping into this area. Although retention of the technical material covered during the training had a rapid decay, the relationships people built through communication during the series of classes has proven to be long lasting and the major benefit of the training intervention. In the end, the goals of the change management initiative were exceeded, and people succeeded in creating an effective social fabric of collective experience. Future business objectives will be more easily met because the personal channel of the Communications Matrix is primed. People are willing, ready, and able to benefit from each other's experiences.

The case study of Jeff Bukantz shows the importance of reflection. Faced with a life-changing event, Jeff must remake himself. In Part III we will discuss reflection in greater detail, but for now think of it as a form of self-communication. In other words, by reflecting on his personal experiences in the form of stories, we see how Jeff discovers new insights and turns them into learning. He succeeds in creating a new vision and mission for himself. The same stories that catalyzed insights also become the template for Jeff's new role. These reflective principles made possible by the functions of stories and their unique effects operate on the level of an individual, as in the case of Jeff, and for groups as well.

Case Study: DTE Energy ITS Knowledge Builder Initiative (January 2002–December 2004)

Knowledge Builder has been instrumental in upgrading the technical skills of the IT department. An additional bonus has been the spirit of collaboration and cohesiveness that has carried over into the culture of the department.
—Lynne Ellyn, Sr. VP and CIO

It is amazing what can be accomplished when you truly focus on the business's needs.
—Osbin Cooper, Project Manager, ITS Knowledge Builder

This case study tells an important story. It is a clear example of the central role communication plays in learning. Collective knowledge is also shown to be a central part of this change management strategy. The results and outcomes surprised everyone.

Detroit Edison was in the midst of a merger with Michigan Gas. A team of which I was part was brought in to develop a change management strategy for the information technology (IT) teams. The challenge was how to build synergy between two IT teams with very different practices, processes, standards, and ideas. Our goal was to enable the new combined IT organization to become a leader in continuous learning, and in the process create a knowledge-intensive culture. (See box for the context of the project as described in DTE Energy's business case.)

Solution

After spending time on-site with a wide range of subject matter experts and gaining a feel for the overall climate, I worked with them to design six classes—the Knowledge Builder Initiative. Cohorts of twenty-four people representing a wide range of functional areas and experiences, and composed of members of both companies were created. These cohorts went through all six classes together. This was instrumental in breaking down barriers between the merging companies, building new relationships, and providing ample opportunities for people to share their knowledge.

All of the classes were four days in length except for the first one, which was only two. Participants were provided with breakfast, lunch, and valet parking at an off-site hotel. Each class included a pre- and post-test as part of the evaluation process. This created some problems in the beginning. We had to help everyone understand that their scores were not being used to evaluate their position in the company. In other words, no one's position was in

---

Description of Business Opportunity

Information and intellectual capital is a valuable corporate asset to DTE Energy. The Information Technology Services (ITS) organization is challenged to become the best of the best in aligning IT solutions with the business goals and strategies. Business solutions with a competitive advantage are becoming more innovative and complex with an increasing reliance on ITS to enable DTE Energy meet business goals. Our employees need to be informed IT ambassadors with the right knowledge at any time.

According to a national IT industry survey dated June 2001, on the "*Top 10 Best Places to Work in IT for Training,*" the overall average training provided per employee is 13 days and $10,000 annually. The company that ranked #1 provides an annual average of 17 days of training per year, per employee, and spends $9,200 annually. Training is also one of the top motivators for employee retention.

Our challenge is to become an adaptable knowledge-intensive organization that ensures the right number of people with the right skills set at the right time. To support this continuous learning culture, we need a training solution that replicates benchmarks from best in class organizations and allows customizable content.

Below are some of the causes and symptoms that hinder ITS from becoming a knowledge-intensive organization:

- Need to build team synergy between Michigan Gas and Detroit Edison Information Technology (IT) groups after the merger
- Need to balance the knowledge inequality between the two groups
- Employees understand their functional IT role, but not how their role effects other IT areas
- Employee turnover must be reduced in ITS due to lack of opportunities for training or career advancement
- Training not offered equally to employees
- Lack of organization-wide strategic continuous learning opportunities
- Lack of knowledge management and rewards for knowledge sharing
- Emerging concepts and technologies are not deployed in a timely manner
- Lack of base-level training for the entire organization
- Lack of mechanism and tools to deploy current and new methodologies to the ITS organization

---

jeopardy. The last class in the series was a performance test using a problematic scenario that participants had to develop a solution as a team and that incorporated key concepts from the other classes in the series. See Table 6.1 for a breakdown of the classes.

Table 6.1

Breakdown of Classes at DTE Energy

Class title	Description
ITS overview	Central to this class was a special presentation and dialogue with Chief Information Officer Lynne Ellyn. A significant amount of time was also spent facilitating processes to help people get to know one another. The remainder of the time was spent discussing current processes and introducing technologies to be discussed in the remainder of the courses.
IT architecture and infrastructure	This class discussed current and emerging hardware, software, and middleware architectures that comprise the ITS infrastructure. Lots of current examples taken from the company, industry case studies, and two workshops done in teams with presentations at the end of them created a dynamic class.
Telecommunications, data communication, and network security	Explored network standards; layered protocol suites, telephony, and data transmission methods used in various local area networks (LAN) and wide area network (WAN) standards. This was the most technical and information-intensive class. Analysis of company's LAN, WAN, and network security topologies softened the technical load and ensured that the information was not just abstract.
Application development	This class contained extensive analysis and discussion of ITS software development life cycle and project management methodologies. Participants were introduced to object-oriented analysis and design. A major theme of the class was how to develop collaborative partnerships with the business. Students gained an opportunity to evaluate the principles guiding new software development in the company.
Internet, intranet, and Web technologies	This hands-on class allowed participants to work with web-based standards and understand how DTE Energy is leveraging these technologies in its architecture.
Capstone case study	Participants were randomly assigned to one of four teams and required to solve a problem in a way that demonstrated command and assimilation of topics covered in preceding courses. Presentations were video taped. In every class one presentation was randomly selected. The team selected gave its presentation to senior management, including the CIO, Senior Vice President, and directors, who attended the last day of every run of the class.

Central to all of these classes were lots of discussions. In keeping with the principles of communication discussed in Chapter 2, participants were treated as collaborators and "learning partners." We had an excellent cadre of technical instructors, but eliciting people's job experiences in the form of stories was central to our strategy. People were encouraged and, at times, gently coerced into sharing their experiences, knowledge, ideas, and opinions. Every class was filled with war stories, success stories, and personal stories. People became very adept and generous in offering current examples and stories from their day-to-day challenges. This kept the sessions energized. Something new and spontaneous was always happening for the facilitators and students. Here are two brief stories to provide an idea of the impact.

1. The DTE Energy ITS Story of John and Andy

John was part of the merger team. He was responsible for handling all of the logistical details of moving people from one building into another. As he was wrapping up the project, John was pulled into a new project to research commercial off-the-shelf web-based products to handle trouble tickets, company suggestions, and a few other workflow type requirements. He selected a product, but he did not have the budget to test it. He needed a robust server, and there was not a strong business case for purchasing one without more assurance of the product's fit with the company's requirements. It was likely that the whole project was going to die before it even had a chance to get started. During one of the classes, John shared his frustration with the group. Andy, who did not know John before the class and was from the "other" company, quickly said, "Hey John, I am in the process of consolidating servers. I have a box with plenty of muscle not being used right now; why don't you come see me next week and we can park the demo on it?" A new friendship was forged, a door between companies knocked down, and the organization ended up implementing the software package that is now a major application in its portfolio.

2. The DTE Energy ITS Story of John and Chang

During one class we were involved in a heated technical discussion about networks and database performance. John was a database administrator with over twenty years of experience. He was struggling to understand how to test for network-related issues that might be impacting the performance of a database. Chang was also in the class and an experienced network engineer. When Chang realized John had never seen a protocol analyzer, which is a tool used by network engineers to assess traffic on the network, he turned to John and said, "Are you going to be at your desk on Monday morning? I would like to swing by and set up a protocol analyzer on one of your database servers and show you how it works. Maybe between the two of us we can figure out what has been causing all of the performance issues."

These are just two examples of new relationships that were forged in the classes. The Knowledge Builder Initiative was filled with moments like these. These moments are what made the intervention a success both while it was happening and long after the classes were over. The "us vs. them" doors so typical of mergers were completely absent. At the end of the six-month series of classes, members of a cohort thought of themselves as one company. Through the life of the initiative there were always folks who were resistant. They were quick to criticize the huge amount of money being spent and argued that it could be used more wisely. However, even the resisters sang a very different tune when they had completed the process.

Key Results

Average ITS training investment per employee cost $7,600 and required twenty-two days of training. Over 450 employees completed the process. Here is a summary of the key results:

- supported the creation of a performance driven environment;
- increased employee morale and motivation by providing high-quality learning and team-building opportunities;
- raised the organizational IQ by giving IT professionals current industry knowledge and a clear understanding of how to support the business;
- created a continuous learning environment;
- established relationships and processes to encourage knowledge sharing;
- enabled ITS employees to become agile knowledge workers;
- fostered operational excellence and efficiency by deploying common knowledge and understanding of ITS infrastructure;
- prepared staff for emerging strategic role ITS must provide for DTE Energy to become an efficient, high-performing organization;
- developed an understanding of how the individual's role contributes to the organization;
- introduced a wide range of technologies that were then adopted into the ITS infrastructure.

Conclusion

DTE Energy employees will retain only a fraction of the technical information they learned during the initiative. Communication was the cement that made this learning and collective experience work. People will remember the stories they shared with one another and the relationships they formed. When we performed follow-up, an overwhelming majority of people were maintaining the new relationships they had created. I heard stories of people beginning work on a new project and remembering that another employee in the class had worked on a similar problem, picking up the phone, soliciting the help of the other person, and being delighted by the person's willingness to share their knowledge and experience. This is only possible because communication was the focus of a guided, dynamic learning process.

Case Study: The Story of Jeff Bukantz

Reflection is a central part of learning. In the third part of this book we will explore in greater detail what we mean by reflection and how it can be cultivated. Working with our personal stories is a powerful way to learn and gain new insights. In this next case study we meet Jeff Bukantz, who falls from the heights of success to the depths of doubts. Jeff works through his personal stories to understand his past, create a vision of the future, and pursue a whole new direction.

Jeff Bukantz was a successful bonds salesman, working in that field for fifteen years. After he had a run-in with the Securities and Exchange Commission, Jeff's license to sell bonds was revoked. Despondent, he approached me for some personal advice. I had known Jeff for a long time. His success was not limited to the bond market. Jeff was a medalist in the Pan American Games in fencing and a member of U.S. teams. Today he is captain of the 2004 Olympic Fencing Team. Before I even knew Jeff was a salesman, I was impressed by his natural abilities as a communicator. A conversation with Jeff is never lacking for rich stories or evocative metaphors. He does it without thinking.

Jeff was trying to regroup. He needed a new career and a fresh outlook. So my first piece of advice to him was to revisit all the personal stories that contributed to his success. Over the next several weeks Jeff amassed a huge collection of stories. In the process he discovered the principles that guided his success, recouped a sense of his self, and discovered how to turn his lemon of a situation into lemonade. Jeff realized that he had a lot to share with other sales people getting started in the business. He felt compelled to help others avoid the mistakes he made and turn his principles into reusable teaching stories. Jeff is now one of the most in-demand financial sales coaches in the country. He travels around the world coaching others on how to be great salesmen. Below is a much-abridged sample of just three of the stories that helped Jeff find his new mission in life and hone his message.

Story Number 1

Telling the stories of my career was easy. Relating these stories in a speech was a whole different ball of wax, as it would be necessary for me to grab their attention. I chose to illustrate points by weaving in real-life anecdotes, albeit with fictitious but catchy names. Without doing so, I'd be just another arrogant speaker droning on about accomplishments that others could never grasp.

I was hired in August of 1979 [by a company that sold bonds]. According to my interviewer, I was the single worst candidate he had ever interviewed. "You had sweaty palms and you seemed nervous as hell," he said. Famous last words, as I became the single largest producer in the history of the 70 year old company.

I had no knowledge of the product; had less than no knowledge of the financial world, yet after a two-week bare bones sales course I was thrown out onto the sales floor.

I was taught how to cold-call and I was given a desk and a phone. My territory consisted of Queens, NY, and the letters A thru L. Of course, when no one was looking, I called M thru Z, as well! Within a month, I had made my first sale, and the snowball never stopped growing. Every single name was eventually crossed off in those Yellow Pages.

Cold calling is the single worst part of being a salesperson. It can naturally bring you down, which thereby hinders your effectiveness. No matter how you cut it, cold calling is a numbers game.

I started cold calling on November 5th, 1979. Despite having the bare minimum knowledge of the product, and having the worlds' [sic] lamest script, I was making draw within a month of being on the floor. That was about $1000 net, or $2500 gross.

The next month I made about $1100. The following month almost $1200, or about $100 increase. After I got my run, I proudly proclaimed to my group leader Mr. Pomposity, "Next month, I'm going to make $1300!"

Mr. Pomposity went on to become a bigwig in the company, but he was anything but a great salesman. However, his response to me turned out to be the most important bit of advice I ever received.

He replied to my boast to increase by yet another $100 increment by asking, "Jeff, why are you setting an arbitrary increase? Why don't you just try to make as much as you can?"

While I hadn't thought of that, I sure made the best of that suggestion. The following month, after consecutive months of $1000, $1100, and $1200, I made $3900, and never looked back!

So, here was a mediocre salesman who was directly responsible for a huge part of my success. This illustrated why you should always listen to others, even if they are not super successful themselves. If you set a specific goal, you are creating an artificial ceiling for success, and at the same time backing yourself into a corner.

Story Number 2

As building relationships is one of the most important aspects of attaining great success, the next segment drove home a real story about how relationships, even with very small clients, can lead to bigger referrals. Again, a true anecdote paints the picture. This time, however, I didn't listen to the advice of a superior. I went with my gut.

The smallest unit of bonds was $5000. It was the quintessential "odd lot." Ideally, you would not want to open accounts with people who only bought bonds in $5000 increments.

However, when I started, I would do summersaults naked on the interstate if anyone said "YES!" to me. At the beginning, I had plenty of odd-lot buyers. There was a brother combo, Bro1 and Bro2, who shared a dental practice. Not only did they buy only in lots of the dreaded $5,000, but often from new issues, where sometimes there was no commission.

My buddy and one-time group leader Dave the Rave, who was not a great salesman really chewed me out over my dealing with such small and unprofitable accounts as the Bro1 and Bro2 tag team. "Get rid of them, and look for some bigger accounts," he barked at me one afternoon.

I had a different view. The Bro Team did not take up a lot of time or effort, and I had developed a nice relationship with them. For those reasons, I decided to maintain their accounts.

Sure enough, that nice relationship I had built [led] to the Bro Team referring me to their tennis buddy, Calvin Good. As it turned out, Good's account produced more commissions each year than the Bro Team did combined in ten years. And then Good referred me to his other friends.

Story Number 3

The story of Big Red is true. He lived by the sword, and he died by the sword. After hearing this real life story, every member of the audience will always think twice before putting all of their eggs in one basket, that's for sure! The fact remains that many have already done so. Those people will leave knowing they have a Sword of Damocles over their head, and that they have been warned of the risk. Those who think that living fat off a big account is the way to go will most certainly reconsider. And those who haven't done so will definitely not do so in the future.

Big Red was a very effective salesman. He was a natural. Early in his career, he got lucky, as he opened up one of the monster accounts of all time.

Monster accounts are never easy to land, and Big Red won the lottery, as his monster was not even an individual account, but rather an institutional account. Big Red developed a relationship with the one trader who was solely responsible for buying and selling all of the bonds for a major stock firm. We'll call the firm Chuck's Discount Brokerage.

Chuck's was a stock house, and didn't really have a bond-trading department. The "department" was mainly one guy who had to call other bond firms to either buy from their inventories or get bids on bonds from their trading department. It enabled Chuck's client-base to do its bond business with the well-known discount stock house, and it enabled Chuck to keep all of the business under one roof.

Big Red was pulling in the "big green," as his day was filled with buy and sell orders from Chuck's. This was the ultimate account, as Big Red was not even in competition!

Naturally, Big Red was spending the overwhelming majority of his time on this plum account. As you can imagine, Big Red was deriving an overwhelming amount of his income from this single account.

No pressure, no cold calling, no worries about cancellations, no need to cajole any clients. We were all envious of Big Red. We prayed for an account like Chuck's. Along the way, Big Red's friends suggested that he broaden his base, as he had put nearly all of his eggs into Chuck's basket.

Big Red ignored them, and reasoned, "Why should I change anything? I'm making a fortune, it is easy business, and the pivot man at Chuck's is my great buddy."

One day, Big Red came to work ready to open his cash register. He called Chuck's to check in with his trader-buddy. And, lo and behold, the trader-buddy was no longer at Chuck's! He was replaced with a new trader.

The new trader cut right to the chase when he told Big Red, "Listen, I know you've handled the account for years, but I've got a friend at another firm, and we've had a 10 year relationship."

Big Red pleaded, "But can't I compete for the business?"

The new trader responded, "You may, but I will give my friend the right to match any bid or offer price, so you will always be behind the eight ball."

Jeff Bukantz has used his own unique brand of storytelling to create a new career for himself. His storytelling had always been a part of the skills he brought to his work. Now, through a period of reflection and self-examination, he found that storytelling was central to his future and to effectively reaching others. His stories are accessible and practical and make him an in-demand speaker and business consultant.

Part II

Interviews

7

Introduction to the Interviews

Part I has given us a theoretical framework. We have examined the ways in which stories function and have adopted them as a metaphor to understand effective communication and learning. In Chapter 3 we used the Communications Matrix derived from identifying targets and channels to establish a framework for organizational communications. Organizations are very good at reaching some of these targets and channels by broadcasting messages. Broadcasts amount to large-scale centralized efforts to push out messages using a variety of tools. However, while we are very good at reaching some combinations of targets and channels, we also discovered that organizations are missing out on 50 percent of the potential opportunities they have for communicating. In order to reach these we have to be much better at listening than broadcasting messages. The strategy of "push-to-pull-to-push" was introduced to describe how we can spend less time concentrating our efforts on broadcasting signals and more energy tuning in to all of the frequencies around in us in order to deliver more messages with fewer broadcasts, smaller bandwidth, less information, and more impact. Stories were shown to be an essential part of executing this strategy. Figure 7.1 illustrates the relationship between how stories function (the subject of Chapter 2) and the Communications Matrix (Chapter 3). Stories are effective in the untapped areas of the matrix because of their unique effects.

We ended Part I by demonstrating that organizational learning and knowledge, which we referred to as collective experience, are not stand-alone entities; they are best understood in terms of communication. Organizational learning and collective experience require us to construct bridges that are built with reflection and communication, which is facilitated by the functions of stories and their unique effects.

The interviews serve three purposes:

Figure 7.1 The Relationship Between Story Functions and the Communications Matrix

STORY FUNCTIONS	The Relationship Between Story Functions and the Communications Matrix	UNIQUE EFFECTS of STORIES
Empower a speaker		Entertaining
Create an environment	The functions of stories enable us to reach untapped areas 7–12 of the Communications Matrix...	Creating trust and openness between yourself and others
Bind and bond individuals		Elicit stories from others

Untapped Areas of the Communications Matrix

Communications Matrix	Target				UNIQUE EFFECTS of STORIES
	Internal	External	Partner	Nonspecific	
C h a n n e l — Formal	1	2	3	10	Listen actively in order to: *Understand context and perspective* *Find the critical point in a system* *Uncover resistance and hidden agendas*
Social	4	5	6	11	Shift perspectives in order to: *See each other* *Experience empathy* *Enter new frames of reference* Hold diverse points of view
Personal	7	8	9	12	Become aware of operating biases and values Creating a working metaphor to illuminate an opinion, rational, vision, or decision

Require active listening		Establish connections between different ideas and concepts to support an opinion or decision
Negotiate differences	**Stories are effective at reaching areas 7–12 of the matrix because of their unique effects**	Think outside the box to generate creative solutions and breakthroughs
Encode information		
Tools for Thinking		
Weapons		
Healing		

Table 7.1

Individuals and Companies That Participated in Interviews

Company	Name	Title
1. CTB/McGraw-Hill	Bernice Moore	Project Manager CTB University
2. DTE Energy	Robert Kraska	Senior Organizational Development Consultant
3. Dreyer's Ice Cream	Sherrie Cornett	Senior Manager of Learning & Development
4. Starbucks Coffee	Marty Fischer	Director, Retail Learning
5. Woodside Priory School	Father Marus Nemeth	Priest/Teacher
6. Cambridge Savings Bank	Paula Dickerman	Vice President of Training
7. Sodexho	Angelo S. Ioffreda	Vice President of Internal Communications

1. They explore to what degree people are aware of stories in communication and learning.
2. They model informal modes of communication with stories.
3. They help us identify competencies people and organizations will need to develop in order to be more effective communicators and learners.

In Part II we will merge the theoretical with the experiential. Seven companies were randomly selected from files and on the basis of the availability of individuals to participate in an interview (see Table 7.1). The interviews were recorded and transcripts of each were prepared. These are not meant to be scientific studies. I treated the interviews as dialogues. I simply wanted to engage in an interactive conversation with people responsible for communication and learning in their organizations. The interviews were guided by a series of questions. At the start of each interview I asked each participant to fill out a short survey (see Figure 7.2). The purpose of the survey was to act as a guide for our conversations. I then suggested, "Before reading the interviews, take a few minutes to review the survey questions and reflect on how you would respond to them. This will enable you to vicariously participate in the interviews, compare your thoughts with the interviewees, and be more analytical of themes that emerge."

Responses from the surveys are summarized in Tables 7.2 and 7.3. One of my main objectives for the interviews was to model a style of communication based on mutual storytelling. I tried to get the interviewees to tell me as many stories as they could. In the process many of them were surprised at some of the insights on communicating and learning that they discovered along the way.

Figure 7.2 **Survey Used in Interviews**

SURVEY

Name:
Company:
Title:
Number of years at the company:

1. Jot down some words that come to mind when you hear the word *story*:

2. On a scale of 1–7 rate the frequency with which you tell stories:

1	2	3	4	5	6	7
never			occasionally			all the time

3. On a scale of 1–7 rate yourself as a storyteller:

1	2	3	4	5	6	7
very poor			fair			excellent

4. On a scale of 1-7 rate the potential role you think stories could play in your organization:

1	2	3	4	5	6	7
none			moderate			very important

5. Are there any prevalent stories in your organization?   YES   NO

> **5a. If yes, what are they?**
> **5b. How do they get shared?**
> **5c. Have these stories changed in any way over time?**

6. Are you aware of any stories that you like to tell?   YES   NO

If so, jot down (1) a few keywords or phrases that will help you remember each one, and (2) why you like to tell that story.

Story	1. Keyword/Phrase/Trigger	2. Why do you like telling this story?

7. Are you aware of using stories in your work?

> **7a. If so, how? Give me a few examples:**

© Survey developed by Terrence Gargiulo of MAKINGSTORIES.net - http://www.makingstories.net

Table 7.2

Responses to Survey—Part I

Name	Words that come to mind when you hear the word *story:*
Bernice Moore	• Legend • Myth • Icebreaker • Teaching tool
Robert Kraska	• Dramatic • Fun • Tragic • Long/Short
Sherrie Cornett	• Analogy • Illustrate learning or talking points • Tale • Convey humor • Engaging the listener • Fable
Marty Fischer	• Moral • Meaning • Role Model • Example • Drama
Father Marus	• What is the message • Teaching • Communicating • Making connections with persons and reality • Driving a point home
Paula Dickerman	• Characters • Illustration • Prose • Interesting
Angelo Ioffreda	• A self-contained narrative that is way to transmit an idea, share information about oneself or a topic or tradition, and engage the listener • Stories are meant to be told and require active participation of both the teller and the listener • Stories help us make sense of the world

Table 7.3

Responses to Survey—Part II

Name	Frequency	Story-telling rating	Potential role	Are there prevalent stories in your organization?	Aware of stories you like to tell?	Do you use stories in your work?
Bernice	5	4	7	Yes	Yes	Yes
Robert	4	6	4	Yes	Yes	Yes
Sherrie	4	4	6	Yes	No	Yes
Marty	7	6	7	Yes	Yes	Yes
Father Marus	6	4	7	Yes	Yes	Yes
Paula	5	5	6	Yes	Yes	Yes
Angelo	4	4	6	Yes	Yes	Yes
Average	5	4.4	6.1	Yes (100%)	Yes (86%)	Yes (100%)

At the beginning of each interview you will find a short introduction along with a summary of its main themes. These cannot do the interviews justice. To get the full benefit, you will want to read the interviews in their entirety. The process of the interviews and all of the stories shared along the way are in fact more pertinent than the major themes extracted from them. The meat of the interviews comes from the stories shared and not just the bullets summarizing them. A short summary is also provided at the end of each interview.

Summary of Major Themes

Here is a summary of major themes across all interviews:

- Stories can clarify a subject being discussed.
- Sharing personal stories brings people closer together, establishes connections among members of a group, and makes a group more effective.
- A masterful storyteller creates a space for the story, which encourages listeners to go along with them.
- Stories need to play a central role in retrospective project debriefs because they facilitate dialogue and because they can be carried forwarded as a valuable resource for later projects.
- Making room for personal and organizational reflection is a key to leveraging the power of stories.
- The length of a story needs to be adjusted for the context in which it is being told.
- "After-action reviews" provide a structured opportunity for reflection and storytelling.

- In order for stories to work in meetings, people need to trust one another, be skilled in interpersonal communications, and know how to ask the right questions.
- In training, people learn the most from dialogue among themselves and with the instructor.
- There is an integral relationship between stories and reflection.
- Stories from our personal lives can be effectively used at work.
- Analogies are stories that help people see things in a new way that may have more meaning for them and that gives them something to hang on to.
- Stories have more impact than any other mode of communication.
- Important messages need to be communicated in stories.
- Stories have intentionality. The teller has a reason for sharing the story and hopes to lead his listeners in a particular direction.
- Storytelling is a two-way street. Listening to stories gives you the context for what another person is trying to communicate.
- The critical role of context in communication establishes a common ground between those who are communicating so that they are focused and directed toward the same thing.
- Stories create a sense of comfort between people, which opens up all kinds of possibilities.
- Storytelling can be as simple as saying the right word at the right time, which can produce a rich set of associations.
- Finding stories requires introspection and reflection.
- Stories help us find the message we want to share and make it relevant for our listeners.
- Stories allow us to communicate more directly.
- Stories we tell should be a part of us.
- Stories connect us to the moment.
- Business leaders who acknowledge the importance of each person for both the role they play in business and for who they are, will be the most successful.

The last part of the book will take the theoretical ideas of Part I and the experiential discoveries of Part II and provide a behaviorally based model that includes a large collection of personal exercises and organizational practices aimed at developing essential story-based communication and learning competencies.

Before concluding, I would like to offer some examples of stories used in Sodexho's communication strategy shared with me by Angelo Ioffreda, Vice President of Internal Communications. Sodexho provides a full range of hospitality services to hospitals, institutions, and a large number of other customers around the world. After the U.S. invasion of Iraq in 2003, Sodexho was in danger of losing many of its U.S. military contracts. As a French-owned company, it was experiencing a backlash of anti-French sentiment, since the French were vocal in their opposition to the U.S.-led coalition in Iraq. Sodexho USA responded with a barrage of ads that used short stories to protect its interests and foster political support. Here is one of those ads:

Three Tours in Vietnam. A Purple Heart. The Bronze Star.

> David Christy defended his country. He never thought he'd have to defend the best company he ever worked for.
> David Christy is one of the 110,000 Americans who work for Sodexho USA. When David heard that some people in Washington are questioning Sodexho USA's work with the United States Marine Corps, he felt they were putting American workers at risk . . . employed veterans at risk. So he flew to Washington to tell the country he served that Sodexho USA supports American workers, businesses, soldiers and their families.

Angelo also shared with me some of the tools he uses for internal communications. One of these is a perfect example of our "push-to-pull-to-push" strategy. The company hosted a back-to-school essay contest for employees' kids. Angelo explained, "We put this contest together as a way of starting a dialogue about the work our people do every day to improve the quality of everyday life. These showed the personal qualities of our people and the difference they make each day as seen through the eyes of their children." Here are two examples:

> My mom is a hard worker at her work. I know it because she treats me well. Also she gives food to people so they won't die of hunger. She makes sure that all of the plates come back. Mom gives them food, so that they can feel much better the next day. I know she will always work at her job because she likes the job she works at.
> The sick people get help and are treated nicely. My mom is a qualified worker. She is nice to everyone in her job. My mom never gives up at her work. She doesn't stop until she is finished. I hope she always is a hard worker as she is now. She treats the sick people like her own five children. I know my mom will always work at a good job like her job right now.
> I hope she will always be happy and be nice to the sick people and everybody at work because she is a nice mom.
>
> —Child #1, 8 years old

My mommy works for Sodexho at St. Luke's Allentown Campus. My mom gets up very early in the morning when it is still dark outside. She gets there before everyone else so she can unlock the doors, turn on the lights, and make sure that everything is in order. Everyone really depends on my mom. She makes sure the food is safe to eat because the people at the hospital are already sick. She delivers the food trays and helps people fill out their menus. They love my mommy because she puts smiles on their sad faces. I love my mommy too.

—Child #2, 6 years old

This simple contest is such an effective tool because it operates on several different levels. Its impact affects the kids, the parents, employees, and anyone that any of the employees or their children potentially comes into contact with and with whom they share their stories. The ripple effect of stories moving within and outside of the company is impossible to measure, but it sets in motion the "push-to-pull-to-push" effect we discussed in Chapter 3.

In the remainder of this part I have selected five out of the seven interviews I conducted to share with you. These are representative of the communication and learning principles we have been discussing. Each interview highlights various aspects of how stories function in communication and learning. Naturally, there is some overlap of themes from one interview to the next. However, each one explores different facets of the relationship between stories, and communication and learning. The interviews also provide a glimpse of how other organizations are approaching communication and learning. The collection of interviews tells a story. Taken together they will construct a bridge between the theoretical material in Part I and the practical material in Part III. I will use the major themes uncovered in these interviews in Part III to identify and define key competencies. Following that, I will present this map of competencies and offer concrete ideas on how to develop these competencies in individuals and groups.

8
Interview with Bernice Moore, CTB/McGraw-Hill

Bernice Moore manages Training and Development at CTB/McGraw-Hill in Monterey, California. CTB develops standardized tests, both custom and shelf product, for a variety of customers. Bernice has a unique perspective. The importance of reflection for individuals and organizations is a theme that runs throughout our interview. Bernice also talks about CTB's work with its Diversity Council, and the structure of CTB University and how it tries to align its learning objectives with the business's objectives.

Here is a summary of the major themes in our interview:

- Stories can clarify a subject being discussed.
- Sharing personal stories brings people closer together, establishes connections among members of a group, and makes the group more effective.
- A masterful storyteller creates a space for the story, which encourages listeners to go along with them.
- Stories need to play a central role in retrospective project debriefs because they facilitate dialogue and because they can be carried forward as a valuable resource for later projects.
- Making room for personal and organizational reflection is a key to using the power of stories.

The Interview

TERRENCE: What was your reaction to some of the questions from a process standpoint? Was it clear what I am asking you about?

BERNICE: I think it was clear. I like stories anyway, so it wasn't confusing for me to have you ask about them. But I guess it's difficult to say how often I use them.

TERRENCE: Okay, so the questions seemed straightforward. Why do think it's difficult to say how often you use stories?

BERNICE: Because I use them so often. When I train, I might tell a story to give an example of teamwork. I've also used them deliberately for historical background in some of the diversity work we've done. I've also used them in a more casual way, saying, "On my way to work today . . ."

TERRENCE: So stories have been a strategic part of your work in training and in facilitating formal communication, situations in which you can choose a particular story for a specific purpose. But when you think about what goes on in casual conversations, have you thought of that in terms of storytelling?

BERNICE: I don't think I've put them in that category officially. I think we all use small vignettes from our personal lives to connect with others, to bridge gaps. For me, I'd say I use them not to tell a "story" so much as to make a joke.

TERRENCE: When you're informally telling a joke or relating a personal anecdote, are you ever aware of what triggered you to do so? In other words, are you conscious of the communicative process that prompts you to use a joke or anecdote?

BERNICE: Sometimes at a team meeting it will strike me as a valuable way to pull together some of the loose ends of the meeting so that we can see how they fit together, particularly if the group has been working on some difficult issues. It can also be a good way to transition to other issues.

TERRENCE: So sometimes there are these disparate themes in a conversation or meeting that don't seem to have a clear connection. But somehow the situation triggers the recollection of a personal story that can help tie those loose ends together—both for you and others.

BERNICE: Yes, the story can clarify what the central subject is that we're all talking about.

TERRENCE: Can you think of a recent occasion when that sort of process took place?

BERNICE: Well, today Erika was talking about an experience she'd had with a boss, which prompted me to tell her a couple of stories about the difficult bosses I've had in the past. Sharing these stories brought us closer together. I work with the Diversity Council, and we often use personal stories as a way to establish a connection among the group, especially if we're talking about tough issues.

TERRENCE: The effect was to allow the group to come to some common understanding.

BERNICE: Yes, because we were seeing a shared type of experience from different perspectives.

TERRENCE: Some of the words you used on your survey to describe stories were "legend," "myth," "icebreaker," and "teaching tool." I'm interested in legend and myth and how, if at all, those come into play in any of your personal communications.

BERNICE: There are people I admire whose lives have a legend-like quality. Edward O. Wilson is one. He helped develop the theory of evolutionary biology and biodiversity while at Harvard, even though his colleagues really challenged him at every step along the way. He's written about how he really loved that challenge, because it prodded him to further develop his ideas. His story of persevering is sort of an example for me. I think of Claire Newark's overcoming her own adversity and creating something that people around the world can relate to as another legendary story that can be an example for folks.

TERRENCE: So there are people you admire who stand out as legends for you in a way, because of their life stories—stories that you are moved to share with others?

BERNICE: Yes, especially if I'm teaching a course where the story is pertinent. All of us deal with adversity, especially people who are successful in what they do. Their stories about overcoming adversity are legendary just because they teach the moral of persistence and what it takes to win against the odds.

TERRENCE: Those certainly tend to be the stories we remember and like to share with others. I guess that's why we are so interested in the stories of sports and entertainment celebrities, so many of whom had to struggle to achieve their success. I remember participating in a program called "Sports Pact" in the Boston public schools, which was about the parallels between participation in sports and life outside of sports, and how you can transfer lessons learned from one to the other. I would tell the students my story as a competitive fencer and how the values of will and drive to succeed were applicable to both my sport and to other areas of life—like school. That was something those kids could understand.

BERNICE: I'm reminded of a man I interviewed for a job. He works for CTB (in another department), and I wasn't able to hire him, but he was successful in sports. And I know the skills he had that made him a champion would work in our business environment. So there is a connection between the two, and kids can pick up on that.

TERRENCE: Yes, they sometimes can. Those kids in Boston weren't necessarily well motivated. A lot of them were at risk of not completing high school. But telling them how what it takes to succeed in hoops or volleyball can be used to succeed in other areas was an important way to dialogue with them about values. So these stories were very powerful.

How conscious do you think you are about using stories? If we consider personal anecdotes and short vignettes to be stories as well, would you change how you rate yourself on a scale of 1 to 10 where 1 is not all and 10 is a lot?

BERNICE: Do you mean how often I use stories consciously?

TERRENCE: Yes.

BERNICE: I think it's still about 5.

TERRENCE: You feel you're a fair storyteller. What do you think makes an exceptional storyteller?

BERNICE: A masterful storyteller creates a space for the story, doesn't rush it but provides a lead-in for it. My problem is that I'm too impatient—I don't take the time to set up the story properly for it to have an impact.

TERRENCE: Storytelling is about reexperiencing. We focus on the word "telling," but it's really not primarily about telling. It's first and foremost about allowing ourselves to reenter the world created by the narrative and to realize that by doing so we're giving something both to ourselves and to our audience—a connection, a place to anchor our experiences.

BERNICE: I think it's so important to make that space that allows for telling stories. Creating room for the story encourages listeners to go along with you.

I know that when I'm teaching, I am often too driven by wanting to cover the material. You can't tell a story effectively with one eye on the clock.

TERRENCE: I know that on those occasions when I'm poorly relating a story, it becomes more of a performance. But storytelling is not really performance. There's a time and a place for performance, which is certainly an effective way for reaching out to people. But the storyteller is different—it might be that awkward person in the back of the room who perhaps hasn't said much, but who for some reason is prompted to speak up and relate a personal experience, a story. He may not speak with ease or have a way with words; his voice may be monotone; and what he has to say may amount to only several sentences. But the impact can be as dramatic as that produced by a trained performer.

BERNICE: That's true. I think it doesn't really matter how the speaker looks or how polished they may be. If someone brings something personal and genuine to their story, people are more likely to listen, especially if that person hasn't spoken a lot.

TERRENCE: What we're saying is that stories don't have to be so stylized as in "Once upon a time. . . ." There are similar phrases too: "Let me tell you a story . . . ," "My mind flashes . . . ," "I can remember. . . ." These can have an effect, of course. But when there is a flow of conversation with intermingled stories, it becomes a rich place for everyone to learn from and much richer than if you're just following the path of a single narrative.

So, you feel stories are very important in the organization?

BERNICE: Yes, and could be used more effectively.

TERRENCE: How so?

BERNICE: We're preparing a retrospective process review—you know, looking backward so we can identify where things went wrong in a project. In designing that review, it's occurred to me how stories could be an effective tool. It would be useful to have people basically tell their story about how their project went. When I consider the work done on diversity, I think we really need to tell the story of that. The people that have been working on it in addition to their regular workload have a sense of appreciation for the journey that they've been on and what they've created. But not everyone else knows that story and may not understand all the hard work it took. I did some work with the Science team, and we developed a story at the end of the project to help people better understand what had been accomplished. Here in a business setting those sorts of stories are very useful. I would like to develop a process in which people can meet informally and have a dialogue about what this business is really all about and how they connect to it.

TERRENCE: How they understand themselves to connect to what they perceive to be the larger story.

BERNICE: Right.

TERRENCE: And then I hear you say that there are many processes that we go through all the time at the end of a project. How is that knowledge and that information—the frustrations, the successes, the incongruities, the things that fell through the gaps—how is all that captured, and is there an established process for it?

BERNICE: I like what we did at the end of the first Diversity Council. We created a document covering all the things we were involved with and asked what went well and what didn't, and how things could have been done differently. It's important for teams to be able to look back and ask those questions. For me the challenge is to take the group's experience and craft it as a collective story that reflects the team's self-understanding.

TERRENCE: You're describing how in a sense there is a retrospective process that you value as much if not more than the formalized measures that come at the end of a project and at the end of a process. You then began to hint at how it's difficult to craft the results of that process—to take all the individual retrospections by team members and come up with a collective story to adequately narrate the group's experience. How much energy do you spend formalizing that story so that it can be shared at large? How important is that?

BERNICE: I don't really know how important it is. I think one problem is that when a team completes its work, its members tend to rush through the post-process review saying "Okay, that's done," and then quickly move on to the next project without thinking about the human interaction and relationships that made that previous project work. That's where creating a story about the project can help, by preserving an account of what worked and what didn't and how people worked together to get things right. This means that the retrospective by the team doesn't just fade away in the rush of getting started on the next project, but the story can be carried forward as a valuable resource for later projects.

TERRENCE: Even when you're able to use the process of retrospection to enable a team's members to take the time to focus on their relationships and personal interaction with others—those sort of things that could certainly be of value to future projects—I would think it's a challenge to get them to provide more than a laundry list of what happened and then what happened next. What I'm wondering is how you get them to tell the broader story of the group's work together rather than simply saying, "This worked here. . . . That worked there."

BERNICE: I think that's certainly part of the difficulty. To avoid producing merely a root cause analysis, you have to structure the retrospective process so people are given the time and feel safe talking about their involvement and the issues they encountered. They need to be reassured that whatever they share with others won't be held against them, that their perceptions— their own way of telling their story—will be respected.

TERRENCE: I think it's important how you focus on the cultural climate of the workplace, on how workers need to be assured of their acceptance. And again you mention how crucial it is to provide team members adequate time for "reflection," which I'd say is the critical notion we're talking about. If the business environment is a safe one, where employees can be confident they're taken seriously and respected, they can develop the unique competencies involved in being reflective. This makes it much easier for storytelling to take place. Nurturing this capacity for reflection often is not something we place a priority on, and yet it is the most important thing. We all know that in learning a skill that could save our lives, such as properly driving a car, if I don't reflect on the feedback mechanism telling me what I'm not doing well and how to adjust accordingly, it could mean my life. Shouldn't the same sort of reflection about what's going on in the organization and our involvement and interactions with others also be encouraged? What I'm asking is why we don't make it a priority in the life of the organization to encourage people to be reflective. After all, it seems to be a natural part of who and how we are.

BERNICE: That's a fabulous question. Reflection as you describe it is so important. And yet, so often in team meetings—even with some of the most highly paid, brightest minds of our business—there's no time or effort given over to reflection. Say you had a meeting of the Technology group but wanted to do something out of the ordinary, like create a space for reflection, what would it take to do that? Certainly, the group would have to be agreeable to the process, and you'd have to ensure there was enough time for it—you can't have people always looking at their watches. And it would be critical that you encourage people to really listen to one another. You might set it up so that one person speaks at a time, and then others share what they heard the speaker to have said. This way people can reflect both on what they understood the person speaking to say and what others made of it.

TERRENCE: You said so many wonderful things. One thing that really struck me was the issue of how we can encourage people to first and foremost reflect on themselves. We talk a lot about the importance of listening to others. But it seems to me that before you can even listen to someone else you have to first be allowed to pay close attention to your own thoughts and feelings. Organizations tend not to encourage individual reflection. The climate is usually one in which the individual is expected to have a more objective relationship to whatever he's doing. He might have to figure out the root cause of this or that development, but how he is personally involved with what happened and what may happen next—how he understands himself to relate to what's going on—that's seldom encouraged.

BERNICE: I agree, and that's one of the sadder parts of corporate life today. Where you stand on the corporate ladder often determines what you're expected to think about, and certainly how seriously others will take what you say. People who rank high in the organization sometimes aren't aware of the power they have to influence the thinking of others, even if those others would exercise better judgment if left to themselves. The solution, as you say, is getting people to take their own feelings and thoughts seriously, to help them trust themselves, which can provide a framework for reflecting on what others have to say.

TERRENCE: And that framework is what enables a story to incorporate more than a single point of view. It's not about relativism, that if we look at the world one way it looks like such and such, but will seem entirely different if looked at another way. It's about being able to recognize multiple points of view at the same time, which in the broader narrative context of the story are both true.

BERNICE: Yes. You might relate an experience that we shared that is quite different than my understanding of that experience, but being part of a broader story enables them both.

TERRENCE: And by being personal about it, by allowing those two very different points of view, you actually can depersonalize it. It's like two negatives canceling each other out so you get a positive. What often happens is that we become defensive about our understanding of how things are and should be—we protect our turf. But things then get personal in a bad way. Suddenly nobody's hearing anyone but himself. On the other hand, if we encourage reflection on the story that incorporates the disparate viewpoints, the conflict may become depersonalized in the sense that those doing battle over who was "right" could say, "Okay, what should we do here? Maybe we can go back to corporate and try to get that line item switched over so that we can just buy servers from Dell and HP. But you know what? On the software licensing you heard the dilemma we're in. Every business is asking for their own licenses because they need to contain their costs that way. Can we go back and make a case together?" Powerful, right? And problems are resolved a lot quicker.

BERNICE: Yes, and it allows people to see the other perspective in a way that informs future work.

TERRENCE: And they also see each other as listening to one another's story, eliciting each other's self-reflection, and then saying, "Okay, let's deal with the messiness and conflicts of the situation by depersonalizing it and moving forward."

So, you've said there are some prevalent stories in the organization. Can you share a couple of those with me?

BERNICE: Well, the story about the company's founding and development is the first one that comes to mind. That's the story of how Ethel Park and her husband began by handing out postcards at schools and then building on their enterprise until selling it to McGraw-Hill. It's not told in the hallways or anything like that, but is more part of the formal history of the company— the sort of thing you'd find in our promotional literature.

TERRENCE: Is it related at annual meetings?

BERNICE: Ethel herself attends the annual meetings, but they mainly use the story in videos about the company and, as I say, in promotional materials.

TERRENCE: How do you think the story affects people who hear or read it? What does it tell them about the beginnings of the business?

BERNICE: I think it stresses the entrepreneurial spirit that's here. The story also gets across a sense of individualism that is also a part of this organization. Ethel is quite an individual. She and her husband had very different skills sets, but through their work together they built the company. They had to really hustle to make a success of things. We still do.

TERRENCE: Are there other stories?

BERNICE: The story I hear most often is about how this is the worst time the company's ever had. But someone's always saying that, it seems—that times may have been bad in the past, but now this is worse.

TERRENCE: So regardless of how the business is doing, there always seems to be a negative story told by someone . . . the grass is always greener. . . . How do people react to negative stories of that sort?

BERNICE: As far as I'm concerned, they don't appeal to me at all, and I don't put a lot of stock in them. They do make me focus on how we're in a period of difficulty, but that's because we're growing. Growing is hard.

TERRENCE: Right. What was another one . . . ? We lost the California contract and laid people off?

BERNICE: Yes. And that was a real low point for the company. You don't ever want to lay people off. You work hard to prevent that. So that kind of story seems stuck on remembering how bad it was.

TERRENCE: Do you think the story expresses some fear that that could happen again?

BERNICE: I think there is an element of fear. Even if we're gaining market share and getting our products and services out there, the bad economic times become a concern for people. There are a couple of other stories. There was a famous researcher who was sent here by the corporate headquarters who turned out to be a very disruptive influence.

TERRENCE: What are some of the stories that you tell your customers around those types of themes?

BERNICE: Part of our mission has been to help the teacher help the child, so a lot of our products are designed with children in mind. That's more than just a positive story; it regularly reminds our customers what we're all about— the concern and care we have. Other stories about our renowned research group can help explain our culture.

TERRENCE: What sort of stories might your customers tell about how they perceive the company and its products and services?

BERNICE: I'm not sure I know enough about our customers to say for certain. But I do know that we do everything we can to meet a customer's needs. In the delivery process, for example, there are stories about how we'll rent a plane to deliver products to a customer if we're running behind schedule.

TERRENCE: Stories are food for our imaginations. I remember a buddy calling me up and complaining about how demoralizing his work environment was. He shared stories with me to help me imagine his situation and compared these with his memories of working for me. He really wanted to know if working in the financial industry was by nature competitive and unsupportive. I said, "Well, I've never worked in that industry but I don't think in any industry it has to be that way."

BERNICE: I think that's true. A man that worked for me several years ago recently called me, unfortunately just before he was laid off. But I was so touched to talk with him and to hear how valuable he found it to have been a part of my team. For me, the hard part of leading a team is being strong enough to be firm in what I expect from team members, but to be compassionate as well.

TERRENCE: Participating in sports taught me a lot along those lines. When fencing, I was at my best if I made my opponent fence his best. That was the ultimate pleasure. The rush of competition pushed us both to be our best. I didn't want my opponent to be less than himself. That's not to say I didn't want to win, or that I didn't want my opponent to lose. Those are external measures that are important in getting a medal or making a team. But in the later part of my career, what kept me participating in the sport was not so much winning or losing but that wonderful sense of competition that comes from pushing the other person to be their best.

BERNICE: I don't have any competitive sports experience, but I do connect with what you say about pushing folks to perform at their fullest capacity. That's what I understand myself to be up to as a team leader. Even when people work hard, they can be challenged to further explore their potential.

TERRENCE: Well, you want to put out your best. So you demand the best from them. What's interesting about our exchange over the last minute or so is how it's been a series of personal stories. This is what I meant earlier about the process of reflection. You were able to respond as you did because you really listened to my stories and were prompted to share a story about your own work as a team leader. When I told a story about how I was complimented by someone I used to work with, you responded by relating a similar experience. Then I talked a little about what competition has meant to me, and though you don't have experience in competitive sports, you were able to tie that into your own experiences of challenging team members to perform at their best.

I'd like to hear now something about CTB University—how it's structured, what sort of activities and courses it offers—that sort of thing.

BERNICE: CTBU is sponsored fully by CTB. The project is still in the early stages. We're very small, a three-person team until this year. I've recently brought on an instructional designer, a project manager starting tomorrow, and a new staff assistant to kind of help us support some of the learning needs that we have. We structure our program so that it really aligns with the strategic goals of the company, especially the Technology group. But we try to stay sensitive to the needs of all the employees at CTB. Hiring an instructional designer has been especially helpful for me because now we have the added expertise of a learning professional, and I don't have to be the only spokesperson for what we're trying to accomplish, whether it's programs supporting adult learning or management programs that develop leadership capability.

What excites me personally is being able to craft and support modules for learning that have a direct impact on the business—improving it. I love the challenge of trying to enhance employees' capabilities and their success on the job. It's really a matter of supporting staff by enabling them to learn the skills they need. Some of those skills are technical, but others have to do with leadership—things that help enhance teamwork. It's what I call "action learning," like what I did with the Science team. We're hoping to teach folks to do more coaching and mentoring; that is something that makes for greater cohesion across the company.

TERRENCE: How do most employees perceive the University?

BERNICE: One of the things I hear through the grapevine is how much people value the training they receive here, and that there's such a strong commitment to learning. I think people realize how hard we work to be responsive to their needs. We are very ambitious about what we try to offer, and sometimes we have to scramble to keep up with our strategic planning, but I think folks still view us well. We're seen both by business leaders and by employees as learning consultants who target our efforts at what staff members personally need to do their work as best they can. You know, when we first started this, people were dragged kicking and screaming to classes that they didn't like and didn't find valuable. We've really worked hard to change that.

TERRENCE: Are you able to respond to an expressed or perceived need for learning in a timely fashion?

BERNICE: We do our best to respond as soon as we find out about a need. If there's a burning need that is brought to our attention that's crucial to the business, we redouble our efforts to handle the problem, especially if several people bring it up. Otherwise, we do regular surveys and take them seriously.

TERRENCE: How often do requests come in to you? And can you give me some examples of recent requests?

BERNICE: Fairly often. We have an e-mail address that people use, and they can also leave a request on voice mail. One recent request was to help non-native English speakers improve their written English. So we had to identify the appropriate learning cores and find the right instructors. We also recently had a request from Research for more leadership training.

TERRENCE: Let's say a project manager is getting ready to kick off a project and he or she is looking at the resources and maybe sees there are some gaps in terms of staff members' knowledge or experiences. Do they come to you and say, "Look, I've got a team of x and I think there may be some possible problems down the road. I've already talked to these individuals, and I think they could maybe use something to get them up to speed in this area." Do you have that kind of relationship with management as well?

BERNICE: Not so much at this time, though I'd love to see that kind of work relationship be developed.

TERRENCE: What about when the company announces its quarterly objectives, for example, or its targeted goal for the fiscal year? What process does that kick off from the learning standpoint? Is there a connection between them?

BERNICE: The budgeting process is a part of strategic planning, so the budget we receive for our training programs is part of the company's broader plan. It's an interim process.

TERRENCE: It seems that learning has to occur. That perhaps you're going to have to give people information or learning and training in order to hit those. And try to align those two.

BERNICE: Especially with the big things. I think that the sales is one area where we haven't really supported them in every way that we could. But with program management, ETR [Enterprise Technology Transfer], those have been our main focuses for the last year. And with our three-person team . . . now we're supporting the software development cycle. The instructional designer helped design the program for learners, but that's part of that ETR strategy. It will probably continue as we deploy the scoring and new technology for scoring. My boss is Monica Casey and she's on the executive team, so that comes forward. I shape funding to sponsor and support different initiatives. I think it is seen as an enabler for team strategy.

TERRENCE: And so you have your own budget.

BERNICE: Right, and I think this year I'm not sure that's the perfect model. Or the model I want to stay with forever. It's the model we're working with now. I think they're going to give us more of the departmental budgets for training is what I understand, and how that will work is that we'll have to design systems that treat the departmental needs clearly. So we're tracking that by department, which we haven't done until this year. The funds are part of our budget, and then we manage it. The funds are sort of like I thought, in trust to us.

TERRENCE: That does make it hard sometimes to get that partnership.

BERNICE: I think that it's not the most ideal model. I think the two biggest initiatives have gotten most of our dollars and so there are areas where we need to put some resources like sales, and we're helping them. Research, we just provide them training and software packages. It would be nice to help more with that training to better meet their needs. I think having another instructional designer also. If we move toward the model where we're designing more training at CTB, we'll really need another instructional designer.

TERRENCE: Yes, especially if you develop nontraditional approaches to learning that blend standard one-day or three-day classes with online learning, and so on. That's when it is particularly important to get people out of the mindset "Here I am sitting in this classroom being trained." They need to see what they're doing as empowering themselves and the company to meet personal and organizational goals.

BERNICE: Right. And that's a hard mindset to shift.

TERRENCE: How do you measure your program's accomplishments when you have to justify its budgetary allocation?

BERNICE: Accounting for exactly where the dollars went is a big part of it. That's a matter of good record keeping. We've also done a couple of ROI [return on investment] analyses to demonstrate the return value for every dollar invested. The Science team, for example, developed a model using ROI to show how the investment in the team improved the quality of its production.

TERRENCE: Do you see stories playing any kind of role in this process?

BERNICE: I think the story about the Science team's use of an ROI analysis is useful. As I said, it found a strong correlation between the number of dollars allocated and the quality of the work produced. And I think a retrospective about the work and effectiveness of the CTBU would be great. It could evoke stories about people's different experiences with learning programs to provide a connection among them.

TERRENCE: Tell me about the diversity project.

BERNICE: We have a Diversity Council that we started a couple of years ago after some difficult experiences that resulted in some people's leaving. Since then, we've been in the process of developing diversity leaders and coming up with a strategic plan. Our goal is to create an inclusive organizational culture that hears every voice and in which everyone makes a difference. And we also support our customers with multicultural assessment needs.

TERRENCE: Right. Engaging that diversity. Learning how to negotiate those differences. I think we have a habit of looking for some artificial common ground.

BERNICE: Well, I do think it's more important to talk more about how we're the same than about how we're different, but not in a way that demeans the differences. I shared stories about our families; it's a way to celebrate our diverse heritages.

TERRENCE: And again, just reflecting on how each person is different—just as every tree and every leaf on a tree is unique—it helps us get past the exclusive focus on race, ethnicity, creed, gender, whatever else.

BERNICE: Every person is unique. But people sometimes say, "Well, I don't look at you as a woman." Hah! Well look again! What are you missing about me? That's a lot of who I am, that's part of my uniqueness. An understanding of diversity is especially important for leaders. I just read a report about diversity training for managers so they will understand the importance of including everyone's perspective. Without making the managers consciously aware of the different perspectives among staff members, the diversity programs fall flat.

TERRENCE: Stories can bring to consciousness those differences.

BERNICE: Yes, they do. And it's also important to see different perspectives without judgment, as you said. You don't change people's minds; you change their hearts. Hearing a person that you respect tell a story about how they've been oppressed by the organization motivates folks to keep working to improve the situation. Better hiring practices, better management skills in place— these are ways the business can remedy what's happened in the past, and that will benefit all employees, regardless of color, ethnicity, gender, and so on.

TERRENCE: Let's talk for a minute about the process of recruiting. Recruiters often don't take the time to figure out the story of the person being interviewed; they're just looking to have a set of criteria for hiring be met. They're not taught, for example, how to read a resume as a story, how to reflect on who that person might be and what they can contribute because of their uniqueness and diversity.

BERNICE: It's a combination for me, I think. You have to consider an applicant's competencies and capabilities, but you also want to think of them in terms of how they might help create a diverse team. We really need to work with recruiters and improve the process, which often seems too mechanical.

Observations

Right from the beginning Bernice demonstrates an acute awareness of stories in communication and learning: "I think we all use small vignettes from our personal lives to connect with others, to bridge gaps." The challenge, she confesses, is being aware of how pervasive stories are and being more conscious of using them more effectively. As the interview develops, we begin communicating more with stories. I ask questions to elicit stories, and at first Bernice responds with a description of an experience but not the actual story. When I offer a few personal experiences, Bernice begins to reciprocate. There is one point in the interview where we share a string of personal stories. At this point the conversation becomes more dynamic. This flow of short personal stories interwoven naturally into conversation exemplifies the fluid nature of stories. Bernice and I are able to cover more ground and explore subtle nuances. The stories were not tangential or entertaining. Bernice believes stories are how we connect with each other and create a collaborative space of richer understanding.

Reflection emerges as a central competency that needs to be developed by individuals and inculcated by organizations. Bernice asserts that we do not make reflection a priority. Working with the functions of stories and their unique effects facilitates reflection. Stories become a way in which we can be engaged in self-reflection. Since stories are a tool for thinking, they can be used as symbolic constructs through which greater abstraction can occur. Despite the existence of a story line, working with stories can be done in a nonlinear manner. Stories enable us to mentally and emotionally rotate the information contained in them. In this sense, stories act as packages filled with items of potential insight and learning. These cannot be as easily explored if they are discussed sequentially. Stories offer us the benefit of working with them in tandem. Bernice also notes how reflection and stories relate to negotiating our differences. Her work with CTB's Diversity Council has shown her how stories allow people to listen more actively to one another, depersonalize their differences, and find common ground while respecting differences. Chapter 15 explores the relationship between stories and thinking, and offers concrete practices for strengthening reflection.

9

Interview with Robert Kraska, DTE Energy

Rob is a manager of training and development at DTE Energy, a utility company based in Detroit, Michigan. From the case study in Chapter 6 you know I worked closely with DTE Energy's Information Technology Services (ITS) team to facilitate synergies in the Information Technology teams during a merger. Rob's facility with language makes this interview a treat. It is full of lots of rich examples that examine the different facets of stories in organizational communication and learning. Rob shares some stories about the company and its cultures that you will want to read.

Here are some of the major themes:

- The length of a story needs to be adjusted for the context in which it is being told.
- "After-action reviews" provide a structured opportunity for reflection and storytelling.
- In order for stories to work in meetings, people need to trust one another, be skilled in interpersonal communications, and know how to ask the right questions.
- In training, people learn the most from dialogue among themselves and with the instructor.
- There is an integral relationship between stories and reflection.

The Interview

TERRENCE: Tell me a little bit more about some of the words that came to your mind when asked to think about stories.

ROB: Well, I guess "dramatic," "tragic," "funny," "long," and "short" came to mind. Stories can be dramatic in nature, like when they're about a tragic event of some kind. Often they're funny and are used as a way to break the ice. Jerry Seinfeld creates humorous stories out of simple, everyday situations. I think as listeners we tend to judge stories as being short or long. For example, I was out to lunch with five co-workers today and told a story that I consciously tried to make short and sweet. Then another guy told a story in which he included every last detail. It was a great story, but you could tell the others felt it dragged on for too long.

TERRENCE: So the context helped you determine the appropriate length and detail of the story?

ROB: Yes. I think many storytellers consciously assess their audience and their environment to determine how long a story should be and whether, for example, to stress a dramatic aspect of the story.

TERRENCE: Typically there is some drama; it doesn't have to be tragic, but some type of motive energy that captures our attention as listeners and sort of ropes us in. Is that kind of what you were driving at when you spoke of stories' being dramatic?

ROB: Yes. There's usually a sense of risk and drama to the stories we tell here. Many of them tend to be about emergencies like severe storms or our recent blackout. Others concern dramatic possibilities like the business merger or the threats surrounding Y2K, although nothing much happened then.

TERRENCE: During a workshop that I was facilitating today, people told stories about their pride in the leaders of this company during a major blackout—how they stepped up to bat and presented the company in a very positive light. I was actually quite moved to hear people say things like, "Well, you know, I don't always necessarily agree with the leadership and everything they say, but I was really proud. I was really proud of what Tony Earle said and how he responded to the situation." Those sorts of stories will probably remain part of the organization's culture.

Something else that you said really triggered my thoughts about how we often take a utility company for granted. I walk in my house, turn the switch . . . and it's there, light. If it weren't there, I'd be the first one to get on the phone and complain. But because it is almost always there, I don't even consider how mysterious it can seem that you turn a switch and light happens. Again, we take it for granted. Maybe that's why it's important to have stories about storm outages and the people in the field who go well beyond the call of duty to get power back on and defend the public from downed lines. Those stories are a counterweight to being taken for granted.

Rob: I think that for major companies like Motorola, for example, a lot of their dramatic stories surround new product launches—say, whether they were able to successfully release the next great phone before Nokia could. That kind of rallies the folks at Motorola, but, for us, we don't really have the occasions to celebrate how we'll be getting electricity to your home next year. We do have a lot of new products that can really help businesses and private homeowners, but we don't make much noise about them. Generally, we're just always in the background, providing a necessary product that people don't think about too much.

Terrence: The metaphor that comes to my mind about how utilities providers are ignored by the public is an obvious one. So long as we eat three meals a day and get eight hours of sleep a night, our bodies run on autopilot. Yet you start taking away one of those meals and begin to sleep only half as much—suddenly you notice.

You have a facility with language, and you seem to think in terms of analogies and metaphors.

Rob: Well, you have the opportunity to do a lot of storytelling as a facilitator or trainer in the learning environment. But as my responsibilities have become more varied, I guess I don't have the chance to tell stories quite so often.

Terrence: So where you once had a forum for encouraging stories as a facilitator, and you certainly used them in that capacity, it now feels like there's less opportunity for storytelling, or maybe that it's less appropriate.

Rob: It seems less appropriate. Our conference meetings are usually one hour in length, and there's a lot that has to get done in that one hour; time-consuming storytelling just doesn't fit in. The situation is different in our Learning Leadership Program, an eight-day program that includes nineteen learning modules. Trainers who facilitate that program are in a good position to be storytellers and share anecdotes about leadership that is a helpful part of administering the program.

Terrence: Right. I think it's especially valuable when those stories and anecdotes are dramatic. But I also wonder whether even in the more succinctly drawn lines of a conference meeting, when as you say there's only an hour or so, there is still a role for stories? Is there another way of thinking about stories other than time-consuming tales?

Rob: Actually, here at DTE we have just begun experimenting with the sort of storytelling you're asking about. It's what we call an "after-action review." After completing a planned activity of some kind, everyone involved comes together and answers four questions: What was intended to happen? What happened? What did we learn? How can we improve in the future? Now this review could last as long as twenty-five minutes as part of a formal debriefing after a blackout, or it could be used at the end of a conference meeting as a two-minute review of what the meeting accomplished. It's been great to do this storytelling and reflection in an organized fashion.

Terrence: That's great. It allows narrative to play a natural role in addressing those four questions, encouraging people to give their sides of the event and getting a better idea of what actually took place. But what about that one-hour meeting that doesn't involve an after-action review? Can you envision how stories might have a place in that setting?

Rob: I think it would require a few conditions. First, the meeting would have to be of a group whose members knew one another fairly well and trusted one another. Second, the individuals in the meeting would need to be skillful in interpersonal communicating, knowing how to ask the right questions and advocating for their own positions. They'd also need to know how far to go with certain stories. What you wouldn't want are stories that become merely critical in a negative way or that rehash old issues. It would require a skilled meeting facilitator to keep things on track.

Terrence: I hear you describing the importance of trust and a group dynamic that is sensitive to the boundaries of when and where a story would fit. Another really important thing you said was not allowing storytelling to become a downward spiral of negativity that recounts only what went wrong. Not only does that take time away from core agenda items that need to be covered during the meeting, but also it doesn't move the group forward in a positive direction.

I want to push the point in yet another way. What we've been discussing all sound to me like stories even if they're very brief. In fact, as part of my research I hypothesize that stories may be a single word, a single association, a metaphor, or an analogy. Today in class we were talking about something when someone just sort of blurted out the title of a movie. Boom! Suddenly everyone was on the same page. The same thing can take place when people are trying to understand another perspective and someone comes up with a succinct analogy or metaphor to make it clear. I would consider

these to be stories that can have a significant role in one-hour-long conference meetings, or even in communications that happen between people as
they pass each other in the hall.

ROB: You obviously use the word *stories* to cover a very broad range of
communications—including such things as metaphors and models. I think
modeling takes place in our workplace a lot. Let's say a group that is talking
about an issue gets stuck for a while on a certain point until finally someone
goes up to the white board and is able to successfully illustrate his or her
point in a way that the others understand. In that case a picture really is worth
a thousand words.

I think corporate culture often values the ability of company leadership
to be able to tell stories. Steve Ewing, our president of Energy Gas, is a
master at being able to give presentations about the business while weaving in analogies to books or to what's going on in the world, including
anecdotes about the experience of other companies. Of course, if you over-
use analogies and metaphors, you run the risk of not being understood by
some of your listeners.

TERRENCE: Yes, I agree with you there. It's funny your saying a picture is
worth a thousand words, because I have a saying: "If a picture is worth a
thousand words, then a story is worth a thousand pictures." But I see no
reaction on your part. That doesn't work for you?

ROB: No, it's just that your definition of *story* is a little different than most
people's.

TERRENCE: Yes, it probably is, but I don't want to define the word *story* so
much as to explore whether we can think of stories themselves as a metaphor
for understanding effective communication and learning. That's one of the
reasons why I'm very interested in seeing the different ways that people talk
about stories. That's really more what I'm driving after.

ROB: Stories can be ineffective too. Or they can be a negative part of an
organization's culture, like a painful family story about a situation that was
never resolved but that nevertheless keeps being told.

TERRENCE: Yes, definitely.

ROB: So I think stories could sometimes be used in communication effectively but at other times ineffectively.

TERRENCE: Right. Storytelling itself is neutral. It depends on how it's used. . . . Let's see, when asked how you assessed yourself as a storyteller, you responded with a rating of 6, probably being a little modest there. You rated the potential of stories to have a positive influence within your company as moderate. What was your thinking there?

ROB: I think DTE is probably right in the middle. We have a history of being quite business focused, engineering driven, and process oriented. Sort of a traditional business environment. But we're starting to do some creative things like the Learning Zone, the DT2 project, and the Project Floor. We're trying to capture the new spirit of how we do things that was part of the merger. During that time we really focused on how the impact of things was felt by the employees. So we're starting to loosen up.

TERRENCE: Earlier in our conversation you mentioned how you put communicating on two levels: one the level of the longer narrative, and the other level comprising more of the smaller communication exchanges, perhaps using visual modeling. We raised the question whether the latter could also be considered stories, and whether metaphors and analogies and other sorts of quick visuals or word pictures could be as well. How do you get people to improve these less formal communication skills?

ROB: The most important factor is to have a formal structure of some kind in place, some framework that can actually help the more informal communications take place. Take the operation system that's part of our leadership training program, for example. One of its basic principles is the practice of transferring organized knowledge and reflection. That's part of the structure of the worklife here. But then there's the tool I talked about earlier—the after-action review—which organizes the approach to the less formal dialogues that take place, like reviewing our success or failure in responding to a situation. That kind of dialogue is a great source for learning. For instance, participants in our training sessions often say that the part of the training they get the most from is dialogue among themselves and with instructors. I really think we need to develop other frameworks to support that dialogue.

TERRENCE: I see what you mean—structured opportunities that open up the space in which these dialogues can take place. . . . A couple of times in this last set of comments you used the wonderful word *reflection*. You spoke of the importance of having time to reflect. Can you tell me more about that?

ROB: Well, I mentioned how the underlying principle for our operating system is the transfer of organized knowledge and reflection. That is a process we all contribute to in some way; it's how the organization functions. Reflection is also part of our employee development program, especially for those who exhibit high potential. In fact, the ability to self-reflect was recently added to the factors that make up our talent planning process. We want to build up the confidence of our employees that self-reflection requires. And that includes leaders and managers as well. A leader needs the confidence to self-reflect when a mistake is made, and the objectivity of self-reflection when something good happens, because it's part of his job to help employees understand both mistakes and successes.

TERRENCE: Do you see a relationship between self-reflection and stories? If you do, how would you say they're connected?

ROB: There is a definite relationship between them. Part of the process of self-reflection is to formulate the lessons already learned but that you haven't had time in the bustle of work to consciously understand thoroughly. You need to take the time and create the story that communicates what's been happening on the job—what's worked and what hasn't. But that story can't come to you unless you make the space for self-reflection.

TERRENCE: One of my favorite little mottos that I coined is, "Meet less; lunch more; do less with more thinking." As you said earlier, we spend a lot of time in formal meetings where there isn't much, if any, storytelling going on. There aren't many real linkages between people in this setting. It seems to me that the best opportunities for these kinds of connections are more informal—over lunch, say, or standing in the hallway having a cup of coffee. We don't have to be so frenetically and, I think, ineffectively busy all the time. By reflecting a little bit more on what we actually are doing and need to accomplish, and by developing our skills of informal communication, we can really accomplish more while doing less. That's the gist of my little motto.

You said there are some prevalent stories within the organization. Will you share some of them?

ROB: Most of the stories center around emergencies, naturally enough, usually bad storms. We had two catastrophic storms this year alone. The first was a major ice storm in April that produced a blackout affecting hundreds of thousands of people. April is the worst month for ice storms in Michigan. And this one kind of came upon us without much warning. I was directing a training session when someone came by and said there was a huge ice storm headed our way. That night many of us throughout the company—not just field operation people, but those in human resources and finances—went out on public storm duty to guard downed lines. It was pretty dangerous, with trees and lines coming down. But it was also fun, a sense of being part of the team.

I'm sure the recent blackout will generate many stories as well. I happened to leave Detroit two hours before it all started, but was able to follow it on television. I later found out that everyone had their own story about the blackout—my neighbors, fellow employees. . . .

TERRENCE: Sorry to interrupt, but I just want to say that what I particularly love about your account of the storm in April is the commonality of viewpoint. What I mean is that regardless of the functional area that folks worked in, everyone came together and connected with the core mission of the business—providing for and protecting the public. That's a unique story about a rare experience not many companies can give their employees.

ROB: Yeah, it happens maybe twice a year, and for two or three or four days. It is kind of neat. People group together, but there's also hard work there. At the time, I don't believe we even think of it as team building. That realization doesn't come until later when you reflect back on the experience.

It may be two or six months down the road until you notice how a shared event like an ice storm has changed relationships at work, has changed the way people think about one another and the work they do.

TERRENCE: Yes, there's a synergy that happens.

ROB: There's another story that usually gets told as part of our new employee orientation. It's about how Thomas Edison and Henry Ford worked together early on, just before Ford created the Ford Motor Company.

TERRENCE: See, I didn't know that. Please tell me a little bit more of the story. Sounds interesting.

ROB: Well, to be honest, it's one of those things that are more lore than historical fact. It is about how Ford and Edison's early interest in using electricity to make things move later developed into Ford's interest, along with that of other entrepreneurs like Firestone, in producing electric cars. The real story is probably embellished, because we don't know how interested Ford really was in making an electric car; but that doesn't matter for the purpose of the story, which is the fundamental role played by electricity. Our vision statement today is oriented more toward our being a premier energy company, but it used to be "We energize the progress of society." I think that was pretty powerful.

The merger with MichCon has generated other stories. It was one of if not the first large merger either organization had experienced. The merger was actually an acquisition—Edison acquired MichCon. In any case, a lot of dialogue and conversation came out of it, and continues to this day. People still talk about whether it was a good decision or a bad decision, and which company was more creative with the more dynamic organizational culture and higher profits. Because I started during the middle of the merger, I have no personal allegiance to either of the original companies. But people will still ask me, as I introduce myself, whether I'm MichCon or Edison.

Sarah Sheridan is another subject of organizational storytelling. She was one of the company's first female directors. It was her original idea to give our customers light bulbs so they would use more electricity. That spawned a lot of innovation in marketing strategies across the country. We honor her by giving someone the Sarah Sheridan Award each year.

TERRENCE: We've talked a little bit about the mechanisms for communication. Can I hear a little bit more about the informal method at DTE?

ROB: My perception, again I've only been here for three years, is that the informal network is pretty good. We have a company of 11,000 people, most of whom live in southeast Michigan, though we're getting bigger every day. Still, one of the main mechanisms we have for informal communication about the company is our tradition of relatives working here—children following their parents in becoming employees; sometimes three generations of a family will be employed at the company. We also have a history of people meeting their spouse here, and then both of them having a full career with the organization but in different departments. There are also a lot of company-sponsored activities, many of them at the boat club that the company owns and which employees can become members of. And then there are golf leagues and those sorts of activities where people can meet informally outside the workplace. These informal mechanisms for communication and the more formal ones, like what takes place during the training programs, have really developed over recent years to be part of what we like to describe as the "fabric" of the company.

TERRENCE: So becoming part of the company is being woven into the fabric of the organization's traditions, becoming first a listener to and then a teller of organizational stories. Another way to describe this is to say one is "socialized," as opposed to "institutionalized," within the cultural ethos of the company. But that's a dynamic thing, and the culture is always changing, so the stories change.

You mentioned there are a few stories you personally are aware of telling. Can you share a couple of them?

Rob: Well, one story I often relate, and I mentioned this earlier, is how when I meet people in the field while doing leadership training, they often ask, "So are you MichCon or Edison?" And I respond, "I'm DTE Energy." That shocks them a little because they think anyone in a leadership position must have earlier been with either MichCon or Edison. I explain that I have no allegiance to either company, and so much of the bantering back and forth between former MichCon and Edison workers is lost on me.

Another story I often tell is about the big ice storm we had. That first night a co-worker and I were up in Pontiac, Michigan, trying to find a downed power line, and of course could hardly see anything because all the lights were out. And when we did find the line, we had to figure out where best to put the car so the trees wouldn't fall on us. It was all fun and exciting, and I won't forget it for a long time.

The last story I'll relate here is one I tell during our employee engagement training. There was a new leader recently appointed for one of the work groups that I dealt with. She started in January, and her employee engagement action plan wasn't due until August. So she calls me up one day in February and says she's ready to submit a new action plan. My immediate response was to point out we don't do that until August. She said, "Well, I've already finished it. I made some changes to the previous plan, which is in pretty good shape as it stands. So we're ready to submit the revised one. Do you think that's a good idea?" I sat there and I thought, well, on the one hand you're not supposed to do that until August. But on the other hand it seemed ridiculous to make her wait when she was so obviously wanting to make continuous improvements to the plan and do a great thing for her team. I said, "You know? You're way ahead of the rest of us in thinking of our planning in terms of a continuing process. It's something leaders of all our teams should be doing every day, not just in August." I like to share that story during training. It's a great way for trainees to understand how we can sometimes lose sight of what's really important about what we do.

Terrence: That's a great story to help people stay focused on the "what" and the "why" of their work. Sometimes we forget, to use a cliché, to keep our eye on the prize. These structured activities, these processes, these practices that we adopt—are they really the ultimate goal? No, their only use is to help us get somewhere.

ROB: The story also tells us that even as so-called experts we can get trapped by what we know, or at least what we think we know. It can leave us blind to the very thing we're trying to teach.

TERRENCE: It tells of a wonderful beginner's mind. It was the new leader's fresh energy, together with your ability to listen that made such a great insight possible.

Tell me a story about your action review process.

ROB: I was part of an after review for a disjointed project in our department for the creation of an online training catalog. We had a team that didn't really understand its purpose. No one really understood their role or their responsibility. So the result was a very noncollaborative two-month struggle to get this thing up and running. And the leader said that we got the training catalog implemented two days after we hoped it would be successful. But also, along the way, had a lot of destruction, and people working overtime and on Saturdays and lots of bad communication. We used the after-action review process to share our stories about what had happened during the project. As a result we were able to reflect without complaint and create an action plan for this year that we hope will get us into a better place with future projects.

TERRENCE: That's a neat demonstration of the power of stories. Typically, bumpy projects involve a lot of natural finger pointing, but that is never productive for anyone. No one is able to hear the lessons to be learned, no one walks away necessarily feeling good about their participation or contribution. Yet when it becomes a story, and each person is adding their perspective, it depersonalizes it and it becomes a virtual working space where the things to be celebrated can be celebrated, and the things to be garnered and taken forward in the future can be brought forward in a positive manner and safe environment.

ROB: The facilitator actually had us put on cards the series of activities from our perspective that occurred, and we posted them up on a wall. It was truly interesting to see what each person's perspective was at different key moments. It was a safe way to talk about personal differences. The facilitator had people put what their inner dialogue was on cards. Not your external dialogue, what's going on inside, and you put that up on the board and you shared that in a safe way. It is a wonderful process to use with teams when you're really trying to tap into diversity of the group.

TERRENCE: People build this story, and you get this subtext around the story, which is that thought process which each person is having as they go through reviewing their involvement on the project. You begin to actively hear and imagine all the other personal and organizational perspectives involved. The subtext is all these different perspectives. Then the next layers are the personal perspectives—the fact that you and I each process information differently. We're reflecting on it differently, we're emotionally experiencing it differently. We have a set of different experiences that filters what's happening to us in the present in different ways. So how do all those come together in the future? What happens? That's very powerful stuff.

ROB: It's interesting how over the years we've tried different OD [organizational development] tools to do it. But this after-action review is really being accepted. Maybe it's because of its credibility from the military or maybe it's the simplicity of the four questions. It's truly being used, embraced, and socialized into the fabric.

TERRENCE: I think it's the directness. It's the simplicity. I think it's also probably a certain amount of the associations that we have with a military briefing . . . we've GOT to get to the bottom of this. But yet it has within it the elbowroom for those who feel comfortable to share their experience more as a narrative. You don't bring to the table your bullets for those four questions. With just a little bit of relaxation and a safe environment the story process can occur. It takes very little to create that safe environment. If just one person starts sharing a personal narrative, suddenly a floodgate opens up, and everyone has one they want to share. It's very easy. The four questions are pillars to tie the narrative to. It's very powerful.

I'd like you to talk a bit about learning and organizational development, and specifically about the Learning Zone.

ROB: First of all, some time ago we identified some core values for the organization, and among them was "learning." Then, of course, we were faced with how to go about making this value part of the fabric of our company. One of the first things we came up with was the notion of a career development center. Because of a changing business environment—deregulation, increased competition, and mergers and acquisitions—we felt it was necessary to provide employees with the opportunity to better prepare themselves to meet those challenges, both within and outside the company. But once we got down to actually planning the sort of things the career development center would offer, we quickly realized that our approach had to be much broader, because of all the connections that career development had with such matters as technical training, leadership, diversity, and interpersonal skills. So then we started to investigate the possibility of what we initially called a "university," which would offer learning in different areas throughout all levels within the company. But one of the union leaders at a planning session pointed out that the connotations of the word *university* might give the wrong impression—that it wasn't meant to be for all employees or that it was only for those who passed some kind of test to get in. Many of our employees don't have a lot of education, and we wanted them to be comfortable about the learning opportunities we were trying to put in place. So the union leader came up with the "Learning Zone."

There's a fairly wide array of opportunities the Learning Zone offers—career and leadership development, diversity learning, communication skills, and technical training. After four years, we're still trying to expand what we offer, adding more pieces to the puzzle. It's been fun. And we've reached the point where we don't have to spend a lot of energy selling the program to folks; now we just do it. That's a big milestone in my work here.

TERRENCE: Looking ahead to the next three years, what do you see as being the major challenges that you'll face?

ROB: I think one will be continuing to integrate computer training with technical training; they're still kind of separate, and we need to unify them as part of a systematic approach to training. Another key for us will be to continue and to expand our leadership development program. A third will be to better integrate new types of learning, like e-learning and self-directed learning. We've run some pilot programs along these lines, but they're still pretty far from being part of the fabric. A final major challenge we'll have to deal with is growth. Subsidiaries can tend to take on a life of their own, and our task will be to ensure those employees feel that they're a part of the company.

TERRENCE: Are you set up as a profit center?

ROB: No, we're part of the budget for Human Resources. But when we've found ourselves in a situation where more funding is needed, the organization has been willing to negotiate with us.

TERRENCE: Does management seek you out as a way to help achieve quarterly and yearly objectives?

ROB: I think we're still headed toward that point, but aren't there yet. We've gotten good reports and solid testimony about the success of our programs, and each day I think we are coming to be more respected for what we accomplish.

TERRENCE: On a scale of 1 to 7, how would you rate senior management for how well it appreciates learning as a strategic advantage?

ROB: I would say that at this point in time they rate a 5 or 6. For example, even in the face of a lot of budget cuts this year, the president of Energy Gas has committed to our continuing to do leadership training for all supervisors this year. Depending on future business conditions, that rating may fall to a 4, but I don't think it will get any lower than that.

TERRENCE: How have you communicated back to senior management your value to the organization in the sense of a positive return on investment?

ROB: The main way we do that is by doing good work. Recently we received approval to hire three more consultants based on the successful work that previous consultants had done. And our leadership development program is now being adopted enterprise-wide. In this culture, if you exhibit value from what you're doing, senior leaders are apt to notice. We also have a pretty great leadership team within our own group. Our director and managers are good relationship builders not only with the consultants we bring in, but with the organization's senior leaders. A third way we demonstrate our value is by submitting quarterly reports and program evaluations.

I just remembered a great example of a very effective story Lynne Ellyn the senior VP of ITS used during one of our Leadership retreats. She called the conference "orbiting the giant hairball." It's based on a book that she had read about a guy who used to work for Hallmark, who spent his thirty-year career figuring out ways he could stay in the creative zone. He had to orbit the entanglement of the corporate structure without losing his creativity. He found this practice of orbiting kept him alive and happy while at Hallmark. We use that as a metaphor in the workshop to have the leaders identify what are the hairballs and then to come up with solutions on how to orbit them.

Observations

Rob points out that the teller should adjust the length of a story based on the context in which the story is being told. Given his background as a facilitator, Rob uses stories extensively in training. However, he finds it more difficult to see how stories can be used in less formal settings such as conversations, and structured ones like meetings. DTE Energy's use of stories in after-action reviews is a step toward incorporating them in other venues besides training.

In order for stories to be used effectively in other settings, Rob explains that three things are necessary. To begin with, members of the group have to trust one another and know each other well. "Second, the individuals in the meeting would need to be skillful in interpersonal communicating, knowing how to ask the right questions and advocating for their own positions." And, lastly you need a skilled facilitator to keep things on track. In the beginning of the conversation Rob points out that I am using the word *story* in a much broader manner than he and most people are accustomed to. Rob also observes that stories can be used ineffectively. As the conversation develops, Rob demonstrates his facility as a storyteller by offering a wealth of personal and organizational stories that are full of insights.

Reflection emerges again as a key competency required by effective communicators. Rob explains the relationship between stories and reflection in the following way: "Part of the process of self-reflection is to formulate the lessons already learned but that you haven't had time in the bustle of work to consciously understand thoroughly. You need to take the time and create the story that communicates what's been happening on the job—what's worked and what hasn't. But that story can't come to you unless you make the space for self-reflection." DTE Energy's adoption of after-action reviews in their organization is a good example of how organizations can encourage reflection in a structured way. Rob's experience of working with after-action reviews also highlights the role stories need to play as part of that process. Without creating a safe environment for eliciting people's stories, the effectiveness of after-action reviews is significantly diminished.

10
Interview with Sherrie Cornett, Dreyer's Ice Cream

In Chapter 4 we explored Dreyer's Ice Cream's Grooves. These are the cultural values that guide Dreyer's employees' behavior. Lots of companies adopt admirable tenets, but few succeed in the way Dreyer's does in truly actualizing them. This is bottom-up and side-to-side communication at its best. At Dreyer's, the Grooves are living, breathing, and evolving values that are taken to heart by the employees. In this profile, I spoke with Sherrie Cornett, who is one of the lead Grooves facilitators. Our dialogue began with an examination of stories and her responses to the survey questions and then naturally evolved into a discussion of how the Grooves are supported and spread through the organization. The Grooves and how they are inculcated is a perfect example of the communication and learning principles we have been discussing. Dreyer's has been successful in tapping into the personal channel of our Communications Matrix (see Chapter 3) to advance these values.

Here are a few of the major themes:

- Stories from our personal lives can be effectively used at work.
- Analogies are stories that help people see things in a different way, which may have more meaning for them and give them something to hang on to.
- Stories have more impact than any other mode of communication.
- Important messages need to be communicated in stories.

The Interview

TERRENCE: I am curious about the relationship of our personal stories to how we use or don't use stories at work. You seem conflicted about this in your own case. On the one hand, you are aware of using stories at work, but on the other hand you're not sure how you use them personally. I kind of feel the same way. But what I want to better understand is the relationships that may exist among how stories are used personally, how they are used personally at work, and how they are used in a concerted, organizational way.

SHERRIE: Well, I think there is some relationship. The connection I see is that, although I don't necessarily use stories in my personal life, I do relate events in my personal life for purposes at work. For example, when I'm facilitating a Grooves workshop and talking about learning a new set of communication skills, I want to get across that those skills can be used outside of work as well. And to make that point, I share a story about when I did volunteer work in Seattle. I worked with a nonprofit organization and chaired their annual fundraiser each year, which was run by all volunteers. These people weren't paid to be there, but by using the communication skills I had developed, I could help keep them be engaged, help them feel like they were really contributing. So I've used that story from my personal experience to illustrate the value of these skills in workshops.

TERRENCE: Okay, and that sounds like it happens a fair amount in training situations for you. How do you find people in training responding to these stories?

SHERRIE: I think they bring concepts alive. It gives them something to really hang on to and say, "Oh, that's how you would use that. That's how that applies." So particularly for training purposes a story like that can help illustrate the value of what you're learning. Sometimes just talking about the raw concepts underlying the new skill that is being taught leaves people asking, "Well, how can it be used? How could I use that?" And stories help answer those questions.

TERRENCE: So you're pretty much down the middle of the rating scale in terms of frequency with which you tell stories. You also rated yourself as a fair storyteller. Why do you perceive yourself that way?

SHERRIE: Well, probably because I'm aware that it's not something I do consistently. As a trainer, it's a skill I've learned that has its value in terms of my becoming a good facilitator for learning. But in other aspects of my work life, I don't know that I really use storytelling. And I think this is why I rated myself "fair." When I plan to use a story, I think I do it well. However, that takes place in a fully conscious way as part of my plan for a training program. But that's different from incorporating storytelling into my style of communication or leadership. I think I'd have a fair ways to go to do that.

TERRENCE: If you rewound a tape of the day's events and interactions, do you think you would ever find yourself responding to someone with a short personal experience or anecdote, or would you communicate in a fairly straightforward fashion without using a lot of analogies or illustrations?

SHERRIE: As part of my general communication, analogies don't come easily to me. I am good about sharing a personal experience, but if I had to make up a story or come up with an analogy or something to help convey a learning point—well, I'm not able to do that extemporaneously.

TERRENCE: So it helps you to really script out a story. For example, you might know a metaphor that's worked well in a previous training situation and you're able to use that effectively.

SHERRIE: That's right; and I'll steal shamelessly from other trainers. When I hear them effectively make a point about one thing or another, I have no qualms about thinking, "Wow! That really worked for them. I'm going to try that myself." But as I said, I just don't have a brain that can come up with analogies. However, I think I do a good job of drawing out people's personal experiences and observations, but for me that's a tangible thing in a way that analogies and metaphors are not.

TERRENCE: Can you give an example from a recent training when you saw something happening either during the training or before because you had worked with that person? Was this planned, or did it happen spontaneously?

SHERRIE: I don't know if this is what you're asking about, but I did a Train the Trainer workshop recently in which I was walking through one of our Grooves . . . the Groove of "Ownership." I remembered back to a previous training workshop that took place about two years ago in which one of my facilitator candidates had come up with a really wonderful way to illustrate that particular Groove. It was a different approach than any I was familiar with, and so I shared it with the group. I've used it several times since, and I always credit her. It was a great learning experience for me as well. Is that the sort of thing you're talking about?

TERRENCE: Yep. And then when you are facilitating a two- or three-day workshop, do you bring other such comments, experiences, observations, responses, and behaviors from previous training to your work with the present group?

SHERRIE: Yes.

TERRENCE: Do you think those are stories? Would you have thought of those, before today, necessarily as stories?

SHERRIE: No, I would not have thought of those as stories. I would've thought of that as just linking back to something that someone else had said that ties into what you're talking about right now. I look at it more as a way to acknowledge the contribution of past participants and to illustrate the learning. But that's an important part of facilitating, especially for a multiple-day program. You have to be able to link back to past training for observations and comments and different approaches that can enrich the present work.

TERRENCE: For a minute, entertain this notion of linkages, associations, and connecting experiences as all ways in which stories function. Does that change the number of instances that you would qualify as storytelling?

SHERRIE: Yes, it fits one of your definitions of making stories. Absolutely.

TERRENCE: I am interested in understanding how stories facilitate linkages and associations. In this sense, stories are more like small nuggets of communication facilitators, which is not how we traditionally think of stories. Let's take Dreyer's "The Birth of Rocky Road" story:

> Dreyer added walnuts (later replaced with almonds) to his chocolate ice cream and, using his wife's sewing shears, cut marshmallows into bite-sized pieces to make the first batch of Rocky Road, a name that gave people something to smile about in the face of the Great Depression.

Now when you look at the story on the [Dreyer] website, it's just a sentence. It's not a long drawn out narrative, yet the imagery is rich and generates associations. What if I wanted people to get the message that sometimes the company has been on "Rocky Roads"? Couldn't I use this story as a working metaphor and guide people's imaginations to make an association? Something like, "Hey, we're getting ready to go through a merger process and while it's an exciting time, and we're all behind this 100 percent, it could be a rocky road. Each of us may have to find our little nuggets of responsibilities like those original marshmallows and throw them in to sweeten our success." I'm just role-playing here. But sometimes, excuse my French, there may be only a fine line between bullshitting and storytelling. But the idea is that it comes via an association.

One of my hypotheses is that much of what we learn is through linkages and associations. We relate something to something else. What I want to learn is whether, when you broaden people's sense of what makes for storytelling, that changes how they consciously use stories, when they use them, and the impact the stories have. So I'm really happy that you used those words *linkages* and *associations* because that's really more of what I'm interested in. Let's see, on a scale of 1 to 7, rate the potential role you think stories could play in your organization.

SHERRIE: Now having a more broadened sense of how you're looking at stories, I would bump that up to even a 7. I was thinking of stories as "Let me tell you a story" or "Here's a story about. . . ." If we are thinking about them as "Here's how that relates" or "Here's the association" or "Here's the connection as I see it," then I would absolutely say those are ways of storytelling too.

TERRENCE: Do you make a distinction between the words *analogy* and *metaphor*?

SHERRIE: That's a good question. I've never really thought about it before. Off the top of my head I can't think of how I would define them separately. Both of them mean to me something like, "Let's look at X in terms of Y."

TERRENCE: Could an analogy be a simple word? For example, if you weren't sitting in front of this microphone and I was trying to describe its shape to you, I might say it's like a drumstick. That's a simple word, but it has an image associated to it. Sometimes I've heard people use word pictures as analogies and metaphors.

SHERRIE: That is one of the values in using analogies, I think. It does paint a picture. It gives you a visual to hang on to that maybe is more tangible than trying to describe something in words. It helps people see things in a different way that may be more meaningful for them.

TERRENCE: So, for example, if you know that someone's a golfer and you relate the concept you are trying express with golf, that analogical framework becomes a powerful way to link ideas.

SHERRIE: Right. And the person will be more likely to remember it.

TERRENCE: Why do you think that?

SHERRIE: I think people often get more meaning when they can visualize something. I haven't read the book myself, but I've heard people talk about Timothy Gallwey's work the *Inner Game of Work: Focus, Learning, Pleasure, Mobility, in the Workplace* and the analogies he draws between tennis and work. Now, I'm not a big tennis player and haven't played since I was in high school, and I won't tell you how long ago that was, but that approach is apparently successful in reaching a lot of people. But you do have to know your audience. For example, it wouldn't do any good for anyone to use a golfing analogy with me. I'm not a golfer. I wouldn't have a clue what they were talking about. Broader-based analogies are probably better than those drawn from sports.

TERRENCE: Do you find yourself trying to determine what might be useful metaphors or analogies that would speak to a particular group? As you're going through the training and learning about the members of the group, do you put these items on a mental peg to be used later on?

SHERRIE: No, I don't, at least not with the degree of specificity you describe. I may do it unconsciously with people that I know fairly well.

TERRENCE: Now what about the word *experience*? How would you define it? I know it sounds like I'm asking for the obvious, but I'm interested again in how it might relate to some of the ideas we have already discussed such as how stories facilitate linkages, associations, and the use of metaphors and analogies.

SHERRIE: I think of experience generally as all the things that happen to me. But then there are those events or moments that really stand out for me in some way such that I later remember or harken back to. We have experiences every day. And although some we'll never remember because there just wasn't anything notable about them, there are some that will stand out, perhaps because they remind you of other experiences. I think these are the kind of experiences that get turned into stories, as I've already shared.

TERRENCE: You used a wonderful word a moment ago. You used the word *harken*. Now what made you put that word together with experience? What were you thinking?

SHERRIE: I guess I was thinking that harken describes how an experience becomes available for me to recall even if it was lost in the vastness of all my other experiences. Something harkened it back to me. It's a very old-fashioned word.

TERRENCE: I don't think it is old-fashioned at all. When we harken, we call something back to ourselves and gather the unique gift it offers us. When something is harkened, there's a sense that we listen to it in a fundamentally deep way. It's come back. And maybe before, as you said, it was just a passing moment, but another event takes place that causes that earlier experience to return and in the process we garner a new insight. In this sense it is like an epiphany.

So, why do you think stories could play a more important role in the organization? As you look around and assess how things presently are at this company, where would you say the company is on a storytelling scale of 1 to 7?

SHERRIE: If a 7 is the best, I would say we're not there. However, I would also say there are people here who are very good at using stories. As an organization I think we value stories without fully understanding that's what they are. If we were to ask people here about the value of storytelling or using stories, I bet a lot of them would have the same reaction I did. They wouldn't think of all the links and the associations we make every day. So I think that organizationally we're probably better than we might think we are. We're probably somewhere between a 5 and 6.

TERRENCE: And why do you feel that it could play even a greater potential role in the organization?

SHERRIE: It is such a powerful way to help people learn, and a powerful way to communicate. Again, learning is more effective if you can get people to visualize what you're talking about, or help them understand a new concept in a different way, or lead someone to see the benefits of some behavior or offer a better way to remember something. I think stories can have more of an impact in doing these things than other modes of communication.

TERRENCE: If we think about all the memos and other forms of communication that an organization uses to reach both its employees and its customers, do you think stories would have to be used as frequently as these more traditional forms of communication? If an organization was going to consciously use the story approach rather than the traditional means of communication, would the same level of effort be required? What might be different, if anything? Maybe nothing would, what do you think?

SHERRIE: My initial response is that I think stories are more effective in informal communications. It's when we're communicating with a person one on one, or even in meetings, that stories come into play the most. In written or more formal communications, I think they have to be carefully used and not overused. If you're communicating to several thousand people, it's very difficult to make sure that your story is going to speak to everybody. So the smaller the group, the more you can tailor the story or customize it, and relate it to peoples' experiences and work.

TERRENCE: What do you think it would take to invigorate a company to use stories in informal communications? Think about all those small communications that happen constantly in an organization between people. What would you need to do to get people more engaged in consciously using stories as a form of communication?

SHERRIE: One thing is for sure—you'd have to help them understand all these aspects of stories that you have brought to my attention, things like making linkages and associations. But I can't imagine that anyone who considers themselves to be a good communicator or someone who wants to be more effective as a communicator would say that the use of stories or analogies or making associations isn't important. Anybody who has even halfway good communication skills certainly recognizes the value of relating things to one another and to people's experience, particularly in business. For them to see it as storytelling would require some education about the broader meaning of *stories* as you use it.

TERRENCE: The curious thing is that, as you said, stories are so prevalent. It is common sense. The word *story* is so much a part of our everyday vernacular, but we use it aimlessly. What's so groundbreaking here? No one would disagree stories are effective, but when we listen to our conversations and look at our forms of communication, we notice that for some reason we're not really using them, and certainly not very well. But that can change once we become conscious of it. What else do you think holds you back from using stories more consciously and frequently than you do?

SHERRIE: As I said before, my brain doesn't always work that way. You're going to think this is an odd coincidence, but I've been working with a consultant friend of mine in redesigning some materials and procedures, and I've been talking to her lately about having trouble thinking up analogies. Then just this weekend I was doing some personal reflection and I came up with two that relate to my personal life. I was so excited and asked her whether they made sense, and she said, "Yes, they're very good." But because I don't come up with them extemporaneously or in the moment when I'm in a conversation or a meeting, I think that keeps me from using them more often.

TERRENCE: Do you realize you just told me a short little story about reflection? In it there were lots of little associations and epiphanies. Let me relate a brief story that comes from my reflection on my drive here this morning. Driving across the bridge, and trying to remember all the right exits and being unfamiliar with the route, I felt myself becoming anxious. Then I started to daydream about a scuba dive I am planning to do this weekend. It's going to be a very deep dive in an area I'm not really familiar with, so the topography will be unique. Despite the depth and the new topography, I know I can't afford to be anxious—it's imperative I stay calm and relaxed. In that moment I realized that my feelings on the highway could be guided by the same principle. Reflecting on one story enabled me to rewrite the story of driving on the highway unfolding right then. The reason why I use that little story is that I find that while most of us are very visually dominant, there's an aspect to stories that is kinesthetic.

You used the word *reflection*. I am curious to know how you articulate your sense of that word. And when you do reflect, what do you think or see yourself doing?

SHERRIE: Reflection for me is the quiet time that I spend with myself in introspection. It's part of my process of evaluation, whether it's about how I'm feeling, sizing up a challenge that's in front of me, or contemplating a big decision. For example, I may not be happy with the way something is going and want to do something about it. That for me is what I do in reflection. But it can also be about taking time to enjoy the good things that have happened in my life. Those are important for me to recall and think about as well.

TERRENCE: How does the image of a mirror work for our discussion of reflection? We stand in front of a mirror because it reflects ourselves back to us. Do you feel sometimes like you're standing in front of a mirror but you're in the dark, because you haven't made the effort to turn any lights on? We have mirrors around us all the time. The people around us, the events of a day, our reactions to these events, how these relate to events in the past—aren't these like mirrors? Do we really make an effort to switch on the lights to see our reflections in these other sorts of mirrors? If you were to play with this metaphor, where would you find yourself in it?

SHERRIE: I would take a little bit different approach. Maybe I see myself going through life avoiding mirrors. I know they're there, but I'm not stopping to look at them.

TERRENCE: You need to use mirrors when you drive a car, right? When I used the metaphor of mirrors, I did not mean to imply we only use mirrors to look at ourselves. We also use mirrors in cars to see behind us and from side to side. I wanted the metaphor of mirrors to include reflections of things other than ourselves. For example, I am frequently on the cell phone when I am driving and need to change lanes, but I don't always take the time to check and see what cars might be coming up behind me. So I am guilty of not making the effort to direct my attention to one of my car's mirrors. In this way I am missing a vital source of information. I would never advise it, even though I do it. If we can agree it is not advisable to do while driving a car, would we advise doing the same in our lives as part of an organization? The question to ask is, "Are we looking in our rear and side view organizational mirrors for information?"

This is pretty heavy stuff. Let's shift gears. Tell me a story about the Grooves.

SHERRIE: Back in the late 1970s, before they bought Dreyer's, our CEO and former president had been in the restaurant business together. They are the first to tell you that they failed miserably at it. But what they were successful at was creating a work environment that people enjoyed. In fact, when they bought Dreyer's, a large number of the restaurant employees came to work for them because of the closeness and loyalty they felt. They started with a very small business of about thirty to forty employees. As the business grew, however, they realized they ran the risk of losing that shared sense of closeness that had made it a special place to work. So the company executives and key employees went on a retreat to focus on those things about the organization that were most valuable to them. Then they set about the task of deciding what to call them, how to label them. The hot business book at that time was *In Search of Excellence,* and somewhere in that book Tom Peters talks about being "in the groove." So that term was adopted for our guiding principles.

One of our Grooves, I think it's "Respect for the Individual," came from a principle followed by the Nordstrom Company. Back in those days Nordstrom would give each new employee a business card on the back of which was printed their principle "Use your own best judgment at all times." We borrowed that value to create a Groove about respecting others' ideas and opinions. My point is that we didn't just make up the Grooves; some were borrowed from other sources. But they all are ways of labeling these powerful principles that were and still are the foundation for our success.

I am reminded of our organizational story that I mentioned on the survey about "One Trip Around the Track"—that you only get one trip around the track in life so you better enjoy it. You hear that story so much at Dreyer's. It's very much ingrained into the culture of this place, including even job interviews: "If you come to work at Dreyer's, we want you to be making a good choice for yourself. It isn't just about our trying to find the best candidate. We want this to be the right company for you too, because you get one trip around this track and what's the point if you're not enjoying it?" Any time when someone is here and not having fun, we say to them, "Go and God bless you. Life's too short. Go find what makes you happy." I think that's a wonderful approach.

This is another story that I like. Our CEO talks about how when we hire someone new, we've got the perfect employee. We've got somebody who's enthusiastic and excited to be here. Our main responsibility is not to suck that out of them. They've got the perfect attitude on Day 1. So we want to create an environment that fosters that Day 1 attitude and keeps people encouraged, involved, excited, and empowered. We want them to feel that every day what they do makes a difference. We want them to be excited to get up in the morning and come to work. That's what the Grooves are intended to help ensure. I think that's one of the things people most misunderstand about the Grooves. They're not just warm and fuzzy, but there are powerful business reasons behind each of them that are part of our strategic planning.

TERRENCE: See how from an analysis standpoint there is a series of brief stories in which each triggers the next? From an observer's perspective your energy changed. Your engagement level changed. Let's go on to some of these other stories you mentioned on the survey. Tell me the one about Dreyer's successful product launch of Dreamery.

SHERRIE: That's become a big story for us because it signaled a business shift for the organization. About three years ago, we had a distribution agreement with Ben and Jerry's Ice Cream. One day, I think it was in August of that year, Ben and Jerry's gave us notice that they were terminating our distribution agreement. Under the terms of that agreement, I believe they had to give us one year's notice. Of course, we were disappointed and discouraged; we had enjoyed a long-standing relationship with Ben and Jerry's, and they suddenly decide to try to build their own distribution network. Our immediate response was, "How can they do this to us? We're going to lose volume." But within hours we started changing our tune and said instead, "Hang on a second. This could be a huge opportunity for us." In the distribution arrangement that we had with Ben and Jerry's there was a noncompete clause that prevented us from developing, marketing, and selling our own super premium product. But that wouldn't apply in a year's time. So our whole business focus shifted. The next day our marketing and research and development people were brought together in a conference room and given the task of developing a product that could compete in that category. Even though this was a new niche of the ice cream industry for us, we later had our most successful launch ever of a new product. Ironically, after a year trying to develop their own distribution network, Ben and Jerry's came back to us. However, this time when they signed an agreement with us, there was no noncompete clause in the contract. We had our own super premium ice cream that we distributed along with theirs.

TERRENCE: I'd like you to tell me more about the Grooves. I am especially interested in what your role is with them.

SHERRIE: The Grooves are really the guiding principles of our business philosophy. There are ten of them, and they go back to the very origins of the organization. In the early 1980s, when we started distributing outside of the Bay Area, there was a concern that as we grew we would lose our unique working environment. So it became very important for us to formalize what made that environment so special. A lot of work was done to clearly articulate and define the Grooves. We had to get them down on paper in a way that would make sense and be understandable to different people joining our organization.

Our early efforts involved very little in the way of formal training. We relied on all the informal communications that naturally occur in the life of an organization to get the message of the Grooves across. But the mid- to late 1980s were a time of great growth for us; that's when we went national. We were expanding at a rate of anywhere between fourteen and twenty new markets a year, and it was decided that we needed to begin training people in what it was we as an organization were all about. So we began to work with a consultant to put a training program together about the Grooves. I believe the first Groove class was held in 1991. However, at that time there was no specific department dedicated exclusively to training employees in the Grooves. And though there had at first been a great push to get training materials out there, there was no formalized program for what to do next.

The scores of our Groove surveys in the mid-1990s started to level off. Although the scores hadn't dipped, to our executives' credit it was a trend that disturbed them. A task force was formed to try to understand the reasons for that trend, and a key conclusion it drew was that we needed a person or department focused solely on Grooves training. As a result of that finding, in 1998 Dreyer's formed a department that was then called "Leadership Development." I was transferred from our Washington office as one of two people who were tasked with developing not only leadership development programs but reenergizing the Grooves training throughout the company. During my first year we hosted a conference with folks who had been doing our Grooves training, asking them "What is it that you need to be able to do this more effectively and what are your current best practices?" A number of wonderful recommendations came out of the conference. One was that the trainers felt unprepared to deliver the training. They had just been asked to do so. And in many cases they were not trained facilitators themselves, but had gladly taken it on because they were committed to making the Grooves work. A second thing we discovered was that the materials were outdated. They really needed to be looked at again in terms of the learning design model and how they were presented. We took that review on and in 1999 distributed brand new materials for Grooves training. We also created a certification program that trains our trainers specifically for Grooves programs.

We typically find there are many people in the organization who have a great deal of passion for the Grooves. One of the exciting things about our program is that the door is open to all members of the organization to become Grooves trainers—everyone from sales representatives to production workers in warehouses to division managers. Survey results told us that people really appreciated the new materials we developed and found the skills training to be better communicated and, what I think is most important, consistent. Our goal is to have a network of trainers out there who consistently communicate what the Grooves mean. We want to make sure everyone in the organization is on the same page. To ensure that consistency we continue to tweak and fine tune our materials based on the feedback we get from surveys.

One of the factors of the Grooves' impact on the organization is the expectation that every new employee will receive Grooves training within their first six months. I've actually had people in Grooves classes their first day on the job. I don't think that's necessarily the best thing, but timing-wise, that's how it worked out. If you are a manager, we love it if you receive your training within your first three months of employment, because you're responsible for helping to create and maintain a Grooves environment for others. We also have an expectation that every eighteen months to two years, you go for some sort of regrouping process to get back in touch with the Grooves.

TERRENCE: How many trainers do you have?

SHERRIE: Right now we have 119 trainers for over 6,000 employees in the organization nationwide.

TERRENCE: Tell me some more about the Grooves certification program.

SHERRIE: The certification workshop is three days. We have some material that goes out to people before the workshop to prepare them for what their experience is going to be like. There is a little bit of reading to introduce them to the ideas of competencies and perfected facilitation, and also to prepare them for the fact that they will be delivering presentations on the Grooves and receiving coaching and feedback. When they arrive at the workshop on Day 1, we first discuss the purpose of the workshop and their expectations. Next we spend two to three hours carefully going over facilitation competencies. For example, we want to ensure that people can write clear directions for activities. As for communication competencies, we focus on different aspects of the communication process, for instance, the use of examples and analogies. Do they summarize points and make clear transitions? What is their level of knowledge and can they fully articulate it? There are drills that are used to assess and develop these competencies; after working through them, each person does a teach-back to the class. We also ask each person on the first day to prepare a five-minute presentation about their favorite Groove. That not only enables me to assess whether they understand that Groove, but its real purpose is to have folks begin to get used to being in front of a group—to get rid of some of those nerves. At the end of the day we go over the homework assignment. They have to be prepared to facilitate right from the Groove materials the next day.

TERRENCE: How big is the group?

SHERRIE: Usually around six trainees. If you have any more than that, you can't get all the presentations in and the coaching done. When we do have more than six, I assign a second trainer and the presentations are split between the two. On Day 2 we first introduce the feedback model because immediately following the individual presentations, each person must expect group feedback reinforcing things that were done well and identifying areas for improvement or opportunities missed. Then we move on to the next presentation. At the end of the day I will sit down with each person for some one-on-one coaching based on what I observed. I like to give them different things to target for their round 2 presentations.

TERRENCE: At that point they've seen what you're looking for in terms of how to engage the people they will be training. It's just a function of applying it.

SHERRIE: Yes, and they've seen the flow. They've also seen the activities that go with it. We talk about what they're learning throughout the process. And sometimes somebody will stumble, and we'll talk about that and say, "You had a little problem at this point. Here are some tips and ideas to think about when you go to deliver this the first time." It is a very interactive and engaging process. I remember what's it's like to be certified. It's hard. It's a lot of work and it's exhausting. It really pleases me that, almost without fail, people complete their training so energized and enthusiastic about the Grooves, and about this new opportunity they're being given. I think it's important to stress that the folks who become Groove trainers in the organization are not professional facilitators; it is not their full-time job. They take this on in addition to their regular duties.

TERRENCE: Have you had learners that said they just couldn't do it?

SHERRIE: No.

TERRENCE: Why is that?

SHERRIE: I think the answer to that lies in a couple of things. First of all, even though they deliver only two of the Grooves during the workshop, they got to see other Grooves presentations by their colleagues. And they're encouraged to observe the presentations from the perspective of a facilitator. The training empowers you to discern what in a given presentation has the greatest impact—what works and what doesn't. The feedback is incredible.

TERRENCE: Do people find these skills they learn in workshop transferable to other areas?

SHERRIE: I have had people attend the workshops who weren't specifically interested in Grooves training per se, but who wanted to gain those skills that they've seen their colleagues to have learned in training. I've also had managers in the workshops say, "Oh my gosh, this is going to help me when I'm leading meetings. It's going to help me be a more effective communicator. It's going to help me be a better coach." They can see the value of these kinds of communication skills because the focus is on the other person, the one they're learning to better communicate with, and not on them as a learner.

TERRENCE: How would you assess most people as facilitators before they begin a Grooves training workshop?

SHERRIE: More often than not, most of the people starting a workshop have never trained before. They have never been a trainer nor done any sort of facilitation of learning. We've all helped a fellow worker learn something new—on the computer, maybe, or by explaining how we do things to a new employee. But that isn't the same thing as the sort of facilitating that we teach in workshops. So, I very often work with extremely inexperienced people. It is rare to have someone with previous training or who had been certified in other kinds of materials. But I want to point out that even if they're inexperienced, most of the folks are there because it's something they want to do. They're usually well thought of in their organization and have a lot of passion and belief in the Grooves. In our organization, that counts for a lot— the passion and commitment for learning and teaching form that connection with the people that they're standing in front of. It's a connection that gives them support.

TERRENCE: That's very powerful. The actual Groove training itself that they deliver. . . . Could you describe that?

SHERRIE: It's an eight-hour day, and again we try to make sure that it's structured to appeal to a variety of learning preferences. We include visual, auditory, as well as kinesthetic learning. We begin by introducing ourselves, of course, and getting those details out of the way, then launch directly into a game designed to make a very powerful point about how important are the choices we make every day and the impact that they can have on our culture and our environment. That gives us an effective way to transition to a conversation about communication skills. For this part of the training, we use a variety of different approaches—videos, informal interactions. Sometimes we break the group up into smaller groups for discussion. We try to have a good mix of activities. In the afternoon we go through the ten Grooves. We begin by asking the group to illustrate with a drawing what being a "Groovy" person at Dreyer's might look like, incorporating the ten Grooves into the drawing. There are only two restrictions: They can't use words and everyone has to contribute to the drawing.

TERRENCE: What are some of the good ones you've gotten?

SHERRIE: Of course, they're all different, just like every group and the people who make it up are different. Some take a broad approach and try to capture the Grooves with one all-encompassing picture. Others draw a person and try to represent each of the ten Grooves individually. One that really stands out in my mind took the broader approach and depicted climbers making their way up a mountainside. It was a really nice job of tying the Grooves together.

One of the best illustrations came out of the last workshop I did. The group was depicting the Groove "Ready, Fire, Aim." Now, usually you get a bull's-eye target with an arrow in the middle for that Groove. But this time the group drew arrows that had fallen all around the target and then finally one hitting the bull's-eye. That really captured what we mean by "Ready, Fire, Aim." You're going to have some misses, but you'll learn from them and get better.

TERRENCE: I would call that working with a metaphor.

SHERRIE: Yes, it's the process of telling a story. And through that I get the opportunity as a facilitator to see whether or not the group and its members pick up on what we're talking about.

TERRENCE: What amazes me is that it's so simple, in the sense of being basic. Now, you could stand in front of the group and talk about the Grooves very formally, and perhaps on the evaluations they might even rate you as being "excellent." But aren't people more likely to better remember the illustration they helped create?

SHERRIE: It's interesting. I've never ever had anyone refuse to participate. They're hesitant sometimes, but every group ultimately gets into it. And some pretty remarkable stuff comes out of it. Our plant in southern California posts the drawings throughout the building. They're great.

TERRENCE: What a wonderful reminder of the power of that process.

SHERRIE: Yes, and it's valuable for new employees. They may not know what the drawings are all about at first, but they can tell they're important. And when they are in their own workshop, I can tell that some of them are thinking about how their art is going to be posted like the others.

TERRENCE: On a much larger scale, are you involved in any other aspects of training here?

SHERRIE: We're decentralizing, and so we're not really a top-down training organization. But there are corporate programs that we sponsor and we provide to the organization. I don't go out and do that training myself, but we help provide the resources and guide the training. One of the corporate programs we provide is our Leadership University program, which we deliver in two sessions with the help of an external consultant. When we first started this program back in 1998, the idea was to direct it to the top 100 leaders of the organization. But after only the first session, they found it had such an impact that it was decided to include more people in the organization. Since then, we've offered it to more than 600 people. It's not a program you can enroll in yourself; you have to be asked to participate. We believe it's had a very powerful impact on the organization.

TERRENCE: How large a group do you support here in Oakland?

SHERRIE: Our Oakland staff is probably pushing 250 people.

TERRENCE: And how many other places in the field?

SHERRIE: We have eight plants including Alaska.

TERRENCE: They eat ice cream in Alaska?

SHERRIE: Yes, it actually ranks higher than any other state for per capita consumption of ice cream.

Observations

Sherrie is aware of using stories in a training event. She recognizes the potential of incorporating stories as an integral part of one's communication and leadership style, but finds it difficult to actualize. Sherrie struggles with what many of us have difficulty understanding in regards to how to work with stories. We assume that if we cannot think quickly on our feet and come up with analogies or stories to land our "learning points," then we are failing to utilize the communication power of stories. Nothing could be further from the truth. To leverage the power of stories we need to be effective at eliciting them from others and using them to facilitate reflection. There is a value to using stories to land "learning points," and in Chapter 2 we saw how stories can be used to encode information. We understand this way of working with stories well because it is one of the principal ways we use them, but it is not the most powerful one. About halfway through the interview Sherrie uses the word *harken* to describe how certain experiences cause her to stop and reflect. This kind of deep listening implicit in the word *harken* is the subject of Chapter 15. In that chapter we will look at how stories facilitate this type reflection. Reflection is a very personal thing and Sherrie reminds us that is not something everyone either wants to do or share with others. As the interview progresses, Sherrie has a wealth of stories to share about Dreyer's Ice Cream and the role of the Grooves.

11

Interview with Marty Fischer, Starbucks Coffee

You might want to grab a cup of coffee while you read this interview. Marty Fisher is director of Retail Learning at Starbucks. He is a gifted storyteller. This is a guy who understands the power of stories and makes it a part of his work. In all honesty, going into this interview I had no idea that Marty was a natural. I also did not realize the extent to which Starbucks has made reflection and stories a part of their corporate culture. You'll have to read it for yourself to discover what I mean.

Here are some of the major themes:

- Stories have intentionality. The teller has a reason for sharing a story and hopes to lead his listeners in a direction.
- Storytelling is a two-way street. Listening to stories gives you the context for what another person is trying to communicate.
- The critical role of context in communication establishes a common ground between those who are communicating so that they are focused and directed toward the same thing.
- Stories create a sense of comfort between people, which opens up all kinds of possibilities.
- Storytelling can be as simple as saying the right word at the right time, which can produce a rich set of associations.

The Interview

MARTY: I was in New York on September 11, and that morning was on my way to a meeting. We were preparing to kick off a new training program, and our regional office in New York City is on Fifth Avenue and 33rd Street, a block away from the Empire State Building. I was standing on the corner of 34th Street and Madison Avenue at a quarter to nine that morning when the first plane to crash into the World Trade Center flew right over my head. I guess it was a defining moment for everyone, but it's something that I will never, ever forget. The sound of the impact and explosion . . . then the billowing smoke. . . . Anyway, what we did for the rest of that week really convinced me that I was working for the right company. The first thing we did was shut down our stores across North America. We didn't know what the implications of the attack involved, and the company wanted our partners to be home with their families and loved ones. It may not have been the best business decision, because we lost a lot of money that day, but it was a decision made out of respect for the people of the company. Then when the Starbucks in New York reopened on September 13, it was just great how we pitched in and helped support the rescue effort. We donated coffee and food to the rescue workers twenty-four hours a day. And people in the city, our regular customers, said, "Thank God! Where have you been? We need you." I tell you, I get chills thinking about it. Folks needed a place to go to connect with each other, and there just aren't a lot of places like that. We have become the world's front porch, where people can interact with one another.

TERRENCE: I think it has that porch-like quality you mention even internationally. When I'm at home, I meet with my friend once or twice a week at Starbucks. It's a setting I associate with relaxed conversation. And then when I'm on the road, even in an international location, the Starbucks I come across connect with that experience and I know I can expect to find a comfortable social atmosphere there.

MARTY: We're really conscious of that. We want to make sure that people make that sort of connection about our stores. But we want to provide that comfortable feeling and be flexible too. Some of our stores have music playing, some even have live music; other Starbucks are quiet. But the fundamental idea is that it's a respite from the world. I grew up in New York, and whenever I'd go to a Starbucks, it was like shutting the door on all the noise and rush of the city.

TERRENCE: I have to ask you. . . . Before we get into some other topics I'd like to talk with you about, how do you respond when people say Starbucks is the big bully driving the corner café out of business? That's been a common criticism of Starbucks over the years as it has established more stores.

MARTY: Our focus is on being a real member of the community. That means giving back to the community, not just taking over. In fact, there are a lot more other good coffee shops throughout North America than there were fifteen years ago. What we've done is provide a market for these other shops. But back to your specific question, every one of our stores is involved some way or another with working for the good of the community. In San Francisco, for example, we do a lot of AIDS work; and in the countries where the coffee we use is grown, we have programs for the education and medical care of the coffee growers and their families. As a good corporate citizen, we aren't looking to take away from the community, but to help improve it.

TERRENCE: I think what you say about Starbucks's enabling the growth of this market niche is true. Throughout the country, even in areas where the folks who lived there would not have thought of a coffee shop as figuring into their daily routine, stores like Starbucks are popping up.

MARTY: That's truly the difference we've tried to make, because before coffee was a commodity, and our job is to make it an experience. It's a product, certainly, but our goal is not just to sell coffee but to create uplifting experiences that enrich the daily lives of people. Everyone in the company shares that goal in whatever position they fill. For example, I don't work directly with customers every day, but I have lots of interaction with others inside of the company, and my goal is to do whatever I can to help them out as employees.

TERRENCE: I'm always struck by how Starbucks links products to different times of the year. Now it's summer, and there are these wonderful chilled coffees and cappuccinos. Then during the holidays, you offer products tied to the season.

MARTY: Yes, we think it important to build in change or variety so there's something new or different for our customers, or at least provide a number of options. Customer service? We don't even talk in those terms; instead we speak about Customer Care and Legendary Service. What can we do that's going to make your day memorable? Sometimes just a smile will help.

TERRENCE: I'll tell you a great Pike Market story. Last time I was here in Seattle, I went to this one place that sold grilled halibut sandwiches, and after ordering one, just stood there salivating while I waited for it. It didn't take long to prepare, and when the young woman behind the counter handed it to me, she took a moment . . . locked eyes with me . . . and said, not in a flirtatious manner but simply making a connection, "I'm so excited for you." She could see how much I was looking forward to eating the sandwich. And so guess where my wife and I went today for lunch. Right back to that same place, because my experience there really stuck in my head. It's those kinds of experiences, and our stories about them, that we retain.

MARTY: You see, her job was not just to hand over your sandwich; her purpose was to connect with you. That's so rare today.

TERRENCE: Yes, it is, and this fits right into the work of Csikmihalyi. He wrote about the flow of the work we do, how it's something that becomes an end in itself. He first started looking at a group of assembly line workers who seemed to get more satisfaction out of their jobs than many of the white-collar employees making much more money. What he discovered was that the assembly line workers had found a way to constantly challenge themselves, and as a result they put more of their hearts into their work—it became a creative act.

MARTY: And that's a two-way street. That's the connection that we really try to cultivate. Merely passing a drink over a bar to me would not be a satisfying job for anyone. But handing over a cup of coffee when you've invested yourself in whether and how much I'm going to like it, well, that makes all the difference.

TERRENCE: Let's change our focus a little bit, if that's okay with you. You know my primary interest is in stories and how they are a part of our professional as well personal lives. So, I'm interested in what comes to mind when you hear the word *story*? What does it mean to you?

MARTY: The first word that pops into my head is *moral*. So what's the moral to the story? There's an intentionality to storytelling; there's a point to be made. The problem for me is that if the teller of the story isn't very skilled, I find myself wondering after a bit, "What's the point of the story? Why are you telling me this story? I don't get it." So the moral is a really critical element for me. If I see where you're taking me, or what the point of the story is, I'm more apt to listen carefully.

TERRENCE: Okay, so there's a sense of broadcasting a specific message through the medium of story, so that intentionality becomes really important. The story is used to encode a specific point.

MARTY: And, depending on the skill of the storyteller, it's usually clear right away whether that person has a point to his story. Sometimes you can tell that it's going to drag on and on, and you're left with asking, "Why did you tell me that?" But other times the point of the story is clear. That's what I hope is the case with my kids when I tell them a story about something that happened to me so it doesn't happen to them.

TERRENCE: Is it possible for a story not to have a point?

MARTY: Absolutely. And even a good story, if it's told well with lots of drama and action, doesn't have to have a point. But I think in the end I'd still wonder why the person told me the story.

TERRENCE: So, intentionality really comes into play for you. Let me ask you this; is it possible to use the same story on different occasions with different purposes?

MARTY: Yes, absolutely. The same set of facts, the same story line, can be used by a skilled facilitator to lead different people each to his or her own conclusions. So by telling you the same story that I told others, I'm prompting a different thought process than before, because now that process is in your head.

TERRENCE: Maybe what the storyteller is doing is trying to spark a specific set of connections on the part of his listeners in order to help them come on their own to a specific point the storyteller wants to make.

MARTY: And I think it's a lot more effective to lead you in that direction with a story rather than just flat out telling you the point I'm trying to make. It's a much more engaging way to learn.

TERRENCE: Definitely. So we agree that stories are important for broadcasting a moral or making a point. They have intentionality. But what about storytelling when the aim is to tune in to where the other person is, to get a fix on what she's thinking, on where she's coming from?

MARTY: That's a good question. I guess stories in that case are meant to gauge someone's reaction. Is that what you mean?

TERRENCE: Well, in part. . . . I think all of us have a very good sense that as communicators, stories are very effective. They're more effective than communication in the form of bullets of data or information. They certainly can have drama and carry with them an encoded message. What I'm wondering is whether, in the process of communication, it's more important to tell stories or hear stories?

MARTY: I think both are really important because storytelling is a two-way street. What I mean is that telling stories allows people to share the context of where they're coming from, or on the other hand, listening to stories gives you the context for what the other person is trying to communicate. I use storytelling for this purpose all the time in interviews I have with people. I'll ask, "Tell me what really makes you happy in your job. Think about a specific time when you made someone else happy in your job. What did you do?" I'm not necessarily asking about the person's job experiences; I want to know what and how they think about that experience. The story they then tell by way of narrating an example of something that happened to them on the job helps me gain an insight into that person's personality.

TERRENCE: Well, I think you're right on target with that. What's communicated in those bullets of information may not always match precisely to what's communicated in storytelling—there may be incongruencies between them. And listening to someone's story can be a way of uncovering what those incongruencies are.

MARTY: It's amazing what types of things have come out in that kind of situation. A person can tell you a story indicating what they really value about the work they've done that is completely different than what they had earlier told you about themselves.

TERRENCE: Let me share an anecdote with you. We've been hiking, when suddenly we realize we're lost. It's getting late in the day; the sun's going down; and we're asking one another, "Does anybody know how we're going to get off this mountain?" No one's got a clue. So finally someone is rummaging in their backpack and they find a map of the mountain. So the whole night we work our way down the mountain through the snow. We finally make it just as the sun is rising, only to discover the map wasn't a map of the mountain at all. Is there anything in this anecdote about the map that resonates with what you've said about your use of stories?

MARTY: I'm not sure. . . . Don't make assumptions, I guess.

TERRENCE: What I'm thinking is that it's sometimes more important to generate some sense of context than it is for that sense to be necessarily the correct one. For those folks on the mountain, when they found the map, it gave them a sense of context, it provided them with an idea of where they were and where they had to go to get off the mountain. This raises questions about how context is created—is it always imparted by one person to another?

MARTY: Absolutely not. No; but what it does is spark conversation. To me, that is the critical role of context in communication. It establishes a common ground between those who are communicating so that they are focused and directed toward the same thing.

TERRENCE: Right. Think of those people on the mountain. Before finding the map, each one would have been saying something like, "Well, I think we really need to go this direction," or "We need to go in that direction." Everybody would've been pulling and pushing in all directions at once. But when they found what they thought was the map, they suddenly had purpose and confidence. Even if the context it provided wasn't really the "correct" one, it worked. You earlier intimated something that's really important—something about being both a teller and a listener of stories. Isn't that how we really establish rapport with another person, to share a part of ourselves in such a way that the other person is comfortable enough to share something about himself in return? Even if a story I'm telling someone has a point in the sense that I want to communicate something, its main function may be nothing more than an attempt to establish that rapport.

MARTY: Yes, what you're saying is that stories create a sense of comfort between people, which opens up all kinds of possibilities.

TERRENCE: Do you think a story must have a beginning, middle, and end? Or do you think they might consist entirely of a single metaphor, maybe an image or concept, that is communicated between people?

MARTY: I think it's best to narrate a story in segments. In fact, one of the strategies we use in our training classes is to start relating a story to explain about something, and then say, "I'll finish telling you about that later." It grabs the attention and interest of the trainees; they want to hear the rest of the story.

TERRENCE: *Lord of the Rings*, Part III.

MARTY: Exactly!!

TERRENCE: I love that sense of people wanting to hear more, even if they don't ever hear the whole story. But notice what I just did: I used the single phrase "*Lord of the Rings*, Part III" as something like a story to create a connection between us. We can use that connection to communicate with one another, even to exchange information and ideas. That kind of storytelling can be as simple, then, as saying the right word at the right time, which can produce a rich set of associations.

MARTY: Sometimes less is more. I'm a big Hitchcock fan, and one of the reasons I love his work as a film director is that after he provides the context of the story, he leaves a lot to your own imagination. Like the shower scene in *Psycho*. He doesn't show everything that's happening, but that has more impact because you're led to imagine it.

TERRENCE: You don't need to see what's going on in the shower for the story to have an impact.

MARTY: No, you don't need to see it. But the same sort of thing happened when you said, "*Lord of the Rings*." You were able to communicate with me through the connection that that phrase set up.

TERRENCE: Right, and it didn't need to be a perfect connection. . . . I mean, I didn't know exactly what "*Lord of the Rings*" might've meant to you. . . . The tendency is to think of storytelling in the traditional sense of a single narrator who is trying to convey a single bite of information or a single story line; but we seem to agree that sometimes all you have to do is say the right word at the right time and you can elicit a whole cascade of associations in other people. And that can enable them to begin connecting with one another.

Of course, it's also important to create the sort of space that encourages storytelling. And it seems that's what you're aiming at with the posters saying, "Come and have a conversation."

MARTY: That's right, and what's funny is that when I was growing up in New York, people never made eye contact when walking down the street. If someone asked, "How are you doin'?" you were taught not to answer them.

TERRENCE: Right.

MARTY: One of the things that I've noticed about the city now is that if someone asks another person how they're doing, they can expect a conversation.

TERRENCE: There has been a change, yes. I think in part it's due to 9/11. That's a story that connects everyone in the city and around the world really. But what about the stories that connect folks at Starbucks? What are some of the prevalent stories that make up its organizational culture?

MARTY: I guess the main story about this place is the one told by Howard Schultz, who is the visionary behind Starbucks. I've heard him tell his story many times, and am always impressed and motivated by it. Howard talks about growing up in a blue-collar household in Brooklyn; his dad, who was a truck driver, broke his leg, but didn't have any health insurance. So there he was—unable to work, no health insurance, no way to take care of his family. Howard looks back on that time as the turning point in his life; he became determined that he would only work for a company or organization that would never leave one of its employees behind the way his father was. The sort of company he envisioned was one whose goal wasn't just to make money, but one in which people helped each other be successful. I use Howard's story as a guidepost in my own job, to make sure I'm really helping folks and not just checking off items on a to-do list. Like I said, I've heard Howard tell that story a number of times, but I always pick up a different nuance of it each time.

TERRENCE: That's really interesting. There is richness to some stories such that when you return to them and reflect on what they're about, you find they always have more to offer.

MARTY: When my kids were little, they would want to read pretty much the same stories every night—one in particular, "Mr. Bell's Fixit Shop." It was about a guy who says he can fix anything, but discovers he can't fix a broken heart. The kids can recite that story to me today almost word for word, we read it so often. I asked them once what the story meant to them, and they told me it means there's nothing beyond repair, nothing that can't be fixed. So even if things are bad, they can get better. I said, "Wow, you got that out of the story?"

TERRENCE: Sure, and they probably experienced it in different ways every time you read it together. I've been reading "Goodnight, Moon" to my five-month-old son, and every time I enter that little book and see the woman who sits in the chair with the bowl of mush and says, "Hush," I get drawn into the story deeper and deeper. It's like standing in front of a painting in a museum, and suddenly you begin to feel a part of it; and even if you've often gone to the museum and seen that picture before, each time you come away with a new appreciation of it, because you've experienced something different about it. What we're really talking about is being reflective—reflecting on the stories to glean something new about them. Being more thoughtful, more attentive, reflective—that's something that should be a part of our lives within organizations. How can we use stories to achieve that goal?

MARTY: I think the key to it lies in the company's values and culture. What ultimately matters most to the company? If bottom-line sales figures are the only thing that are important, then the kind of storytelling you're talking about probably won't take place. That moment for reflection will get lost in the rush to produce measureable results.

TERRENCE: I take a utilitarian standpoint. Say there's this huge rock that six guys are trying to move. Five of them immediately start pushing and straining, huffing and puffing, but get nowhere. The sixth guy's standing back the whole time, carefully looking at the rock's shape and the slope of the ground. After the others are all tired out and have given up, the sixth guy steps up and carefully places his hands on a certain spot, puts his foot on another, and slowly rolls the rock out of the way. From a utilitarian standpoint, which of the guys do you want to work with?

MARTY: Well, it's clear I'd want the guy with the more thoughtful approach. He wasn't driven to produce results immediately, but looked at the problem, took a step back and reflected on it, and then decided how to handle it. I think that's the better approach in the long run for the company and its employees. But it's not always easy to train employees to be reflective in that way. One of the things that we're really working hard on is to instill discretion on the part of our employees. Our approach has been to use stories and role models to illustrate the sort of employee behavior we're seeking. As a result, storytelling becomes a big part of customer service. It provides a context for the employees' use of discretion, as they can ask themselves how best to apply what they heard in a story to the work situation they find themselves in.

TERRENCE: I think it's important to make the point that the crucial aspect to this is not just hearing stories that have Starbucks's guidelines for employee behavior embedded in them, or being able to watch model behavior on the part of a colleague. Until I can personally connect in some way with that story, have the time to reflect on it so that it elicits my own set of stories that I can work into the mix, only then will I be able to exercise the discretion to reenact that modeled behavior that the stories communicate.

MARTY: It seems to me that the connection you're talking about depends on the establishment of a genuine relationship between the storyteller and the listener. We just introduced a program to Starbucks called "Servant Leadership." I don't know if you're familiar with this.

TERRENCE: A bit.

MARTY: A man by the name of Robert Greenleaf wrote a treatise in the 1970s in which he said that the whole idea of leadership really amounts to being of service to other people. As part of his argument, Greenleaf identifies five basic ways of being—like being authentic and being present, and so on. Well, we introduced this material at some training sessions in the spring, first at the store manager level and above, and then later to operations personnel. At each step of the training program, in which we'd consider what Greenleaf says about one of the various ways of being he identifies, storytelling became a really critical element of what we were doing. We asked each person to come up with a personal story that was an example of their own servant leadership. And people really seemed to connect, so long as the stories were personal and relevant.

TERRENCE: Right. It's the personal element that makes them powerful.

MARTY: We start every one of our meetings at this office by reading a customer letter. And for me, that's storytelling to the nth degree: It involves the personal and specific experience of someone who went to one of our stores, an experience they want to share with us. We can never forget that we're not a marketing company. We're Starbucks Coffee Company, and ultimately what goes on in our stores is the most important thing for everybody here. So, we start all our meetings here by reminding ourselves what our customers are saying about us. What do they like? What don't they like?

TERRENCE: What's wonderful is that you're able to consistently keep sight of what really matters to the organization—the customers.

MARTY: The man who originally oversaw all the Starbucks stores recently retired, and he had a little saying that I've often borrowed from him: "We're not a coffee company serving people, we're a people company serving people." The focus is on the people we serve; coffee helps us fulfill that mission.

TERRENCE: That's wonderful. . . . What are some of the stories that you tell as a facilitator?

MARTY: One of my favorites is about my own experience when I first started with this company. I was hired as director of training, and the first thing I did was go through the training program as any newly hired person would do. This gave me the opportunity to do two things. First, I could get a sense of what our management partners in the various stores go through. Before I start training them, I thought I'd better get an idea of what their experience has been like. Second, I could gauge the training program that I was eventually going to be responsible for. I needed to see the quality of the program. I was living in Florida at the time, and that's where I had my first two weeks of training. Orlando was a real new market. Starbucks hadn't really had the chance to make much of an imprint on the market there; but I thought it would be interesting to compare it to what I saw in Seattle, which is the heart of Starbucks.

TERRENCE: Between the epicenter and the . . . what? . . . the farthest ripple?

MARTY: Yeah. Literally the first day I went to a training class called the "Starbucks Experience." The purpose of that class is to connect new partners with the company . . . to help them get a broader understanding of the company they belong to now. It's meant to instill some pride and excitement in the new employee. So, on Day 1 of my career at Starbucks I take my seat in the class only to discover it is led by a guy whose facilitation skills were so bad . . . well, horrible would be an upgrade. He made every possible error that a facilitator could make: jingling keys in his pocket, not looking at the class, reading from written material while holding it in front of his face so you couldn't hear him, and so on. It was obvious his heart really wasn't in it. During a break I went over and talked with him, hoping to get an idea of whether he knew how ineffective he was as a facilitator. He told me that he had started with the company in Seattle and had been an assistant manager of a store there, and because of that experience in Seattle, he was asked to open this new market in Florida. That's when it struck me that just because he had experience with the place where the company was born—Seattle—that didn't ensure he would really get what the company was all about, what it was trying to do in training new employees.

TERRENCE: He didn't pour it out from his heart. He couldn't get that exuberance across; he couldn't get others to feel that.

MARTY: That's right. During my training I kept a journal, and that was one of the important things I noted learning early on. A second story that I often tell is about my further experience during my training, when after two weeks in Orlando, I moved on to Chicago, sort of working my way westward. So, here I was in Chicago, and I'm lucky enough to train at the store in the Sears Tower, which is an incredibly busy store. They open at six o'clock in the morning, and thirty seconds later there's a line that runs the length of the store. Well, I had already gone through the program for training baristas in

Florida; "barista" is the person that serves you coffee in the store. And I'd also already learned how to work the cash register and operate the espresso machine. I knew the recipes . . . in short, I was pretty cocky, like, "Okay, I've been through my training and I've got it down!"

TERRENCE: So they put you on the floor of the shop at the Sears Tower at six o'clock to see how well you do.

MARTY: You know exactly where I'm going with this. It's Tuesday morning, literally my twelfth day with the company, and I had to be at the store at five o'clock, an hour before opening. I showed up on time, trying to be as cheery as our partners were, though it's awfully early for me, and in about fifteen minutes the phone rang. In a minute or so the shift supervisor came out and told me that somebody called in sick, and he's going to need me to fill in. I pointed out to him that I'm there just to train, and he says my training that day would be working the bar. Now, part of me is saying, "Okay. I've been hired as the director of training for Starbucks. I've been through the training, so I'd better shut up and say, 'Yes, I can do that.'" But another part of me is saying, "Are you kidding me? I'm not ready to do that!" In the end, of course I said yes.

There aren't many things that make me nervous. I love to speak in front of a group and have no fear being on a stage or that sort of thing. But my knees sure were quivering at six o'clock when the store opened, and by 6:01 there was a long line of customers. Now, again, I could handle making one drink at a time; I already knew the various recipes for our drinks. But when I saw a line of cups on the bar waiting to be filled with this or that order, I kind of lost it. I was so nervous that I forgot all my training. So I went to the shift supervisor and told him I'd do anything else he wanted me to, but I was just not ready to work the bar yet. As you can imagine, he was *not* happy with me and, in fact, made a little scene in front of the customers (which he and I talked about later). So he jumped in and I went back to doing less-skilled tasks.

The lesson I learned that morning was how important it is to be confident about your ability to deliver. I had all the knowledge I needed that morning to work the bar, I just didn't have the confidence. And during our training classes for district managers, that's one of the first stories I tell. I ask them to reflect on whether they're helping their partners develop the confidence they need to carry out their tasks effectively.

. . . You know, the memory of that morning is still so vivid for me, and every time I tell the story it seems the liveliness of it for me helps make connections with the folks I'm telling it to.

TERRENCE: One of the simplest but most fundamental things for us to learn and to teach is that the quickest way to connect with people is with a story. But that requires that the listener really "hear" the storyteller and be actively open to what is being said. Being fully present in this sense to the story and the storyteller elicits one's own stories in response, though one must always be attuned to what is appropriate to the context. I really do think this kind of listening and elicited response can be taught. And the reason it can be taught is because it's innate. It's something that we naturally do already if we're able to just slow down and open our eyes to our inborn processes of learning and communication.

MARTY: Fascinating. . . . That bit about opening our eyes reminds me of another Howard story, one about how he got his vision for what would become Starbucks. He was working as a salesman for a Scandinavian furniture company at the time, and during a trip to Italy with his wife, they couldn't help but notice all these espresso bars and cafés throughout Italy. People would sit and read a book or chat with one another; it was like the front-porch meeting place that we talked about earlier. When they returned home, Howard realized that there was really no place like that in the United States, and was convinced that an incredible opportunity existed to create them. So, some time later he went to work for Starbucks; there were only three stores at the time, and the company only sold coffee beans, tea, and spices, but no drinks. He tried to convince the owners of the opportunity that existed if they'd set it up more as a café, but they weren't interested. But Howard's tenacious. He eventually raised the capital to buy the company and turned it into his vision of how people can be connected sitting together over a cup of coffee.

Observations

Marty communicates very effectively and naturally with stories. It is interesting that the first word he associates with stories is *moral*. Like most of us, Marty looks for the point of a story. This is a good place to start, but stories do not work in isolation, nor should they be relegated to simply transporting single messages. Even when a story is used to encode information, it also functions as a tool for thinking. Hearing a story triggers our own experience and a set of associations. This explains why when we revisit a story it can take on different meanings. It is not that we are constantly crafting relativistic interpretations to justify our current model of the world, but rather that stories activate our imaginations. They prompt us to look for new insights. In Chapter 15 you will see how the competencies of reflection and synthesis work and how they clarify this aspect of stories.

While Marty believes stories generally have intentionality behind them, he points out that they do not need to have a purpose: "The same set of facts, the same story line, can be used by a skilled facilitator to lead different people each to his or her own conclusions. So by telling you the same story that I told others, I'm prompting a different thought process than before, because now that process is in your head."

Marty also highlights how stories should be viewed as a two-way street. Stories allow us to exchange information, "telling stories allows people to share the context of where they're coming from, or on the other hand, listening to stories gives you the context for what the other person is trying to communicate."

Marty's sense of what constitutes a story is fluid. He had no difficulty acknowledging that stories do not need to have a beginning, middle, and end. A story can be a short phrase or word. The movie name *Lord of the Rings*, Part III, became shorthand for capturing this idea and an example of how succinct a story can be when used in the right way and at the right time.

Throughout the interview Marty shares a wealth of stories. A great deal of the interview is an exchange of personal and work stories. These stories enabled us to cover a lot of ground, find common points of experience, and enjoy a conversation full of interesting insights that are worth revisiting.

12
Interview with Father Marus, Woodside Priory School

I must confess that this interview is my favorite for many reasons. I am a graduate of Woodside Priory High School, and Father Marus continues to this day to be an important mentor and spiritual advisor in my life. Hungarian by birth, during the 1956 Russian invasion of Hungary, Father Marus was one of many to flee his country. Eventually he found his way to Portola Valley, where a community of Hungarian Benedictine monks was in the process of building a school and monastery. His life has been a pilgrimage of service to others. This interview is extraordinary because it captures some of the most important values in a simple and beautiful manner. The values found in this interview transcend faith or ideological creed. They are tenets that are sure to help us succeed in business and grow to be more self-actualized in all aspects of our lives. I encourage you to look for these tenets and not get caught up in any stories that do not fit within your belief system.

Here is a summary of the interview's main themes:

- Stories help us find the message we want to share and make it relevant for our listeners.
- Stories allow us to communicate more directly.
- Stories we tell should be a part of us.
- Stories connect us to the moment.
- Business leaders who acknowledge the importance of each person for both the role they play in business and for who they are will be the most successful.

The Interview

TERRENCE: What comes to mind when you hear the word *story*?

FATHER MARUS: Well, the first thing I do is ask a question: "What is the message?" What is the story trying to tell me? I don't mean I immediately start to formally analyze it, no. I use it as a guide in my own reasons for storytelling—to make things clearer, more interesting, more immediate. These are all part of my work as a teacher, because stories allow me to communicate more directly, to connect with what is real for my students.

TERRENCE: What it sounds like is stories help make things more relevant.

FATHER MARUS: Precisely. And that's important for any kind of teaching, even or especially if you're trying to get across concepts that may seem a little dry. Let me give you an example. I teach a class right after lunch, and one day last week I think they must have eaten too much, because they were just kind of sitting back half-listening to what I was saying. Finally I said, "Look kids, I'm even willing to make an ass out myself just to make it interesting." With that they started to laugh. They started to wake up. I got them to see I'm not only teaching the subject because it's written in a book, but I'm teaching it because it means something to me personally, and I want to present in a way that it might come to mean something personal to them as well.

TERRENCE: I think part of what you're saying is that we can sometimes tell stories simply by being an example to others with our behavior, just as you showed the class your commitment to what you were teaching.

I'd like to share with you something I may or may not have ever told you. You may recall that I came back to visit you after I graduated from university; that was a time, as you know, when I was seriously pondering what it meant to be a servant leader, and whether I had a vocation for the priesthood. I'd always felt that I might, but in my heart of hearts I had by this time begun to realize that perhaps the priesthood wasn't my vocation. But my trip back to see you was still very important to me, because I really wanted to talk with you about how we go about doing God's will. How do we really serve? During my visit, I never actually asked the question because you already answered it by your behavior. When we were in your office, two students had to do a makeup test, and I watched how you were careful to give each individual all of your attention and care, your presence. It struck me then and there that that's what it means to serve. And you showed it through your example. To this day that's an anchoring story for me.

FATHER MARUS: Well, I appreciate it . . . but it's truly not even something I'm intellectually aware of. To be there for someone, to be present—that's neither calculated nor planned. One of my students might say, "Oh, Father, you must be too busy for me right now." But I always tell them that if they need me, that's what really counts. I can correct the papers later or tomorrow, or if they're not corrected for several days, fine. Being there for that student is part of the person I'm trying to be.

I think the stories we tell have to be a part of us, too. Not just the philosophical stories we relate, but the silly jokes as well, which I use to grab my students' attention. Sometimes I ask the kids, "What's the matter with you guys today? You are not alive. Look at me. I am sixty-five years old and I'm full of life and you guys are all falling over." And they'll say, "Ohhhhh, we had such a hard weekend. Father, it is Monday." Now, when I hear that, I know that later in the week they'll be saying, "But Father, it is Friday." So I tell them the story from the *Peanuts* cartoon when Lucy or Patty or one of them tells the others, "School is really not that difficult, you know, because Monday teachers don't expect too much of us because it is Monday. Then comes Tuesday, so the teachers are expecting us to get in gear. But Wednesday is the middle of the week. Let's celebrate. It's already the middle of the week. And Thursday we'll have to start thinking about how the next day is Friday, and we never do anything on Friday." I say to them, "You guys are like that."

Other times I take the time out for a spontaneous two-minute sermon and relate one of the parables that Jesus taught, linking it to whatever we're talking about at the moment. These kinds of storytelling have to connect to the reality of where my students are at that moment. For example, I hired a new physics teacher, and after a while kids would come to me and say, "Mr. No Name is not like you. We can't talk to him." "Did you try?" I'd ask them. "Well, not really. But we feel we can't talk to him. And he's mean, and doesn't show us respect." So I'd tell them, "Why not try asking, 'Mr. No Name, 'Do you have a few minutes? You know, we have a hard time talking to you.' You know he probably doesn't intend to be mean." . . . But maybe we're off the track here.

TERRENCE: No, I think we're very much on track, because people often miss the fact that stories aren't always rehearsed, that they arise in the moment. You just described another instance of being present, being tuned in to the kids and what they're experiencing. And part of that is giving them some alternatives for handling their problem.

FATHER MARUS: I do a fair amount of counseling, and we all know how important it is in that situation to listen, but the reason for listening is to "hear" the person—where is the source of their pain? How is it a part of their present reality? Only by really hearing them in this way can we help them realize they're not so alone with their guilt or anger. I sometimes share something of my own experiences that are similar to what the person is facing or dealing with, even if our situations are not exactly the same, because I consider it very important that the person I'm sitting with should not feel utterly alone, that their unresolved problems will work out.

TERRENCE: So the extemporaneous response from your own experience opens the possibility for that person to realize they're not alone.

FATHER MARUS: Exactly. And that their problem, however serious, can be dealt with. Every problem has a solution. Students especially are prone to thinking that as individuals they are all alone in the world with their problems, that no one faces the difficulties they do. The point is not to make them feel that their problems are a dime a dozen, but rather to make them feel that they're not alone. We're there to somehow lighten their burden and assure them that they have fellow students who are facing the same difficulties, and that a resolution of those problems is always possible.

TERRENCE: When a person feels so alone with their feelings, bringing your own personal experience to bear on the situation is like a beam of light illuminating the darkness. One is no longer trapped in that dark place alone, but can begin to see that there are possibilities available to them and reasons to hope.

We've been talking about your life as a teacher and counselor, which is part of your vocation as a spiritual leader and priest. But someone might say that all this has no relevance to them as a business person. Now, I know you've been very much involved in business matters as the manager of a large organization encompassing maintenance personnel, kitchen employees, the accounting office, the teachers, and so on. I'd like to explore how, whether you're dealing with a student who has a problem at home or with an administrative issue, your guiding principle is the same.

FATHER MARUS: It is absolutely the same, whether you see yourself as in the role of priest, teacher, spiritual leader, organizational leader, or whatever— the principle always applies that we should fully be present for the other person we encounter in the moment. I think that is the true measure of success, not dollars and cents. You earlier used the phrase *servant leader*, which coincidentally is the topic of my sermon tomorrow. The gospel reading is about when Jesus was walking with his disciples toward Jerusalem and he told them, "You know guys, the Son of Man will be handed over to those who are going to kill him." They continued walking, and after a while the disciples fell a little behind and started to ask themselves, "What is he talking about? He's going to be killed? That means one of us is going to have to take over. Will it be you, Peter?" Now, Jesus knew what they were talking about among themselves, though they didn't come out and ask him the question, because they were afraid. So Jesus said, "You're missing the point about who will be the leader by asking who wants to be first. To be a real leader you have to be willing to come last, to be a servant for all your brothers." And he took a little child and said, "Look at this child. If you want to really be blessed, you have to be like a child." He didn't mean childish, but child-like. A child depends on and trusts those around him. Servant leadership is just that.

TERRENCE: A sense of dependency . . . the other wonderful thing about a child is that they have to learn to be vulnerable and to be imperfect.

FATHER MARUS: That sense of dependency is ultimately the trust we place in our Father in Heaven. But the same sort of trust and dependence is part of the ethos of any group—disciples or business organizations. And in business settings it is not confined to any particular level but permeates throughout the organization. From the CEO down, all should each in his own way be a servant to the others.

TERRENCE: You're right to point out that this notion of servanthood is not only a religious concept. In the *Republic*, Plato describes the just man as one who has and does what is natural for him, who makes a specific and unique contribution to the body politic, just as we all bring our uniqueness to the body of Christ.

FATHER MARUS: But the hierarchies that necessarily exist in the political organization or in business, unless they are correctly understood, can be sources of oppression. I deeply believe that in any successful company the leaders are apt to understand that they are really there to serve, not to be served. This they do by encouraging all those who are under them in terms of the organizational hierarchy to achieve all they can profession-ally and personally. They must acknowledge the utmost importance of each person, both for the role they play in the business and simply for who they are as a person. Business leaders who can do that will be the most successful of all. Again, in the context of the classroom, I want the kids to truly know that I'm there for them, but I also emphasize that I cannot do it alone; we have to be there for one another. You learn from me, and I learn from you. We accept each other implicitly. The experience is not easy for me to put into words.

TERRENCE: I'm suddenly reminded of what a wonderful gardener you are, and wonder if there is some parallel to what you just said and the experience of growing things. In my garden, I have to attend to the plants I grow, to their needs, by giving them water and keeping them weeded. But in partnership with them and through my care they yield beautiful flowers or fruits or vegetables. In the garden there doesn't seem to be a servant, just as there's no leader; there's simply the ethos of caring. So when you said how it's difficult to describe the experience you share with your students—well, to me it's clear that yours is a story about being attentive to the ethos of the milieu, the environment, and what needs to be done to cultivate it.

FATHER MARUS: There are so many beautiful stories in the scriptures. Sometimes kids will ask me, "Oh, Father, why did you become a monk? You've sacrificed your whole life." And I answer with questions of my own. "What do you mean by sacrifice? What is sacrifice?" "Throwing your life away," they'll say. So I'll ask, "Do you think Christ threw his life away?" And they usually don't answer that one. Then I'll tell them the story of how Christ died so we might have life. How his death has saved us. And from that we learn that sacrifice doesn't have to be a negative thing. So, yes, I am a storyteller, but not a professional storyteller.

TERRENCE: Well, we're not here for entertainment. . . . I'm interested in themes surrounding storytelling because the word *story* is so much a part of our everyday vernacular. Everywhere you go someone says, "Let me tell you a story" or "Here's the story of the day" or "What's your story?" But, especially from the standpoint of communication or learning, people often want to craft storytelling in a contrived way—formalize it as something predictable and controllable. There was something you said earlier in our conversation about each of us having unique personalities and communication styles, all of those wonderful differences that make up our world. You or I may be more animated than others when we tell a story about our personal experience, and that's fine. Someone else might be more methodical or relate their narrative in almost a whisper. But if it's still from their heart, if it's still from their experience, the delivery doesn't matter.

FATHER MARUS: The question is whether we are willing to really share ourselves—our stories and reflections—with one another.

TERRENCE: Or what we can do to encourage others to share their stories with us. Extemporaneous stories emerge out of a person's attentiveness and mindfulness in the moment, when they are fully invested in the situation, both in the sense of being present for the other person but also allowing for self-reflection on one's own experiences. For Christians, of course, Jesus is the exemplar of this way of being.

FATHER MARUS: Again, it is important to emphasize the role of trust. I must trust you and you have to trust me if we are genuinely going to commune with one another. It's not something that can be forced, but must be grounded in this radical trust of the other person, radical because it frees each person up to be who they truly are as a unique individual.

TERRENCE: The image that comes to my mind is of pitchforks. You take a pitchfork and hit it against a hard surface so it begins to vibrate. Then I come along with my own pitchfork and place it alongside yours, and soon it will pick up the rhythmic pattern of your fork and the two will be in sync.

FATHER MARUS: Storytelling can help bring my students and me into sync like that, especially when I'm teaching difficult or complex concepts. Like just last week, we're beginning to cover cytology, and our book describes all the parts of the cell and how they function and all that, but the class seemed a little flat. So I made up a story, and asked the students to imagine a medieval city with a big wall surrounding it. "Why the wall?" I asked. They said, "Well . . . to protect the city against the enemy." And then I tell them that every cell is protected in the same way by the cell membrane—it keeps the unwanted guys out and keeps safe those who are inside.

TERRENCE: But you need a town center.

FATHER MARUS: Yes, but even before that you have to imagine that just as the town needs a wall for protection, it must have gates for food to be brought in and waste taken out. So, back we go to the cell, and talk about how its membrane is semi-permeable. Right? Then, we think about the town some more, about what goes on inside it and the importance, as you just mentioned, of the town center. And again, we can use that part of the story about the medieval town to talk about the nucleolus of the cell, the DNA, and the mitochondria.

TERRENCE: And the crucial thing is that you have them participating in the story you're telling them, opening their imagination to make connections and linkages between the story and the topic under review. That's what learning is really all about.

FATHER MARUS: Well, doing that is something I really love, but as I said, I'm not a professional storyteller.

TERRENCE: You're better than a professional storyteller.

FATHER MARUS: Again, it's being open to the moment. There are so many occasions that offer openings for telling a story, for making connections with another person's experience. But it isn't premeditated. It is just something we have to be open to.

Observations

This interview is powerful because stories are shown to be a tool aligned with a value system. Although the value system may have its roots in institutional ideologies, it has applicability to anyone. From a utilitarian point of view, being fully present and attentive to others is the best way to produce long-term results. These results are sustainable, and they also have the ability to continue creating new and unexpected ones. Father Marus clearly shows how stories facilitate the synergy between communication and learning and how this synergy leads to the most productive outcomes for everyone.

Father Marus's response to the first question highlights the dual nature of stories, "Well, the first thing I do is ask a question, 'What is the message?' What is the story trying to tell me? I don't mean I immediately start to formally analyze it, no. I use it as a guide in my own reasons for storytelling— to make things clearer, more interesting, more immediate." Stories' greatest communication capacity lies in the opportunities they afford us to listen in the form of reflection—even when we are telling them.

The interview flows as a series of interconnected stories. In this interview the values implicit to effectively working with stories cannot be mistaken or disguised. Stories will make organizations more effective, but more importantly they will make them a richer and more fulfilling place to be.

Part III

The Competency Map

13
Introduction to the Competency Map

In this part we will discuss how to develop personal competencies to become a better communicator and learner through stories. Let's review what we have covered up to this point. We began by laying out a framework for how stories work (Chapter 2). Next, we showed how the principles of stories apply to organizational communication and learning. At the end of Part I we established the relationship between communication, learning, and collective experience (see Figure 13.1).

Communication was shown to be the cornerstone of how people learn and share knowledge. We used our model of how stories work to enrich our understanding of some subtle but key aspects of communication. Using a simple framework composed of channels and targets (see Figure 13.2), we identified a number of gaps that exist in how organizations approach communication (Chapter 3).

We showed that by employing the functions of stories and their unique effects (see Figure 13.3) we could bridge these gaps in communication. By using a variety of techniques for pulling stories versus pushing them from nonspecific targets and personal channels, we discovered we can deliver more messages with fewer broadcasts, smaller bandwidth, less information, and more impact. We continued our analysis of stories and communication by examining the role of stories in the arena of organizational learning. Reflection was argued to be the foundation of learning. Organizational learning was explored in terms of how collective knowledge gets shared in the organization.

We understand that effective organizational communication and learning is demonstrated to be a result of strong individual capacities. Initiatives that aim at changing an organization must start by looking at the skills and strengths of its people. Changes to organizational structures and practices are secondary to efforts focused on developing capacities of employees. Part II was a tour of several different organizations. The dialogues illustrate the central

Figure 13.1 **The Relationship Among Communication, Learning, and Collective Experience**

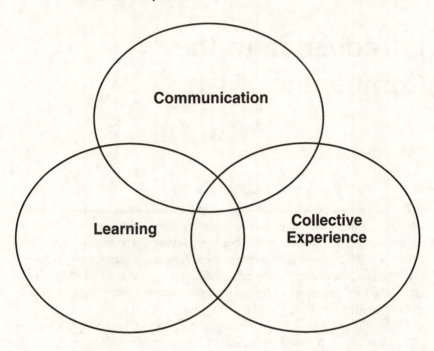

Figure 13.2 **Untapped Matrix Combinations**

Untapped Matrix Combinations		Target			
		Internal	External	Partner	Nonspecific
C h a n n e l	Formal	1	2	3	10
	Social	4	5	6	11
	Personal	7	8	9	12

Note: Quadrants 7–12 represent communication gaps. See Chapter 3 for more detail.

Figure 13.3 The Relationship Between Story Functions and the Communication Matrix

The Relationship Between Story Functions and the Communications Matrix

The functions of stories enable us to reach untapped areas 7–12 of the Communications Matrix...

STORY FUNCTIONS	UNIQUE EFFECTS of STORIES
Empower a speaker	Entertaining
Create an environment	Creating trust and openness between yourself and others
Bind and bond individuals	Elicit stories from others
Require active listening	Listen actively in order to: *Understand context and perspective* *Find the critical point in a system* *Uncover resistance and hidden agendas*
Negotiate differences	Shift perspectives in order to: *See each other* *Experience empathy* *Enter new frames of reference* Hold diverse points of view Become aware of operating biases and values Creating a working metaphor to illuminate an opinion, rational, vision, or decision
Encode information	Establish connections between different ideas and concepts to support an opinion or decision Think outside the box to generate creative solutions and breakthroughs
Tools for Thinking	
Weapons	
Healing	

Untapped Areas of the Communications Matrix

Channel \ Communications Matrix	Target			
	Internal	External	Partner	Nonspecific
Formal	1	2	3	10
Social	4	5	6	11
Personal	7	8	9	12

Stories are effective at reaching areas 7–12 of the matrix because of their unique effects

Figure 13.4 **The Competency Map**

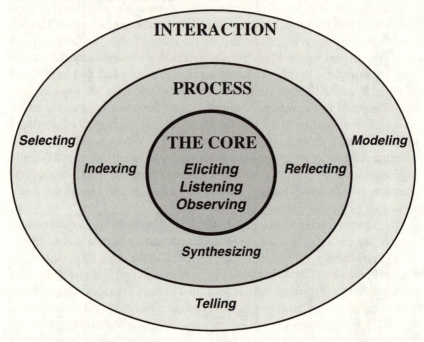

role stories naturally play in how we communicate and learn. Leaders agreed on the power of stories and their applicability to their organizations. Confusion rested in their uncertainties of how to develop the requisite competencies to effectively use the principles of stories. This part of the book provides a map of these competencies, offers practical ideas on how to develop them, and highlights organizational initiatives to support the ongoing development and use of these competencies (see Figure 13.4).

Here is a breakdown of the map. There are three rings and nine competencies. The three rings are:

1. The Core
2. Process
3. Interaction

The nine competencies:

1. Eliciting
2. Listening
3. Observing
4. Indexing
5. Synthesizing
6. Reflecting
7. Selecting
8. Telling
9. Modeling

A description of the Competency Map can be found in Table 13.1. The rings represent three levels of personal story competencies related to communicating and learning. Each ring consists of three competencies. The outermost ring of Interaction characterizes the competencies we use to engage with the external world. Many people mistakenly assume that using stories well requires little besides knowing what stories to select and being good at telling them. Although these are useful competencies, they are superficial compared to the others. Throughout the book we have explored the importance of pulling stories rather than pushing them. We explored the counterintuitive challenges posed by this idea. We concluded that we can communicate more by eliciting stories than by telling them. Consequently, a greater value is given to the competencies found in the Core than the interaction ones found in the outmost ring of our map. Also in the outermost ring is the competency of Modeling.

The innermost ring of the map is the Core. It contains the central competencies that are at the heart of using stories effectively to be a better communicator and learner. All the competencies found in the other rings build off of the central ones of Eliciting, Listening, and Observing. Listening is the common thread to the three competencies found in the Core; for example, being able to elicit stories demands sensitivity and attentiveness to the stories around oneself. Drawing stories out of others requires astute observation skills. We discover what questions to ask or what stories to tell in order to stimulate the storytelling of others by watching for cues in their words and actions. We must also be equally aware of our own thought processes. Listening ties them all together and involves more than hearing. As we gather information, listening engages our imaginations. What we hear is fused with our experiences. The new information co-mingles with the old to become relevant and immediate; otherwise, it is dead on arrival.

The second ring of the map is the Process Ring. It is characterized by all of the internal things that we do in our minds when we are conscious of our stories and the stories around us. It is hard to discuss the three competencies in this ring in any causal order since these internal processes of Indexing, Synthesizing, and Reflecting happen most of the time in parallel. The reflecting competency is the discipline we develop in stopping to notice our stories. To paraphrase Socrates, "an unexamined story is not worth having." While we gather new insights from our own stories, a highly developed capacity for reflection makes us more mindful of others. We are less likely to react to people. Reflection gives us a chance to behave proactively and continually revise our perceptual filters.

The second competency in the Process Ring is Synthesizing. By reflecting on our stories, we begin to find connections with other stories and other

Table 13.1

Summary of the Competency Map

Ring	Competency	Description
The Core	Eliciting	Asking questions and finding ways to pull stories from others.
Describes how we open ourselves to be aware and sensitive to stories.	Listening	Absorbing stories and invoking the imagination to enter them in a fundamental and deep way.
	Observing	Practicing mindfulness to become aware of the stories implicit in others' words and actions.
Process	Indexing	Developing a flexible, vast mental schema for retrieval of experiences and knowledge.
Describes how we work with experiences to transform them into meaningful and reusable stories.	Synthesizing	Finding patterns in new experiences and creating connections between these and old ones.
	Reflecting	Reviewing experiences with circumspection and extracting knowledge from them.
Interaction	Modeling	Being aware of one's actions and using them to create lasting impressions in the eyes of others.
Describes how we use stories to connect with others and communicate.		Employing a variety of analogical techniques to bring an idea or concept alive.
	Telling	Relaying with authenticity a story that paints a vivid, engaging picture for listeners.
	Selecting	Picking a story that is appropriate to the situation at hand and that clearly communicates concepts, ideas, or feelings.

domains of knowledge. Through synthesis we discover relationships between previously unrelated experiences, ideas, concepts, and knowledge. We take the new pieces of information and transform them into insights. The link between learning and stories is found in this competency. Roger Schank at the Institute of Learning at Northwestern University was one of the first to point this out. Schank argues that the ability to find a story in one domain and apply it by analogy to another is the hallmark of intelligence. Being effective at doing this requires the three competencies of Reflecting, Synthesizing, and Indexing.

The last competency in the Process Ring is Indexing. Our experiences, recorded as stories in our memories, do not fit into neat categories. Every experience can be indexed, reindexed, and cross-indexed in a variety of ways. This is further complicated by the fact that we each develop our own indexing schemes. You and I will not use the same keys to codify our experiences and learning or knowledge that result from them. Developing a rich index enables us to quickly see the applicability of our stories in different situations. We can uncover patterns of relevance and encounter greater resonance between others' experiences and our own by deliberately maintaining a diverse index.

There are two levels to the competency of Modeling. The first level describes how our actions model our beliefs, attitudes, and values. Through our actions we create stories. People are far more likely to remember our actions than our words. Whether they do it consciously or unconsciously, people observe our actions and look for incongruence between our words and behaviors. We have the ability to create stories by being mindful of how our actions affect the people around us. Memorable actions become part of other people's stories. Furthermore, our actions have the potential to cause others to reflect. Purposeful actions leave their mark on the environment and travel quickly in personal channels of communication and reach nonspecific targets otherwise beyond our range. The second level to the Modeling competency is our ability to create compelling representations of the concepts we try to communicate to others. Developing a facility with analogies, metaphors, word pictures, and visuals are a few of the subcomponents of this competency.

During the rest of this part we will go through each ring of the map and its competencies and identify concrete ideas on how to develop them personally and organizationally.

Table 13.2 summarizes the major themes from the interviews in Part II and relates them to the Competency Map. After reflecting on the interviews, I scanned them for any recurring elements. The Competency Map we use is a result of that analysis. This is by no means a scientifically validated model—

Table 13.2

The Relationship Between Themes from Interviews and the Competency Map

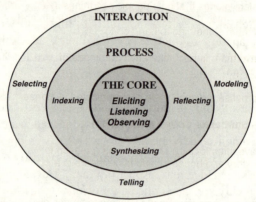

Interview themes	Competency
Bernice Moore—CTB/McGraw-Hill (Chapter 8)	
1. Stories can clarify a subject being discussed.	Modeling
2. Sharing personal stories brings people closer together, establishes connections among members of a group, and makes the group more effective.	Selecting
3. A masterful storyteller creates a space for the story, which encourages listeners to go along with them.	Telling
4. Stories need to play a central role in retrospective project debriefs because they facilitate dialogue and because they can be carried forward as a valuable resource for later projects.	Reflecting
5. Making room for personal and organizational reflection is a key to using the power of stories.	Reflecting
Robert Kraska—DTE Energy (Chapter 9)	
6. The length of a story needs to be adjusted for the context in which it is being told.	Telling
7. "After-action reviews" provide a structured opportunity for reflection and storytelling.	Eliciting/ Synthesizing
8. In order for stories to work in meetings, people need to trust one another, be skilled in interpersonal communications, and know how to ask the right questions.	Listening/ Observing
9. In training, people learn the most from dialogue among themselves and with the instructor.	Synthesizing
10. There is an integral relationship between stories and reflection.	Reflecting

Sherrie Cornett—Dreyer's Ice Cream (Chapter 10)

11. Stories from our personal lives can be effectively used at work.   Indexing

12. Analogies are stories that help people see things in a different way, which may have more meaning for them and that gives them something to hang on to.   Modeling

13. Stories have more impact than any other mode of communication.   Telling

14. Important messages need to be communicated in stories.   Selecting

Marty Fischer—Starbucks Coffee (Chapter 11)

15. Stories have intentionality. The teller has a reason for sharing a story and hopes to lead his listeners in a direction.   Selecting

16. Storytelling is a two-way street. Listening to stories gives you the context for what another person is trying to communicate.   Eliciting/Listening

17. The critical role of context in communication establishes a common ground between those who are communicating so that they are focused and directed toward the same thing.   Observing

18. Stories create a sense of comfort between people, which opens up all kinds of possibilities.   Eliciting

19. Storytelling can be as simple as saying the right word at the right time, which can produce a rich set of associations.   Modeling

Father Marus—Woodside Priory School (Chapter 12)

20. Finding stories requires introspection and reflection.   Reflecting

21. Stories help us find the message we want to share and make it relevant for our listeners.   Indexing

22. Stories allow us to communicate more directly.   Eliciting

23. Stories we tell should be a part of us.   Indexing/Selecting

24. Stories connect us to the moment.   Listening/Observing

25. Business leaders who acknowledge the importance of each person for both the role they play in business and for who they are will be the most successful.   Modeling

which is one of the reasons why I prefer to call it a "competency map" versus "competency model." However, I do not think it is a stretch to say that the nine competencies in the map represent a significant set of skills employees need to develop to become more effective communicators and learners.

We will work our way through the map by starting with the Core. By the time we get to the Interaction ring, you will notice that all the rings are interdependent and that the nine competencies work intricately with each other. In fact, they are tightly coupled with one another. For example, you cannot select a story to tell if it is not well indexed, if you haven't reflected on it, elicited it in the first place, and listened to it. Breaking down the rings into nine competencies is a bit artificial but will provide a systematic method of dissecting discrete areas for personal development. Our prescriptions will be largely focused on individuals; however, in some places we will also suggest organizational practices that have the potential to stimulate inculcation of these competencies. In the end we will put them all back together and observe how they seamlessly flow and interrelate with each other.

Let me preface this part by being clear about one thing. Up to this point we have dealt primarily with theory and a little bit of personal reflection and insights offered by the dialogues in Part II. At the beginning of this chapter we adopted a model for identifying competencies, but without diligence and practice all of this amounts to precious little. If you expect results, you will have to be willing to work at the things presented in this part. Tapping the power of stories for effective communication and learning can only be achieved through experiential application of the principles.

14
The Core

In this chapter we will examine the first ring of the Competency Map—the Core (see Figure 14.1). In discussing the three aspects of the Core, I will offer numerous exercises geared toward honing these communication skills. The final section of this chapter will address how the exercises can be used in the context of organizations.

Observing Competency

I am always struck by how I see what I expect to see or want to see. Our perceptual filters get in our way all the time. We fill in reality to correspond with existing constructs in our minds. We also tune out anomalies that might otherwise shift our perceptions. This is why we can read text when letters are chopped off along the bottom half of words or when paragraphs are missing certain words.

Various researchers estimated the number of bits of information we process per second. Bits here refer to the computer paradigm of the digitalization of information where everything becomes reduced to a dual state expressed as either a 0 or 1. Conservative calculations determined that between all of our sensory organs we receive about 10 million bits per second. From that wealth of data, some brain researchers argue that we are aware of only 10 bits of information per second. In other words, our conscious mind uses 0.0001 percent (that is ten-thousandths of a percent) of the information we receive. We are virtual reality simulators that expend most of our evolved brainpower casting the world in stable, repeatable structures and constructs. Ultimately, it would seem we are not aware of all that much.

Try this quick thought experiment. Carefully scan the room you are in for a detail that up until this point in time you have never noticed. Unless the feature you discover is truly new, your visual cortex has recorded that information time and time again when your eyes passed over that spot in the room, but you have not been aware of it. You have not consciously availed yourself of that information. There is lots of information we constantly skip

---

General Exercise: Simple Observation

Start with the mundane and progress to more complex things as your powers of observation continue to increase. Take an object, a stopwatch, and a pad of paper. Watch the object for at least five minutes and then record your observations. Is there any difference when you increase the time or if you write down your observations as they occur to you as opposed to waiting until the end?

---

over, especially when it comes to people. We can penetrate the essence of objects because they are more understandable; indeed empirical for that matter, but people are ever-changing black boxes full of surprises.

I remember an assignment given to us by a grade school teacher, which seemed at the time inane: We were given the task of describing an orange placed in front of us on our desk. Not so easy. When we center our powers of observation, a world of detail emerges that is otherwise hidden from our routine scan of things.

For our purposes, the competency of Observing can be further subdivided into five key areas:

1. Care/Intention
2. Self-Awareness
3. Sensitivity
4. External Focus
5. Process Dialogue

Care/Intention

It all starts with care. It is impossible to be mindful of the things going on around us or the people we are near if we have no interest in them. Intention is another good word to describe what we are talking about. I will say more about the nuances between care and intention in a moment. If there is ongoing premeditated purpose to our experience of the world, we will feel a sense of ownership for what is going on. The boundary of self softens, and we feel ourselves extending our awareness to include more than a self-defensive cursory scanning of the stimuli in our environment.

Figure 14.1   **Competency Map—The Core**

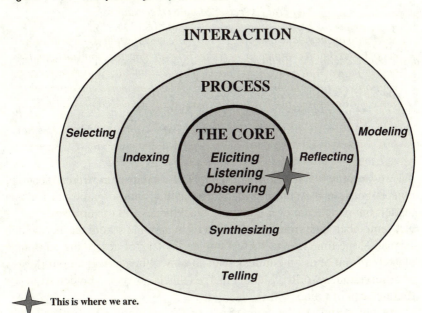

Cultivating genuine care and interest in others and increasing our thresh-olds of patience are necessary aspects of developing keener powers of ob-servation. Power is gained when we cultivate care. Imagine a plant or pet that is part of your emotional landscape. Care plays a central role in imbu-ing it with vitality. The attention you take in caring for it translates into clear directives as to what to do to ensure its healthy and prosperous exist-ence. The care you show it reflects back to you. There is pleasure derived from being a caretaker, and the success of its thriving survival rewards you with prideful achievement.

If there is a pattern of little care about the people around you or your environment, this is cause for some more in-depth soul searching. Typi-cally, as we move our attention away from ourselves, and if we have a strong sense of our accomplishments and unique attributes, other people take on a special glow. We become interested in others. When we are inter-ested, we become more observant. We notice more things because we are receptive and less defensive.

Exercise 1a. Care/Intention—Self-Assessment

Close your eyes for a moment and scan through the various people you inter-act with in your organization. Assign a quick unqualified number from 1 to 7 to describe the degree to which you care about those people (where 1 is the least and 7 is the most).

Now write down a list of people you work with on a regular basis. Next to each person put a number between 1 and 7 (where 1 is the least and 7 is the most) to characterize the degree to which you care about that person. Be hon-est. It is unlikely you care about every person to the same degree. No one is scrutinizing your answers, so be as introspective as you can.

Next to any person with a rating of 4 or less write down a strategy for how you think you could increase your care for that person

Name	Level of Care Rating (1–7)	Strategy

I have grouped care and intention together because they describe two facets of the behavior we need to cultivate to become good observers. Our intentions act as intrinsic motivation that affects our choices. When we care about the things and people around us and we want to have a positive effect, our powers of observations are heightened. Conversely, our powers of observation are also heightened when care turns to malice, and our in-tentions are focused on hurting rather than helping. In many situations, our care and intentions are neutral (see Figure 14.2). This is why our normal powers of observation are weak. We feel no particular stake in what is happening around us or have little investment in the people we are interact-ing with. The bandwidth of our connection is narrow and our speed of processing is slow. Becoming conscious of our level of care and intention and moving them in positive directions will significantly improve our baseline capacity in all of the competencies found in the Core.

Figure 14.2 **The Relationship Between Care and Intention**

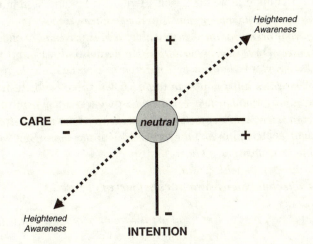

Exercise 1b. Care/Intention—Fostering Positive Intentions

Try this thought experiment. Before walking into a meeting, take a moment to assess your intentions. If your intentions are either negative or neutral, what can you do to feel more engaged? Determine what is in your control. When you changed your intentions to more positive ones, did it change your experience? Did you feel that you were more effective?

Exercise 1c. Care/Intention—Name Badges

Here is a simple way to inculcate more care in your daily routines. Every time you are in a customer service situation and the person helping you has a name badge or verbally tells you their name, make a point to remember it. When you complete the transaction, use the person's name when you thank them. If you are doing this in person rather than on the phone, take an extra second to grab their eyes and smile when you thank them.

Self-Awareness

Developing good powers of observation requires a high degree of self-awareness. Most of us are more self-conscious than we realize. In order to be tuned in to the dynamics happening around us, our attention has to be diverted from excessive self-monitoring and redirected to the external environment. Self-awareness then takes on a different role. It acts as the analyzer and arbitrator of the impressions received, assumptions made, conclusions drawn, and behaviors initiated in response to the things we observe.

From our discussion above we identified the importance of self-awareness as a key to becoming more observant. Here are a few ideas on how to continually invest time and energy in cultivating self-awareness.

Start by taking a look at your habits. James Hillman has a wonderful way of shedding insight on the word *habit*. He points out that *habit* shares its origin with the words *habitat* and *habituate*. Habitats are the places we frequent. We spend lots of time in these known places, which become ingrained and comfortable to us. We should step back and ask ourselves why we find ourselves in these repeating patterns. Which ones are healthy? Which ones are detrimental? How did they evolve? Hillman points out we need to be careful not to get stuck.

Exercise 2a. Building Self-Awareness—Survey of Habits

Take a minute and record what you are aware of about the following:

1. *Habits of speech. Are there any certain words or phrases that you use a lot?*
2. *Habits of behavior. What things do you feel compelled to do over and over again?*
3. *Idiosyncrasies. Do you have any quirks? What about superstitions?*
4. *Predictable patterns. If someone were to describe any aspect of your personality, would they be able to predict how you would respond and react in certain situations? What are those situations? What are the reactions? What are the benefits of those reactions? What are the limitations or potential liabilities of those reactions?*
5. *Awkwardness. What sorts of situations are likely to make you feel awkward or self-conscious?*

Identifying our habits is a good first step toward building self-awareness. These are the visible and more obvious aspects of us. We stand to learn a lot about self-awareness from the various traditions of meditation, yoga, the performing arts, and athletics. Each of these has taught the importance of the breath. The air we take into our lungs is vital energy. As an athlete, performer, and speaker I make a point to practice deep breathing. There is no hocus-pocus behind the effects of deep breathing. Our bodies use oxygen to aerobically perform all of our homeostatic responsibilities. The more oxygen we give our bodies, the better our physical state will be. Breathing is also a good way of becoming aware of oneself. It helps take the edge off of residual traces of muscular tonus and emotional anxiety we walk around with all the time but do not notice.

Exercise 2b. Building Self-Awareness—The Power of Breath

Take five minutes every day to practice deep breathing. This can be done just about any time. It's nice to have a quiet time devoted to it, such as first thing in the morning while lying in a bed, or before going to sleep, but deep breathing can be practiced anytime and anywhere. If the situation you are in allows it, close your eyes and concentrate on slowly inhaling, pause for two to three seconds and then exhale as slowly as you can. If you have your eyes closed, after a few purposeful breaths of this nature take a breath naturally without directing it like the first couple of breaths. Then just observe the sensations in your body and pay close attention to the natural rising and falling of the breath and with it whatever thoughts, images, or feelings that come to mind. Try not to become fixated on any particular one—simply observe them.

Conscious breathing can and should be practiced all the time. With your eyes open, try breathing while stuck in traffic or while sitting in a meeting. Breath is the foundation for all our awareness. It helps center us and makes us more receptive to what is happening in us and around us.

Keeping a journal is another way of developing self-awareness. It is a time-consuming process and one that I am not able to do on a regular basis. However, I set aside several times a year to write in my journal. Vacations, holidays, and birthdays are perfect opportunities. Writing in a journal is a reflective process. We are apt to discover and think about things we have pushed below the surface in the name of efficiency. You do not need to write elaborate prose. You could spend a few minutes writing down several key words or phrases, or maybe drawing a picture. I have known others to use photographs as a way of spending time journaling. The goal is to set aside some special structured time to reflect. The benefit is greater self-awareness and knowledge.

Exercise 2c. Building Self-Awareness—Journaling

Take thirty minutes and begin a journal. Try writing down your recollections of the past year. What things stand out in your mind? What were the major milestones for the year? What were the highs? What were the lows? If you are having difficulty, try taking a calendar and jotting down any words or experiences that come to mind for each month. At the end of your journal session make a commitment for your next date with your journal.

Expert strategists realize the importance of knowing their strengths and weaknesses. As a competitive fencer I had a mental black book on all my competitors with an analysis of their strengths and weaknesses. I made a point to understand how my game matched up with theirs. It is imperative to be honest with ourselves. We cannot be good at everything. And even the things we are good at under certain circumstances can turn out to be liabilities rather than strengths. Developing greater self-awareness would not be complete without an assessment of our strengths and weaknesses.

Exercise 2d. Building Self-Awareness—Strengths and Weaknesses

Take a piece of paper and write down what you believe your strengths and weaknesses are. Feel free to take whatever approach feels natural to you. If you need some structure to prompt your analysis, use the table below to guide you (Table 14.1). These are just a few categories, so add others as they apply to you. Don't stop with your analysis. Ask some of your colleagues, friends, or spouse to give you their impressions. If you have information from any 360-degree feedback surveys that you may have done, be sure to incorporate it in your analysis.

Another tool for building self-awareness is a personality inventory. There are lots of excellent ones out there. Whichever one you use, keep in mind that it is only a tool. I have watched too many people attempt to use information from these psychometric instruments to create predictive models of other people's behavior and charts of how to interact with other personality types. It is infuriating to walk into a workshop and see participants proudly walking around with name tags inscribed with their Meyers-Briggs classification. These tools are useful if they are used to stimulate reflection and dialogue. They are, after all, just another way of catalyzing storytelling. In other words, they are an example of how stories are a tool for thinking. The information offered by the instrument provides a "story framework" to imagine our personality, strengths, weaknesses, habits, and how all of those effect our interactions with others. There are no shortcuts for real self-reflection and awareness, so do not count on any of these tools, as good as they may be, to provide a complete picture.

These are just a few ideas on how to begin to develop self-awareness. Being self-aware requires a disciplined, ongoing effort of introspection and honesty.

Sensitivity

Have you ever watched a dog respond to smells or noises? Think about what life would be like if you experienced it through the olfactory or hearing organs of a dog. We have learned to become oblivious to much of our

Table 14.1

Exercise 2d: Building Self-Awareness—Strengths and Weaknesses

Area	Strengths	Weaknesses
Communication Characterize your skills as a communicator. What things do you do well? Are there aspects of communicating with others that are difficult for you? How would others describe your communication style?		
Interpersonal Traits Characterize the manner in which you relate to others. Do you get along easily with lots of different types of people? Are there certain people you relate to more easily? Are there specific aspects of your personality that facilitate or hinder relationships with others?		
Thinking Style Characterize the way in which you work with information in your head. Are there certain types of cognitive tasks you are better at than others? What is your unique mix of rational abilities versus creative ones?		
Organizational Skills Characterize what you bring to your organization. What set of skills do you offer? What parts of your self hinder your contributions or ability to be more effective?		
Add Your Own		

environment. Evolution has used its better judgment and decided it is in the best interest of our species to be a little less sensitive to various forms of stimuli compared with other members of the animal kingdom. However, if we are going to sharpen our observational skills, we need to turn up the gain on our sensitivity.

Exercise 3a. Sensitivity—Room Awareness

Here is an easy exercise to get started. When you first walk into a room, take ten seconds and perform a quick scan of the general climate. Do you sense any mood? Are you aware of what contributed to that perception? Try to list the various things you observed that caused you to form this impression. Now go one step further. Take another scan around the room and get a read on every person. Use Table 14.2 to record your perceptions.

Table 14.2

Exercise 3a. Sensitivity—Room Awareness

Characterize the General Mood	What Contributed to This Perception?
THE OVERALL ROOM	
INDIVIDUALS IN THE ROOM	

You need to consciously collect enough background information about an environment you enter in order to determine the best way to interact in it. As a facilitator I am constantly taking the pulse of the group. Every question I pose, and especially the comments I make, must be sensitive to a group's dynamics.

Sensitivity is a function of how we direct our attention. Try this quick little thought experiment: Close your eyes and pay attention only to the sounds you hear around you. What do you hear? Are there any new sounds you were not previously aware of? You can try similar experiments with your other senses. Try walking barefoot on the grass or on a beach. Take note of all the sensations. Or take an extra moment and inhale the smells of a good meal, wine, or a fragrant flower. Similar to our physical senses, each of us is endowed with emotional sensors. They are working all the time, but most of us leave them running on automatic. Studies in biofeedback have demonstrated that we have measurable physiological responses to the emotional information we process. For example, if you walk into a room full of tense people, your heart rate is likely to increase. So information is available and is affecting us all the time, but we need to make a concerted effort to pay attention to it.

Exercise 3b. Sensitivity—Sore Spots and Hot Buttons

It is important to know our sensitivities. Are there any things people can inadvertently say or do that cause us to feel or act in certain ways? Take a moment and reflect on all the things that may be sore spots or hot buttons for you. Write down a description of each and the response it elicits from you. (See Table 14.3.) Now do the same thing for the people you work with on a regular basis. What are their sore spots and hot buttons?

Table 14.3

Exercise 3b. Sensitivity—Sore Spots and Hot Buttons

Description	Response
SORE SPOTS	
HOT BUTTONS	

External Focus

Watch a good waiter or waitress. Training, experience, and sensitivity enable him or her to anticipate your needs and respond effortlessly. When we move our locus of attention from ourselves to others, we become sensitive and attuned to their thoughts, feelings, and needs. We adjust our speech and behavior to match the situation at hand. What we sense guides us. There is no need for a script when we are focused on the things happening externally around us.

Whenever I facilitate a multi-day workshop I take a few minutes at night before I fall asleep to imagine the room I was in during the day and all the people I met. If I cannot remember a person's name, where they sat, and a few key stories they told or remarks they made, I know I haven't done a good job of connecting with them. I'll make a point the next day to pay extra special attention to that person.

Exercise 4a: External Focus—Recall

While you are walking down the street or when you are in any public place, try to take notice of every person. Do this consciously for ten minutes or so. Then find a place to sit down, and rerun the ten minutes through your head. How many different people can you remember? What were they doing? Did you pick up on any conversations?

I am always amazed at how difficult it is for people to look into each other's eyes. We are just not comfortable doing it. Yet there is so much we can read and infer from people's eyes. If you are focused on yourself you will find it very awkward to look into someone eyes. Draw a mental picture of a stereotypically shy person. Where are their eyes looking? They are very likely cast down because they are internally focused.

Developing good external focus also requires that we learn how to quickly shift our attention. As a facilitator I practiced moving my attention around a room. There are always some people sitting in a particular section of a room where less of my attention naturally goes. If I do not make a concerted effort to look in their direction and engage them with my eyes and voice, they will not feel as integrated as other people in the room who are more naturally in my direct line of attention.

Here is an exercise that will help you practice shifting your attention and becoming more comfortable looking into someone's eyes.

Exercise 4b. External Focus—Locking Eyes

Spend a day at work and at home practicing making eye contact with every person you come in contact with. Notice when you feel an urge to break eye contact and continue to look in the person's eye. When you are in a meeting, make eye contact with every person during the course of the meeting. Practice moving your attention from one person to the next.

Although we rely heavily on visual information to observe our environment, it is important to learn how to shift our auditory attention. We are easily distracted by multiple conversations. We have all been in a conversation when somewhere nearby we hear our name spoken or we catch wind of another conversation that sounds more interesting than our own; this results in our temporarily disengaging from the conversation we are in. Here is a challenging drill to help us strengthen our concentration and become more purposeful in how we direct our auditory attention.

Exercise 4c. External Focus—Conversation Tracking

Walk into a busy, noisy room with lots of separate conversations going on. A bar is a good place to first try this exercise. Practice moving your auditory attention around the room. Eavesdrop on a conversation until you have enough information to understand what the people are talking about and a grasp of the general tone of the conversation and mood of the people in it; then shift your attention to another one. See how quickly you can do this without becoming distracted.

Process Dialogue

Process dialogue is an internal observational skill that enables us to track how we are forming perceptions. Our perceptions function as theories since we use them to make sense of what we are experiencing. We have tapes running through our heads all the time. The problem is that we have the mute button turned on. We are not aware of our mind's dialogue. We start forming impressions of people based on appearance, voice, and body language in less than one-tenth of a second. If we do not make it a point to pay attention to these impressions and track them, they will automatically be filtered through our black box of attitudes, values, and beliefs. As a result, we react to people and situations versus making conscious choices.

There are two parts to working with process dialogue. First, can we recall the sequence of key events in an experience? Second, do we know what value we attached to each event? Knowing the sequence of events is not just an exercise of memory. There is contextual information that can be extracted from keeping a sequence intact. There may be causal links between how certain perceptions form and the order in which they occurred. For example, events earlier in a sequence may play a more important role in forming our perceptions than later ones. I am using the word *value* to describe the analytical, perceptual, and emotional conclusions we make.

Exercise 5a. Process Dialogue—Conversation Recorder

In this exercise you will practice paying attention to the sequence and flow of a conversation between two people. Find two people who are going to meet. It is best if you do not know either person well. Ask them if you may observe their meeting. Try to also find a meeting that will not be any longer than a half hour. Sit off to the side with a pad of paper and observe their meeting. Make a record of major events in the flow of their conversation. What did they say? How did they say it? What was the flow of the conversation? How did they react to each other? What body language did you observe? Were there any misunderstandings? At the end of the meeting, debrief the people you were observing. Compare your notes with their perceptions.

This first exercise simplifies the two parts of process dialogue. You acted as an outside observer. Since you were not part of the conversation, it was easier to be aware of what was happening. Your perceptions of the conversation were influenced less by your own values than if you had been involved in the conversation. We need to apply the same principles in situations where we are a primary communicator and actor. In this next exercise you will watch what perceptions you form and what catalyzed them.

Exercise 5b: Process Dialogue—New People/New Situations

Find an opportunity to meet a number of new people. Pay attention to all the impressions you form about each person. Watch how your theories of the person change as you gather new information. Pay attention to words, tone, body language, and actions. Try not to give more weight to any particular observation than others, but track how each one makes you feel toward the person. Beware of halting your internal dialogue if you think you have summed up the person. Make a point to keep exploring. If you think you have a strong sense of the person, ask him or her questions with the intent of disproving your current theory. Try to notice what impressions they may be forming about you. What are you saying or doing that might be contributing to their impressions?

You may also want to try this exercise by placing yourself in an unfamiliar situation. Notice how quickly you try to find a mental and emotional reference point. In other words, when faced with a new situation, what past experiences do you draw upon to understand and assess the new one?

The benefit of working on process dialogue with new people or situations is that you are starting with a clean slate. It is easier to observe the inner workings of your mind when you are forming new impressions rather than revising old ones. This next exercise is more challenging because there is more internal and external information to be aware of.

Exercise 5c. Process Dialogue—Group Discussion

Pick a meeting that involves four or more people plus yourself. If it is a long meeting with lots of items on the agenda, start by picking one item on the agenda—preferably a decision-making one involving lots of discussion and different viewpoints. Also make sure that you are one of the contributors to the discussion. While staying centered on the discussion, reserve some concentration to track the flow of the discussion and how it affects your thoughts, emotions, attitude, and perception of others. Afterwards, reflect on some of these questions. Did it feel any differently to be watching your process dialogue while participating in the meeting? Do you think it changed the way you acted? Did you gain any new insight about other participants in the meeting? When and how did past experiences with the group, the topic at hand, or individuals influence your thought patterns?

To do this well is difficult and exhausting. Build up some endurance and then try sustaining awareness of your process dialogue through an entire meeting.

Process dialogues occur naturally all the time. Instead of letting these run in the background we want to bring them to the forefront of our awareness. This will result in a richer connection with others. We may even discover ways to improve our relationships. Old jaded stories or theories that once ruled our behavior will be replaced and invigorated by ever-changing dynamic ones.

We have finished the first competency of Observing in the Core of our map. We subdivided Observation into the five areas of Care/Intention, Self-Awareness, Sensitivity, External Focus, and Process Dialogue and looked at some ways to practice these skills. If you are interested in more exercises in observation that are applied to an organizational setting, take a look at the last chapter in my book *Making Stories: A Practical Guide for Organizational Leaders and Human Resource Specialists* (2002).

Listening Competency

We all want to be listened to, but few of us are consistently good listeners. The heart of the Core ring is Listening. This one elusive competency encapsulates all the others. When we develop the discipline and make the emotional space to quiet our knee-jerk reactions to external and internal stimuli we become effective listeners. This in turn makes us effective communicators and learners. People frequently describe this as "active listening," in order to differentiate it from the act of hearing information but not bothering to do much more with it than make sense of it. *Harkening* is another word that I think gets at this nuance of deep meaningful listening. Also spelled *hearkening*, the word means to listen attentively or to give heed. When we hearken we listen with our full being and take what we are hearing to heart. Sounds, meanings, and patterns are shaped by our emotional landscape and guided by our imagination.

This first exercise is a wonderful demonstration of the relationship between language, stories, and listening. While we may speak in structured patterns formed by the rules and mechanics of language, this is not reflective of how the information is stored or what facilitates active listening.

Exercise 6a. Listening—Life Story

Pair off with another person, preferably someone you do not know. One person will be designated the teller and the other will be the listener. The listener cannot ask any questions. He or she must sit for twenty minutes and listen to the teller talk about her life. The teller has no instructions other than to divulge as much information about her life as she can. At the end of twenty minutes have the listener give a quick capsule. The listener is not allowed to take any notes and the capsule does not have to include every detail shared by the teller. Share the things that seemed important and that really stuck out.

This first listening exercise appears deceptively easy. However, if the teller relies on facts alone, she will not be able to fill twenty minutes. As the teller becomes self-conscious of not having enough to say, she will happen upon a story. A fact becomes transformed into a narrative and suddenly the teller begins weaving a collage of stories. Time now starts to fly. As a listener you will have a hard time recalling all of the details, but some of the stories will stand out in your mind. Try to be aware of how these stories begin contributing to an overall sense of the person. Ask yourself why certain stories stand out more than others.

Music is a universal language. Without words the tones and rhythms of a piece of music can speak volumes. It is easy to get swept away by music without listening to it. This next exercise uses music to practice a more sensitive and deeper form of listening.

Exercise 6b. Listening—Music

Take a piece of orchestral classical or complex jazz music you have never listened to before. Find a quiet place and time to sit down with your eyes closed and listen carefully to the music. Try to follow individual instruments.

Watch how they come in and out of the piece of music. How do the other instruments support and enhance the instrument you are following? Observe how all the sounds blend together. Concentrate on how the piece develops themes. When the piece is finished, sit in silence for a moment and then find someone to describe the piece of music to.

Listening involves sensitivity to sound. Shades of meaning can be construed from tone. The Chinese language is rich in its use of tones to differentiate meaning. A wrong inflection can completely change the message delivered. The way in which sounds move in and out of a piece of music mirrors the way words provide not just meaning through the main text but also through their subtext. The subtext consists of the messages and meanings that lie below the words we speak. We must become adept at listening to the subtext if we are to sharpen our listening capacity.

An essential skill to becoming a good listener is the ability to paraphrase and validate what is being communicated. In this next exercise you will practice summarizing what someone says and then make sure you have understood them correctly.

Exercise 6c. Listening—Paraphrase and Validate

Select a day when you anticipate lots of in-depth discussions both at work and at home. When the person you are communicating with expresses a complex thought or feeling, pause for a second and then recapitulate their point in your own words. Follow your recapitulation with a question to assess whether or not you have understood their point. Take validation one step further by acknowledging some or all aspects of their comment as resonating with you even if you do not agree fully. It is important that you do this with honesty and integrity. Do not attempt to placate someone insincerely since it will be perceived to be patronizing. Words must match intention, otherwise the dissonance between them, albeit subtle, is processed consciously or unconsciously by the receiver and ends up foiling your attempts to be a good listener. It becomes more of a technical display of communication skills rather than a genuine effort to connect with someone.

Restating a person's point is a good way of owning its meaning. The act of finding your own words encourages you to establish linkages between their words and your experiences. Constructs in your head are associated with what has been said. Sometimes you may be able to repeat the information but not really understand the point being made or perspective being expressed. In situations like these it is not enough to parrot back the speaker's words. Clarification is required. Follow-up questions can be used to focus the message, get to the critical point, and ferret out multiple ideas.

This next exercise develops your ability to think quickly and ask good follow-up questions. This skill can be reapplied in more complex communication interactions such as the ones just discussed.

Exercise 6d. Listening—Clarification and Follow-up Questions

Find a friend or colleague who participates in a hobby or activity about which you know very little. Ask your friend to begin explaining it to you. Instruct him to provide a general description but to leave out a lot of details. Let him know you are tasked with coming up with questions to delve deeper into the specifics of his activity. When something is vague, be sure to clarify your understanding. When you are done, find another person who knows nothing about your friend or colleague's hobby and begin to explain what you have learned. Have the first person that explained the hobby listen to your explanation and when you are done provide feedback on the accuracy of your description. Give the first part of this exercise at least fifteen minutes. Inevitably the more you learn about a new area the more you realize there is to know.

Reporters and talk show hosts are excellent at probing deep into areas unknown to them. They quickly create a mental frame of reference. As they start turning their attention and imagination to the topic at hand, their mind generates a flurry of questions. This ushers in a new domain of knowledge and provides a rush to the recipient because it is exciting to learn and we thrive on it.

Most people are much better working with visual information than with oral. Given written directions we are usually able to follow them to complete a task. In the next exercise you will practice working with oral information. Becoming more accustomed to working with oral information will naturally improve your baseline skills of listening.

Exercise 6e. Listening—Following Directions

There are three variations of this exercise you can try. In the first one, ask someone to describe the layout of his or her house. Make sure it is someone's house you have never visited. While they describe their house, draw a picture to represent the layout of it. The second variation of this exercise is for those of you who enjoy cooking or baking. Have someone select a recipe that you have never made before. Without looking at the recipe, have him or her read it to you while you make it. In the last variation of this exercise have someone explain to you how to do a complex task and then try to do it. This could be job related, such as an involved business process, or it could be a home improvement project.

Were you able to keep all the steps straight? How did you manage an onslaught of oral information without visual information to back it up?

It would be nice if all the information we listened to could be measured against a tangible result such as a drawing of a house's layout, a recipe, or the successful completion of a complex task. Unfortunately, most of what we listen to requires interpretation. We need to discern facts from opinions, and feelings from logic. This gets back to the idea of subtext. Sometimes the trappings of how something is said can be misleading from the agenda of the speaker. Politicians are notorious for this. Other times the communication may be unnecessarily convoluted in its jargon, style, or lingo. Professors are guilty of this. Making these split-second determinations when we are listening to someone is a challenge. In the next exercise we break down this skill of interpretation by practicing it with written language before applying the principles to oral ones.

Exercise 6f: Listening—Editorial Interpretation

Take a newspaper or magazine and read one of the commentaries or editorial articles. Read the article once as quickly as you can without pausing to think about what the writer is trying to communicate. Put the article aside and without looking at it, write a summary. Hand the article to a friend or colleague and ask them to do the same thing. Read each other's summary without discussing them. Next, read the article out loud together and discuss it. How does your interpretation differ from your colleague's? Did your interpretation change after reading his or her summary? How did both of your interpretations change when you read the article together?

Our memories are deceiving. When we add hindsight, things have a tendency to look different. This next exercise is a perfect way to get feedback on our communications.

Exercise 6g. Listening—Tape-recorded Conversation

Plan to bring a recording device to a significant conversation. Be sure to seek the permission of anyone who will be involved in the conversation. After setting up the recording device, do your best to ignore its presence and proceed with your conversation. When you are finished, rewind the conversation and review it. If possible, involve the other people in your review process. How does your sense of the conversation differ from the recording? How well did you listen to the other person? If they are reviewing the conversation with you, ask them to assess how well they thought you listened to them. Were there any times when you failed to understand what they were communicating? What contributed to this failure? If you were to have the conversation over again, what would you do differently?

Sometimes in order to listen actively we need to change our frame of reference. Strained relationships are fertile ground for this. Working with someone who has a significantly different world view, personality, thinking style, communicating style, or learning style is apt to cause friction. It can be difficult to work with such a person. This exercise offers some ideas on how to quickly modify your frame of reference to remove any perception biases that are getting in the way of your actively listening to the other person.

Exercise 6h. Listening—Frame of Reference

Try this next time you are in a difficult conversation in which you are having problems listening to the other person or tolerating his or her behavior. Once you are aware of the biases affecting your ability to listen, imagine the person in front of you when they were a child. Imagine every detail you possibly can. What did they look like as a child? What were their needs? How did other kids treat them? How did they react to others? Did you notice any difference in your ability to listen? Try this technique before entering a room full of people. You are attempting to halt all of your perceptual filters from affecting your capacity to listen. A radical reframing of your perceptions in the present will facilitate your receptivity.

We have to be committed to active listening. It takes a lot of emotional energy to do it well. I know after a day of facilitating I am wiped out, but I have learned how to recharge my batteries. Everyone will have different things that work for him or her. Quiet time with a book or a loved one, a movie, listening to music, a good meal, time outdoors, exercise, or time spent on a hobby are just a couple of ideas. If your tank of emotional energy is empty, it will be difficult or impossible to give someone your full presence when they need you. Learning to be fully present with one another is one of the most important things we can learn how to do. It not only makes us more effective in business, it also makes us feel more alive. It is such a simple thing to want, and in principle attainable, but it is incredibly difficult to achieve.

Table 14.4

Three Levels of the Eliciting Competency

LEVEL	NAME	DESCRIPTION
LEVEL 1	Trust	• Building history with others • Creating joint stories • Having shared experiences
LEVEL 2	Climate of sharing	• Willingness to share our own experiences and be vulnerable • Inviting others to share • Demonstrating resonance and understanding of others' experiences • Pacing
LEVEL 3	Attending	• Rephrasing questions • Developing alternative questions • Matching others' language

Eliciting Competency

The last competency in the Core is Eliciting. At first glance it may seem strange to include a competency on pulling information when throughout our discussion of the Core we have focused on listening and observing, both of which have a more passive sense to them. However, one cannot effectively pull information from others without using a variety of active listening and observational skills. To be good at eliciting others' experiences and perceptions in the form of stories, we need to rely on situational awareness and the ability to think quickly on our feet.

The Eliciting competency of the Core can be broken down into three levels (see Table 14.4). The first two layers of the Eliciting competency "trust," and "climate of sharing," are not skill driven. The foundation of being good at eliciting other people's stories is trust. Without trust it is unlikely you will get someone to share much. Gaining the trust of someone stems from two dynamics. The first of the two is time and personality. People vary, but it is safe to say that the majority of us extend trust to others after the passage of time and several positive experiences. The more positive and reassuring our experiences, the more trust we will develop. As trust develops we begin building a history between others and ourselves. Our stories become entwined and it is through shared experiences that the seeds of trust are sowed. Personality also plays a role. We have no control over our own personality or the personalities of others. Sometimes there is a natural chemistry between people, which engenders trust more easily and quickly. The second dynamic of trust is intuition. This is hard to pin down in any satisfying way, but suffice it to say that each of us sizes up others based on a variety of tangible and intangible data points, and each warrants greater and lesser degrees of trust depending upon our evaluations. What we sense about others influences the extent to which we give them our trust.

The second layer of Eliciting is creating a climate of sharing. This builds upon the first layer of trust. Trust is a prerequisite for creating a climate of sharing. Once trust is present, we need to capitalize on it by doing everything in our power to promote sharing. We need to invite others to share their experiences and exhibit a willingness to do so ourselves; in this way we demonstrate resonance, or the capacity to find common ground. If we feel there are similarities between our own experiences and those of someone else, we are far more likely to share more experiences. Pacing is another aspect of sharing. It is not a race and we cannot steam ahead divulging all our experiences at once. It will overwhelm the other person and deprive them of the emotional time and space to process what we share.

The first two levels of the Eliciting competency, trust and climate of sharing, operate on personal and organizational dimensions. We have a lot less control over organizational dimensions than we do personal ones. Through our behavior, and if we are in a leadership position, we can inculcate positive changes. Some companies foster cultures where trust and sharing are key qualities. The damaging effects of widespread negative behaviors are offset by the manner in which we go about cultivating our individual relationships in the organization. However, there are limits to the positive impact of individuals who build trust and encourage sharing. A discussion of how organizations can manage their cultures to develop these qualities is a whole other topic and beyond the scope of this book. Organizations should start the process by doing an honest assessment of the presence or absence of trust and sharing in their organizations, and then ask why they are not more present and if there is a genuine interest in cultivating them. As far as being "politically correct," most leaders buy the rhetoric, but closer examination frequently reveals they either don't really believe in the business productivity merits of trust and sharing or they have a vested interest in abnegating them in their culture in the name of efficiency or competitiveness.

The third level of the Eliciting competency is attending. Attending entails being cognizant of how people respond to the language and questions we use to elicit their experiences and being able to modify them on the fly. Job interviews are a perfect example. Interviews characterized by lots of narrative offer a wealth of information. This first exercise mimics an interview situation to simulate agility with questions and language that stimulates people to share their experiences in the form of stories.

Exercise 7a. Eliciting—Job Interview Questions

Find two people to do this exercise with you. You should know one person reasonably well, however it is best that you do not know a lot about their professional background; the second person should be a virtual stranger. Imagine you are getting ready to interview them for your job. Write down a list of key questions to assess a person's experiences and how they match with the job requirements. Limit the scope of your questions to probing for parallels and similarities between these people's past and your job. Questions of a more general nature about background and summaries of past responsibilities are not in line with the challenge of this exercise. You are trying to get them to tell you stories, not facts.

Underneath each question in your list, write at least two other word-ings of the same question. For the person you know, ascertain if there is any language you can use that will be likely to result in a story. With the person you do not know well, try to be conscious of adapting your language during the interview. Look for opportunities to use short personal stories or other anecdotes to elicit more narrative. To get the full benefit of this exercise, allot 10–15 minutes to develop your list of questions and 30–45 minutes for each interview. Your success in this exercise can be measured by counting the number of stories you elicit juxtaposed to the number of facts.

Next is another exercise that uses eliciting techniques to enrich your interaction with others in a meeting. It can be very important to get a quick read on how people are feeling and what may be contributing to those feelings before diving into your agenda.

Exercise 7b. Eliciting—Words and Feelings

At the start of a meeting, ask everyone to write down a word or two that describes how they are feeling at the moment. You can also have people share their word without writing it down, but most people will respond better if they have a moment to themselves rather than being put on the spot in front of their peers. Go around the room and have people share their words. Pay attention to your reactions to each word. When a particular word from some-

*one strikes you, stop and try to elicit further information from him to probe
his choice of words. Can you get him to tell you what experiences, events, or
mental preoccupations are encapsulated in his word?*

The time you take to perform this exercise can end up saving you time later
in the meeting. If people have a chance to air their feelings and realize they
have been heard, they are less likely to drag these elements into your discussions or decisions during the meeting. You will also gain invaluable insights
and may even modify your own viewpoints. On a related note, another technique I like to use in meetings is to ask someone to bring in one of their favorite
quotes to share with the group. Later on in the meeting the quote may even
become an anchoring device to generate perspective or guidance in the meeting process. I have even gone so far as to have people read the quote out loud
as a group after it has been shared. This serves to unify a group. If you have
ever sung in a chorus or recited text with a group, you will recognize the power
of many voices creating one voice and its effect on participants.

One of the best ways to elicit the richest information from another person
in the form of story is to tell a story. The best response to a story is another
story, and stories are very good at triggering other people's stories. Here is
an exercise that puts this principle to work.

Exercise 7c. Eliciting—Statement–Story—Story

*Make a decision to practice this exercise a couple of times a day until it be-
comes natural and you do not even need to think about it. During a conversation, key into a phrase or statement someone makes. Respond to the statement
with a short story. Be conscious of the context, audience, and receptivity of the
listener and adjust the length and detail of the story you share. The timing of
your story should coincide with the need to gain clarification of a person's
viewpoint, build greater trust and vulnerability between yourself and the other
person, or become a mechanism for uncovering subtleties that a regular conversation would not be able to uncover as quickly as your story can.*

Organizational Practices for the Core

All of the above exercises are geared toward individuals developing these
competencies. Individuals will impact the organization as a whole, but let's
take a brief look at some organizational practices that can support the efforts
of individuals.

The first and simplest thing organizations can do is encourage individuals
to develop these competencies. Managers need to be constantly in dialogue

with the people working with them to assess these competencies and make them a priority. This fits right in with the Observation competency and its subcomponent of care/intention. The time and attention given to these competencies will contribute to an overall ethos imbued with care. Managers also need to find a way in keeping with their unique personalities and styles to balance a certain degree of vulnerability with their employees while maintaining authority and some boundaries. As we saw in the exercise above, building trust and getting others to share requires us to soften the parental image of perfection many managers try to project.

Meetings and project management methodologies should include structures, disciplines, and practices in order for people to work on these competencies. Existing courses should undergo instructional design analysis to be sure they incorporate opportunities for experiencing and practicing these competencies. Evaluation and return-on-investment analysis need to capture qualitative data demonstrating how people are using these competencies to better achieve their organizational objectives. By looking for the relationship between these all-important underlying competencies, the growth and development of these competencies in employees, and how these competencies impact daily effectiveness, organizations will be able to build a compelling case for investing in the ongoing development of them. As with anything else, these are not static efforts, structures, practices, and disciplines, so they will need to be constantly reinvented in order to be aligned with the dynamic needs of the time. Corporate will must be married to flexibility, otherwise well-intentioned practices become black hole efforts that suck up energy and resources but somehow become ends in themselves and devoid of their original intent.

Summary of the Core

We have walked through the first ring and heart of our map. The Core's three competencies of Observing, Listening, and Eliciting are the most important qualities that we need to develop in ourselves to be effective communicators and learners. Observing was broken down into five subcomponents of Care/Intention, Self-Awareness, Sensitivity, External Focus, and Process Dialogue. We differentiated the Listening competency by emphasizing a deeper and more active kind of paying attention. Our last series of exercises examined how to elicit other people's experiences. We ended our discussion of the Core by offering some thoughts on how organizations can encourage the development of these competencies.

15

The Process Ring

The Process Ring is the second area of our Competency Map (see Figure 15.1). The Core deals with listening, and the Process Ring deals with how we work with and store information in our minds. The Process Ring is composed of three competencies: Indexing, Synthesizing, and Reflecting. All three competencies taken together capture the interplay of internal processes that result in learning. Stories are used as a way of codifying experiences. For example, the Indexing competency stresses the importance of consciously developing a robust array of descriptors for our experiences so that they can be easily reused in various settings. The bigger our indexing scheme, the more we have learned from our experiences. A good index increases our capacity to learn in new situations by drawing upon past ones and integrating the news ones into a fabric of knowledge. Our capacity to communicate with others is also improved. Once our experiences have been transformed into easily retrievable stories that have been well indexed and cross-indexed, then we can be sensitive to other people's experiences and converse with a greater range of nuances and understanding.

Indexing Competency

Indexing is how we classify our experiences. The better the index, the easier it is to find information. The problem with an index is deciding what descriptors to use to classify our experiences. Indexes are further complicated by the fact everyone will choose different "key words" or descriptors to classify their experiences. If we cannot access our experiences due to an inadequate index or one that does not match someone else's, our experiences become dormant. They are left in the proverbial warehouse of our mind, available to our unconscious but collecting dust. Effective communicators and learners naturally develop extensive indexing schemes. They draw upon many different experiences and can recall these experiences in the form of stories.

Triggers activate indexes. Triggers are any kind of stimuli that results in a

Figure 15.1   **Competency Map—The Process Ring**

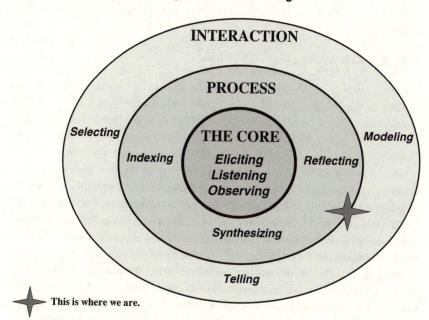

This is where we are.

search of our experiences and in a recounting of them. An item in our index can be stimulated by a variety of triggers. Therefore we need to be vigilant in creating a vast index and become more aware of potential triggers. If we think in advance about what kinds of themes, ideas, perceptions, learning, or emotions are contained in our experience, we will be able to use this awareness to become sensitive to a multitude of triggers. Take a conversation, for example. Thoughts and ideas are expressed one after another. Given the flow of a conversation we can be swept along without ever consciously drawing upon our experiences. We are using them in the background in order to understand what is being communicated, but we are not bringing them to the forefront of our minds. This in turn limits our ability to infuse the conversation with greater depth and energy. The experiences left in the background by our minds generate a base level of understanding, but will cause us to miss vital opportunities to increase our learning and communicate with greater depth. From our previous discussions we have established the complex nature of our experiences, which are stored and recounted to others in the form of stories.

The first step in building an index and developing an awareness of triggers is to reconstruct as many of our experiences as possible. This will result in an active collection of stories, which we can then index and associate with some potential triggers. The next exercise presents a method for building a collection of stories, identifying some major themes, and anticipating potential triggers.

Exercise 8a. Indexing—Personal History

In this exercise you will create a timeline of your life. One end of the horizontal timeline should be marked with "birth" and the other should be marked as "present." Think back upon the years of your life and start scanning them for memories that stick out. As you create your timeline, use the list of eight historical triggers found in Table 15.1 to help you jog your memory.

Be sure you find the stories behind each of these triggers. If your memory surfaces more as a fact, then spend a moment with the memory and try to reconstitute all of the details surrounding it. This will transform your memory into a story. The richness of a story is what lends itself to indexing. Facts get lost. Some people find it useful to do this year by year while others will start randomly filling in their timeline with memories as they occur.

Once you have your timeline filled in with stories, develop a two-columned list for each story that includes story triggers and themes (see Figure 15.2). Your triggers will be any situation or time where you believe your story could have applicability. At the same time, examine your stories for themes. These are in essence things that you have learned and insights you have gained from your experiences. If you are aware of what themes can be found in your experiences, it will help you index them based upon potential triggers.

In order to be an effective communicator and learner you need to possess a wealth of stories. You are mistaken if you think you do not know or have a lot of stories. Our lives are rich with experiences. The trick is, we need to make ourselves aware of these experiences by focusing our attention on them. The Personal History exercise is a sample of how you can recapture dusty memories and shake them off. If you find the timeline difficult to use, I suggest you take a look at my first book, *Making Stories: A Practical Guide for Organizational Leaders and Human Resource Specialists.* Chapter 11 in the book offers a series of topics and questions for each category with the purpose of helping readers build an index of their personal stories.

Let's step back for a moment and realize that the process by which experiences are stored as stories, indexed for retrieval, and then used by us in conversations and learning settings happens all the time. Why not invoke this mental process? We can strengthen this natural phenomenon by increasing its frequency on a conscious level. To do this we must have a solid foundation built. A big, well-organized toolbox of personal stories will get the job done.

Table 15.1

Exercise 8a. Indexing—Personal History (Part I)

History	Description—"In this year ..."
1. Major events	Were there any significant things that happened?
2. Influences	What things had a formative effect in shaping your ideas, beliefs, values, or attitudes?
3. Decisions	Did you make any decisions that had an impact on your life or the lives of others?
4. Changes	What changes occurred?
5. Successes	What were your major accomplishments?
6. Failures	Did you make any big mistakes or experience any failures?
7. Disappointments	Were there any disappointments?
8. Significant people	How did certain key people affect you?

Figure 15.2   **Exercise 8a. Indexing—Personal History (Part II)**

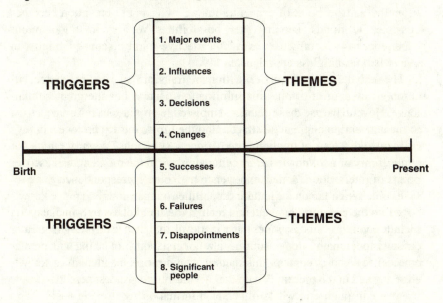

Reflecting Competency

> *The salvation of this human world lies nowhere*
> *else than in the human power to reflect.*
> —Vaclav Havel

We all could do with a little more thinking. Introspection is undervalued and unpracticed. It is another one of those seemingly fuzzy things left outside of the walls of business, yet nothing could be more important to the success of an organization and the well-being of its members. Our ability to reflect is a defining characteristic of being human. So why do most of us prefer our bliss of oblivious autopilot in lieu of a more mindful orientation to the world around us? Perhaps because it takes time, discipline, and commitment to develop this orientation. Given the finite nature of these assets, we do not part with them easily. Socially, as evidenced by our educational system, we do not make reflection a priority. In many instances we go out of our way to discourage it.

Reflection requires focusing our attention in a single direction with circumspection. The image of an hourglass is useful in understanding the state of mind we need to achieve in order to benefit from our efforts. Individual grains of sand pass through a narrow point before they drop into a large collection area. When we concentrate, it is akin to the narrow point of an hourglass. When we review an experience and it yields a wealth of insights, it is akin to the large open collection area into which the grains of sand fall. From that narrow point of concentration a new vista of perception becomes possible. Our minds open up to new possibilities. We are able to look at our experiences in a totally new way. A reflective mind discovers insights in otherwise meaningless experiences.

The insights we gain from reflection are transformed into knowledge, becoming raw chunks of reusable information. Herein lies the greatest challenge. How do we use these chunks? Knowledge provides us with a construct to manage and manipulate abstractions mined from our experiences, but we have to find a way of applying them to new situations. When we look for applicability of our knowledge by being attentive to the moment, we discover points of intersection. A new experience has some correspondence to a previous one. We call upon the pattern capabilities of our minds and move knowledge into the present. This pattern match guides our behavior. Some benefits include avoiding mistakes we have made in the past, exhibiting a greater capacity for empathy, demonstrating new understanding, or acting with greater confidence. When it comes to interpersonal or intrapersonal dynamics, knowledge applied in the present is wisdom. Arguably, the greatest personal power that we can pursue is wisdom. While information by itself is useless and knowledge brings with it a certain degree of influence, wisdom deepens us. The bottom line is that we cannot be effective without reflection. The feedback gained from flexing our internal powers of observation is invaluable and cannot be procured through any other means.

Now that we have established the importance of reflecting, how do we do it? Reflection can be broken down into four parts:

1. Visualization
2. Sitting
3. Inviting
4. Sifting

1. Visualization

Reflection is made possible through the use of visualization. The word *visualization* can be misleading. We need to use all of our senses when we visualize. The more senses we can invoke, the richer our visualizations will be. Saint Ignatius of Loyola wrote a guide for monks called *The Spiritual Exercises.* Although this predates modern psychology, he, like others before him, had an intuitive grasp of how our minds work. The spiritual exercises are a collection of guided visualizations on Jesus Christ's life. Loyola instructs priest to begin imagining a scene from Jesus' life by walking through the sights, sounds, smells, tastes, and feelings of it. The result is a vivid and personal reexperiencing of a story. Athletes offer another perspective on the power of visualization. Mental rehearsals have been shown to result in muscular activity that can be measured. These mental rehearsals enable athletes to practice, learn, and improve motor skills. They can also be used to strengthen cognitive and psycho-emotional skills such as concentration, focus, and stress management. Visualizations are effective because they are not just mental phenomena—they engage our whole being.

In order to reflect on our experiences we must relive them. Visualization offers us this ability. We reenter our past experiences as an observer. Our imaginations fuel our archival inquiry and engage us as active observers. Like the spiritual exercises, we can also reflect on stories outside of our personal experience. Whatever we visualize is projected into a space where we can begin to manipulate it. In this way, reflection has the potential to be more than an analytical rehashing of an experience. Visualization creates a story, while analysis by itself creates a collection of linearly associated data points. If we are to win any insights from our experiences or effectively find connections between our experiences, we will need to work with them as stories.

2. Sitting

Reflection requires us to be still. After we have visualized an experience, we need to sit with it. Here is an analogy to clarify this notion of sitting: Think of a marble suspended in the middle of jar by a viscous medium. The marble just floats. It is completely buoyant. Sitting with our visualizations surrounds them with a rich medium of quiet space. We are enveloping the visualization to become receptive to how it unfolds. Once we set visualization in motion we must resist the temptation to direct it. Reflection will not occur if we repeat patterns. When we sit with our visualization, we are waiting for a new path to appear. The dust settles, and it becomes possible to look for uncharted territory.

3. Inviting

Reflection must be invited. Visualization allows us to relive an experience, sitting with it results in receptivity to discovering new patterns, and inviting is the active process of seeking insights. We must genuinely desire to find insights. Inviting describes an internal process of moving our volition. We go from stillness of mind to movement of heart. In our emotional center we must want to find a new insight even if what we discover hurts our egos. Our self-perceptions can be altered by the things we discover, therefore we must be very sincere in our commitment to uncover new insights. The fact that we are willing to uncover potentially painful things acts as a supportive lattice to buffer our self-image from becoming damaged. Whatever failures we may encounter during our reflection of the past are counterbalanced by the opportunities to turn them into building blocks of knowledge, and hopefully wisdom, in future experiences.

4. Sifting

Reflection engages our analytical mind through the act of sifting. Once we invite insights they will start appearing. This is when we need to review each insight to evaluate its worth and to decide how it is related to our current understanding of things. We turn things over in our mind to examine them. We use our mind as a microscope to probe deeper. In essence, we are deconstructing the array of themes that have been upturned during our reflection process to find the details. Sifting results in the objectification of knowledge and completes the process of reflection. Like a prospector sifting for nuggets of gold in his pan, we need to rigorously shake all the information in our visualization to find what we want to keep. We begin reflection by invoking our imaginations, and we end the process by enlisting our analytical powers.

Reflection is a complex phenomenon. This framework serves as guide. Naturally, there is a degree of artificiality to breaking it down into components, but it enables us to observe what things fit together. The interplay of visualization, sitting, inviting, and sifting is supple. They overlap one another and move back and forth between one another during the reflection process. So while they are presented in a step-by-step manner, discover how they work within you. Every time you reflect there will be a different interaction among the parts. Let's apply the principles of reflection in a few exercises. This first exercise practices visualization. There is a direct correlation between the strength of visualization and the quality of reflection. Strong powers of visualization facilitate reflection. In order to isolate the impact of visualization on reflection, this first exercise incorporates a depersonalized event.

Exercise 9a. Reflecting—Historical Visualization

Select an historical period or event. It can be from any period of any country. Drawing upon whatever you remember of any written accounts or other descriptions, create a vivid visualization. Use all of your senses to enter into your mental fabrication. As the details unfold, sit and watch. Try to observe what you are feeling. What cognitions do you have? Have you ever imagined this scene before? How is it different from other times? Articulate your insights. Compare your insights to any you may have held before this visualization. How difficult was it for you to visualize? Were you able to use all of your senses? If not, which sense was lacking? Were you aware of the other parts of reflection occurring?

In this next exercise we move to the personal. When we reflect on personal events, it is easier to generate vivid visualizations but more difficult to reflect on them. The challenge in this exercise is not to reconstruct memories in the same way we have done in the past. We want to encounter new insights. To do so, we need to be disciplined about using all the other parts of reflection (sitting, inviting, and sifting).

Exercise 9b. Reflecting—Personal History

Go back and look at the timeline you created in Exercise 8a. Reflect on each story in your timeline. You do not need to do these in any particular order. Try starting with the strongest memories, even if these are ones you think you have already done a good job of reflecting on. As you sift through the in-sights, what new themes appear? Take your time; this exercise cannot be rushed. If you do this exercise right, you will only be able to reflect on one or two stories a day. The volume of emotional information you dredge up can be overwhelming. If the story you are reflecting on naturally morphs into another story, let it happen. You may find that as you relive one memory, another one attaches itself to your recollection of the first. This is completely natural and is a good indication of how engaged you are in the reflection process. Allow your analytical mind to explore the link between the coexist-ence of multiple stories in your reflection. If you are coming up short on new insights, try shifting actors in your visualization. Usually we visualize things from our own perspective. In order to stir things up, imagine the story from someone else's perspective. It could be another person in the story or an unrelated observer. This has the effect of moving our attention away from ourselves and encouraging a new perspective.

We want to increase the amount of time we spend reflecting. Reflection can be a natural part of our awareness. This next exercise is one way to build reflection as an ongoing capacity.

Exercise 9c. Reflecting—Daily Rewind

Before you go to bed, rewind the events of the day in your head. Let all your preoccupations fall away. Imagine the details of your day from any starting point. Try to remember all of the interactions, conversations, observations, thoughts, feelings, people, and ideas. As one pops into your mind stay with it until it connects to another or it yields an insight. You might want to have a notebook on hand. A review of the day is likely to produce action items. These are an added bonus of the process, however they are not the goal. You are reflecting on the day to expand your perspective and grow in awareness.

Reflection is a habit we can inculcate. It becomes a discipline, with the time interval becoming shorter and shorter so that reflection is happening all the time and turns into mindfulness.

Synthesizing Competency

The third competency in the Process Ring is Synthesizing. The result of syn-thesis is knowledge and learning. From our discussion above we know that knowledge has the potential to be turned into wisdom if we can succeed in bringing lessons learned from the past into the present.

The ability to synthesize builds upon the competency of Reflecting. Synthesis occurs when reflection moves in multiple parallel directions. We do not work with experiences in isolation. When we are reflecting on an experience, it leads us to recall a past one. During the sitting/inviting phase of reflection, experiences may begin to overlap with one another. As they overlap, a relationship is created between the insights that are arising during our reflection process in the present and insights we have had in the past. We possess a large multidimensional array of associations tethered together as experiences in our mind. Some of these associations are present the moment we go to store a new experience as a story because we are reusing indexing keys and these new experiences line up with them. Other associations are created when we juxtapose experiences with one another. The process of reflection yields insights, which in turn are associated with the original experience. The experience along with the insights is stored as a story in our mind. These stories are filed according to our indexing scheme. Reflections across multiple experiences are woven together to produce insights that result in learning, knowledge, and hopefully, wisdom.

Let's try a couple of analogies. Imagine two strands of rope twisted together. The union of these ropes creates something novel. Synthesis is the bond between them. There is kinetic energy stored in the braids of rope. The connection between the ropes represents a new potential for knowledge and learning. In synthesis, two or more insights are joined together. I liken the process to looking in a crystal ball. The crystal ball is empty until we gaze into its center. A vision appears as our reflection yields insights. These insights are joined by other insights from previous experiences. The crystal ball's foggy vision lifts and we are given an epiphany (see Figure 15.3). If we succeed in using this epiphany, it becomes wisdom.

The power of synthesis rests in its ability to connect insights from totally different domains. We start making connections between previously unrelated entities. We use stories as seen in Figure 15.3 to identify the blocks of information we work with in our minds. When we laid out the functions of stories in Chapter 2, we learned how they encode information and act as a tool for thinking. Both of these functions are at work when we are synthesizing.

Synthesis helps creates an elaborate network of interconnected nodes. The tighter our mesh of nodes the quicker we can reach any point. A flexible mind builds paths between unrelated points. We find a common thread and sew the points together. New connections can be made all the time. We want to strengthen our capacity to see interrelationships between our experiences. When we reflect on one experience in relation to another, a whole new light is cast on the experience. Suddenly parallels emerge. Seizing upon the short-lived connections made between these separate experiences is synthesis.

Figure 15.3   The Crystal Ball of Synthesis

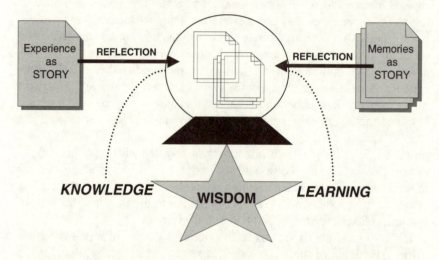

Since our experiences are ingrained in our minds, it helps to practice synthesis by relating an external story to a personal one. We know that stories are a great tool for thinking and that synthesis is a special form of thinking. Stories are used all the time to help us make connections between abstractions of characters in a narrative and ourselves. This is done in a more straightforward fashion every time a speaker uses a story to anchor his message. The themes contained in the story are related to points being made in the present. The speaker uses the story as a bridge. Synthesis is the energy we use to cross the bridge to find new learning. We do not need to wait for others to build bridges between unrelated chunks of information. This is a mental discipline we need to be engaged in all the time.

Let's start simply and simulate the process of a speaker using external stories to promote insights. This first exercise has you look for connections between childhood stories and personal experiences.

Exercise 10a. Synthesizing—Childhood Stories and Me

Below is a list of childhood stories. These are just a few ideas, so add any of your favorite ones to the list. Take a piece of paper and make three columns (see Table 15.2). In the first column put the name of the story and a brief description, in the second column make a list of salient themes, and in the third column create a list of ways in which you connect to the story. The

Table 15.2

Exercise 10a. Synthesizing—Childhood Stories and Me

Story and description	Themes	Story connections

second column contains a list about learning. What do you take from the story? What are the major themes that grab you? Think of the third column as your bridge. How does the story and its dominant themes relate to you? What can you learn from the story? Be careful—we are not looking for moralizing. These are not abstract principles but personal ones. What is the correspondence between the themes of the story and experiences you have had in your life? You are looking for new intersections of learning not rehashing obvious messages. Synthesis will make the story real to you on a personal level. It will guide you to new insights and should trigger a whole slew of other personal experiences from your memory.

    Sample of Childhood Stories:
    Pinocchio
    Little Red Riding Hood
    Snow White and the Seven Dwarfs
    Hansel and Gretel
    Jack and the Beanstalk
    Sleeping Beauty
    Three Little Pigs
    Cinderella
    Robin Hood

    Exercise 10a has the potential to jumpstart the process of synthesis. The childhood stories are a starting point. Once your personal stories are triggered by the themes in the childhood stories, you may find yourself mentally exploring a maze of interconnections. Measure the success of your efforts by the number of new connections you make. If you have new insights, and if you joined previously unrelated experiences in your mind, then you are putting the powers of synthesis to work.

    We begin to see the interrelationship between all of the competencies in the Process Ring. Indexing is being used in the background all the time to find chunks of information that we are referring to as stories, reflection works with our stories to uncover insights, and synthesis connects islands of insight to one another to form new networks of learning and knowledge. When we actualize the learning and knowledge, it becomes wisdom. We said that wisdom is the greatest source of personal power because it is reflected in our behaviors not just our words; because of this, wisdom also has more permanence.

Exercise 10b: Synthesizing—Mind Map of Experiences

Synthesis needs to be an ongoing activity. In this exercise we will use the stories you identified in Exercise 8a and look for how these stories with their themes and insights relate to other ones. If you are looking for a more concrete way to get started, try drawing a mind map of stories and themes. Select a few stories from your timeline. Put each story in a circle. Hang themes from each story off of the story's main circle. Do this for several stories. Now look for intersections. Draw lines to connect themes from one story to another one. Although you are involved in a very concrete task that includes analytical processes, be sure to engage your imagination. Working on paper is meant to be a catalyst and not the main activity. In order for synthesis to occur, your mind will be rapidly moving back and forth between all the parts of reflecting (visualization, sitting, inviting, and sifting) and indexing. When you become more comfortable, you will not need to use a mind map.

There is a sense of accomplishment earned from synthesizing our experiences. Learning is one of the great joys in life. Making synthesis more a part of our mental life is sure to invigorate us and make us more powerful in our organizational communications and actions.

Organizational Practices for the Process Ring

Organizations need to encourage individuals to reflect. We can do with less busy work and more thoughtfulness. People need a chance to stop what they are doing to be retrospective. There are great buzzwords we casually throw around like "lessons learned," "work smart," or "capture best practices," but that is about where it ends in most organizations. Opportunities can be discovered, resources better utilized, more creative problem solving can occur, and new ad hoc communities can form when reflection is made a priority. Group processes can be instituted as part of formal methodologies to facilitate reflection. The "after-action review" discussed by Rob Kraska in the interview with DTE Energy (see Chapter 9) is a great example. Facilitators of any meeting should get in the habit of using phrases like the following: "What insights do you have?" "How does this experience relate to others you have had?" "What experiences have you had outside of work that aid your understanding of this insight?" "How can our organization incorporate this insight into our practices?" "Based upon what you have shared, how will you use this insight in the future?" These simple questions, asked in a formal or informal setting, will yield a wealth of complex information.

Making time for people-to-people connections to occur enables the transfer of knowledge. When we are in the midst of a project, we will leave flip charts hanging up in conference rooms, white board diagrams with "please do not erase notes" next to them, but do we ever keep a running list of project insights in the open for people to use? Do we ever ask people to describe their current experience in terms of past ones? Here's my advice. Let's kill the PowerPoint presentations once and for all at all hands-on meetings and risk opening the floor for people to share insights they have gained over the last quarter. Are we bold enough to risk sifting through irrelevant or self-serving stories to encounter the inevitable gems that would also be shared? As members of an organization, are we willing to take responsibility for any detrimental sacred cows that might be exposed in the process?

We could ask people to create human chains by sharing an insight in the form of a story. The next experience shared will have to connect in some way to the first. Pursue this for a while to create a chain of personal and organizational insights. When the connections appear to be slowing down, shift topics or initiate a new anchor story to start the chain reaction all over again. The intersections will be amazing. Randomly aggregating people into smaller breakout groups and then reconvening the groups to debrief and connect with each other could precede a group process of this nature.

Imagine if we threw away Performance Evaluations, Personal Development Plans, and Key Job Responsibility forms. What if each employee had to reflect on the year and create a communication of their own making that captured a description of their insights? I don't care what camp you fall into as far as personality or learning theories are concerned. Indexing, reflecting, and synthesizing are universal capacities. People will have varying degrees of comfort with orally communicating insights, however every person, regardless of whether they are right-brain or left-brain dominant, or any other psychometric taxonomy, needs to be given ample opportunity to learn. Organizations are stiff; people are not. We are far more flexible and adaptable than we assume ourselves to be. Let's not allow the systems, processes, and structures we create to prevent us from achieving our potential.

I also recommend that companies reduce the importance of e-mail by limiting deliveries to twice a day, and except for very specific purposes, eliminate instant messaging. The constant reactive barrage of e-mail hinders being reflective. As soon as e-mail hits our in-box we feel the urge to answer it. I am just as guilty of this atrocity as anyone else. What if we received e-mail twice a day—once in the morning and once in the afternoon? Do you think you could function? We might have to pick up the phone to communicate, or worse yet, walk over to someone's office. We would have more time to write thoughtful e-mails and increase our other modes of communication. There are other ways to utilize technology without it dictating a frenetic pace. There are shared directories when we need to exchange documents, and there are Intranet portals we can use to post communications. Reducing the frequency of e-mail is a small thing, but represents a potentially dramatic organizational commitment to promoting more reflective behavior.

Summary of the Process Ring

We have walked through the competencies of the Process Ring of our map. If the Core could be summed up with the word *listening*, the Process Ring can be summed up with the word *thinking*. The Indexing competency describes how we store information. The Reflecting competency explains how we turn experiences into insights, and the Synthesizing competency shows how we interconnect our insights to achieve learning and knowledge. For purposes of our model we have discussed each of the competencies separately, but in actuality they interact with one another in a rapid fashion. Taken together, the first two rings of our map can transform us into more mindful individuals. This is a benefit not only to us but also to the success of any organization.

16

The Interaction Ring

We have come to the final ring of the Competency Map—the Interaction Ring (see Figure 16.1). The Interaction Ring contains the competencies that are most noticeable by outside observers. Selecting, Telling, and Modeling describe how we use stories to communicate. In actuality, these are the least important competencies. They demonstrate mastery of the competencies found in the Core and Process Ring without which the competencies in the Interaction Ring amount to little more than showmanship. The Interaction Ring is the icing on the cake. All the other competencies have to be working in concert in order for us to be effective communicators and learners, regardless of how clever we are in selecting stories, how theatrically we tell them, what behaviors we model or analogies we use to explain ourselves.

Selecting Competency

One of the questions I get asked the most is, "How do you know what story to tell?" It's an excellent question. Of course, the setting where a story is to be told has a lot to do with it. Stepping back to do an audience analysis will be instrumental in guiding you. For example, it is more straightforward when you are giving a presentation at a conference in front of a large audience than if you are attempting to select a story on the fly in an informal conversation. When you have advance information about who the people are, why they are coming, and a sense of what you think they want to get out of your talk, then it is easy to use your preparation time to scan a wide assortment of story options. However, when we do not have the luxury of planning, selecting a story becomes more challenging. In these extemporaneous settings you must rely on the Listening competency of the Core and the Indexing competency from the Process Ring. How we select a story is a function of our index. Since we have already discussed this at length in Chapter 15, we will focus on what stories to select.

Figure 16.1 **Competency Map—The Interaction Ring**

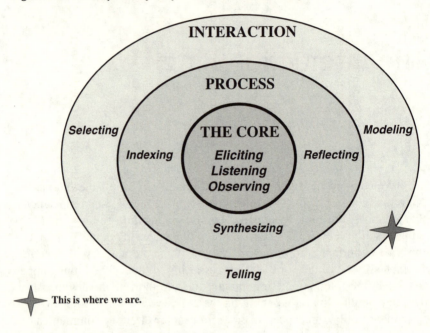

This is where we are.

For the sake of simplicity I am going to reduce the kinds of stories we can select into three broad categories:

1. Personal Stories
2. Other People's Personal Stories
3. Stories from Other Domains

Personal Stories run the gamut from very recent experiences to experiences deep in our past. There is often a quality of vulnerability associated with sharing a personal story, especially ones from our past. We often relate personal stories in the form of a collage. Stories that are well indexed in our mind will be tightly interwoven with one another, and we may feel the desire to share a series of linked stories. Other People's Personal Stories may come from ones they have shared with us. They can also be events we have observed. The major defining characteristic of these stories is that they describe things that have not happened to us. Stories from Other Domains can come from anywhere. Some good examples are books, movies, history, or science. This is not an exhaustive list, but it gives you the sense that these are stories drawn from many different disciplines.

Table 16.1 presents a Decision Matrix and shows you how to interpret

Table 16.1

Decision Matrix for Selecting What Type of Story to Tell

	Intimate	Small	Meeting	Presentation
1. SIZE "How many people will hear your story?"	Usually a conversation involving two people, the nature of the exchange is personal	Several people who share good relationships with one another	More formal setting; there is structure to the group interactions, people may or may not know one another well or have good relationships	Very formal setting, usually large group
	Connect	Teach	Transfer	Entertain
2. INTENTION "Why do you need to select a story?"	You need to build stronger relationships and bond with your listeners	You need to elucidate, explain, or help others conceptualize new ideas or concepts	You need to communicate key pieces of information	You need to break the ice, empower yourself as a speaker, or make people laugh
	Listen	Insight	Reaction	Plant
3. TRIGGER "What is prompting you to select a story?"	You want to hear what a person is thinking or feeling, so you share a personal story to create an opportunity for reciprocity	You need to share an epiphany or while you are listening you suddenly realize something new	You need to respond to another person's story or comment; you may also be responding to group dynamics	You need to deliver a very specific message or invoke a specific mood
	COLUMN VALUE = 1	COLUMN VALUE = 2	COLUMN VALUE = 3	COLUMN VALUE = 4

SCORE	WHAT KIND OF STORY TO SELECT
3-6	Personal Story
6-9	Other People's Personal Stories
9-12	Stories from Other Domains

your score. Use the matrix to determine what type of story to select. There are three steps to the process. First, select a word from the row titled "Size," which describes the size of group you intend to select a story for. Second, select a word from the row titled "Intention." Last, select a word from the row titled "Trigger." At the bottom of each column there is a number indicating a value. Add up the values of your choices from each row to determine your overall score.

Here is how to interpret your score. For example, if you selected "Intimate" for "Size," "Connect" for "Intention," and "Listen" for "Trigger," your score would be 3. The best category of story to select from would be Personal Story.

There is some overlap between the categories' scores to account for situations that naturally could fall into either one. This is meant to be a guideline. You may end up with a score of 12 and decide that selecting a personal story is still the best option. As a general rule, I place a higher value on personal stories, however they are not always appropriate.

The key to selecting stories is having plenty to choose from. While it is possible to get a lot of mileage out of a few stories and reuse them in a variety of settings, this is not optimal. Reviewing our categories of stories, we know personal stories require a rich index. These are your most important ones. If you find yourself coming up short on personal stories to share, then you need to spend more time reflecting on them. Another good source of personal stories are recent experiences, since they are current in our minds. Beware of sharing a story to simply vent or boast. Stories used in a self-serving fashion do not resonate well with others. They have little impact and communication potential. For sharing Other People's Personal Stories, recent experiences are also effective. If we have recently heard another person's story, we are likely to remember it. This story can be used when we do not want to share a personal one or when it is inappropriate to do so. Stories that really strike us stay with us. We are bound to have a collection of stories we have heard from others that are not recent ones. They need to be well indexed along with our personal ones.

Stories from Other Domains is our last category of stories, and it provides an endless assortment of potential stories. These come from lots of different sources. Movies and books are a good place to start. Who are your favorite characters? Look for stories and characters that you have a strong connection with. History and science are another place to look since they are filled with exceptional stories and personages. After a while you will notice a pattern. Without thinking much about it, you will find yourself repeating certain stories over and over again.

Research is another facet of knowing your audience. In regards to your communications with others, think ahead and plan accordingly. The advent of the Internet has made research easier, albeit more time consuming when we wade through all the information. Try to find as much background information on your audience as you can and use it to imagine your audience, whether it is one person or a large group. For example, when I facilitate in foreign countries, I spend time reading folktales from the country I will be visiting. In all likelihood I will not use one of these stories, but they give me a feel for the country's culture, its values, and the ways in which these values have been encoded in stories. If the occasion calls for it, I may use one of the stories to break the ice, but more often than not the stories activate areas of my index, alerting me to potential themes and sensitizing me. Anticipation is an integral component of being responsive in the moment. If I am well prepared with a finely tuned index developed through reflection and discipline, good research, and some forethought, I can trust my mind to select an effective story. Based on people's reactions I can adjust my strategy.

This next exercise puts the elements of audience analysis, research, and working with your index all together.

Exercise 11. Selecting Competency—Communication Plan

Make a list of major meetings and conversations you plan to have during a week. Take a moment to imagine each one of these. What are the key things that need to be communicated? Use the Decision Matrix in Table 16.1 to determine what kinds of stories might be appropriate. What kind of research can you do to prepare yourself? Write down the stories that you think might work. Try the stories. Did they work? What effect did they have on others? What effect did they have on you? Did you tell any stories you did not plan to tell?

Whether we are planning a communication or responding extemporaneously, selecting stories requires indexing from the Process Ring and all of the listening competencies found in the Core.

Telling Competency

The only reason I have included Telling as a competency is that many people are not comfortable sharing information orally. Maybe you are shy or self-conscious. I am not concerned with turning you into an award-winning orator. There are great resources out there that have a lot to offer in that arena. The ability to dramatize a story for purposes of entertaining is an art form, but does not concern us here. If you find it natural to spin a yarn or be the center of attention, there are other subtleties to being an effective communicator through stories that you will want to master.

You must believe your stories are interesting. This is the first hurdle. People love to hear stories. Without stories our conversations are dull. Worse yet, very little can be communicated without them. Transmission is encapsulated in language; understanding is transferred through stories. Isolated islands of abstractions leave us wanting. We listen awkwardly, waiting for some way to connect to the speaker. As soon as an illustration enters the conversation, we breathe a sigh of relief. Finally there is something we can grab on to. Stories are fundamental to how we communicate.

When telling a story, expand and collapse the amount of detail you include. There is a time and place for stories to be told in long, rich detail, however most organizational settings require us to be concise. From our discussions earlier in the book we know that stories can be as short as a single sentence. While you may parse down the number of details you use, be sure to include ones that will enrich the story for the audience. In the next exercise you will practice truncating details without sacrificing a story.

Exercise 12a. Telling Competency—Movie in Five

Think of one of your favorite movies. Find a friend and ask her to time you while you tell the story of the movie. Make sure you are telling the story and not just describing it. Think of yourself as a projector and your friend as a screen. See if you can recount the movie in five minutes. If you succeed, try telling it in three minutes. What details did you forget? What details could you add? Which details are important to you? Are there certain details that are central to your love of this movie? Did you include these details?

Tell a story by reliving it. Overcome any self-consciousness by connecting to your story. If you watch a story as it unfolds in your mind it becomes more real for you and the people you are sharing it with. Telling a story provides another opportunity to learn from it in one or more ways. As you relive the story you may discover new insights, and people's reactions to your stories may offer you a new perspective. These things are only possible if you engage your imagination.

Recognize that there is no right way to tell a story. Find your own voice. Each person has a unique way of internalizing the world and expressing themselves. Admire what you like in other people's communication style, but do not emulate characteristics that are not in keeping with your own. People respond to authenticity, not to gimmicks. Have you ever been in a group when someone's story grabbed your attention? It's not always the story delivered with award-winning aplomb.

The most important facet of telling stories is frequency. The more you tell the more comfortable you will become. Make stories a natural part of your conversations. Stories are not just for speeches, presentations, or premeditated occasions. Telling stories is an integral part of any conversation. In this next exercise you will identify how stories are occurring in conversations and work on incorporating more of them into your own.

Exercise 12b. Telling Competency—Stories in Conversation

There are two parts to this exercise. In the first part you will play the role of observer. Spend a day taking note of all the times someone uses a story in conversation. Be mindful of all the different ways stories manifest themselves. How did these stories impact the conversation? Did these stories alter your perceptions of the topic being discussed or the person using them? In the second part of this exercise, practice weaving stories into your own conversations. Did it feel natural? Were you aware of what prompted you to tell a story? What did the story add to the conversation? How did the person or people react when you used a story? Did you tell any stories you think you never told before?

We tell stories to invoke rich responses in others. The best response is another story. Sometimes this story is shared and other times it is not. When you tell a story, try to involve the listener. Let them participate in the story. Try inserting questions as you tell you story. But these act as triggers for others to search their memory for similar experiences. If you do this, you will need to be prepared for interruptions. I am always reminded of reading a book to an inquisitive child. As the reader it is easy to become wrapped up in the story and brush aside a child's interruptions. But these interruptions are more central to the story than the story itself. I think the same principle holds true for adult tellers of stories. In fact, if the story becomes derailed and goes in an alternative direction, we may have to abandon the original story altogether. If we are interested in making a connection, we need to give up a certain degree of control. When the setting does not lend itself to interruptions, such as a large group or a brief time period, use rhetorical questions and slight pauses to encourage listeners to be involved in the story you are telling. Doing this well requires us to be less focused on ourselves and more focused on the listener. It is a shame that much of our storytelling in informal conversations has a tendency to be self-absorbed in nature. At first this shift will demand a concerted effort on your part. The rewards are worth the disorientation. The next exercise gives you an opportunity to practice involving your listeners.

Exercise 12c. Telling Competency—Listener Involvement

Go back to Exercise 8a, p. 198, and select a few stories. Review them in your mind and look for places where you can add questions. For example, let's say you have a story about an influential teacher. Consider beginning the story with, "Did you ever have a teacher who completely changed the way you look at things?" Another technique for getting people to interact with you is inviting them to fill in details of your story. This works well if you find points in the story that overlap with experiences you know or think they have had. When you feel comfortable with your preparation, try out your stories. How did people respond? Did your story trigger another one? Was your story interrupted?

Telling stories is the final touch. It is what people see first, but there is so much that goes into having a story to tell. At one point or another most of the competencies from the other rings of our Competency Map will have been utilized. In order to tap the power of stories for communication and learning, concentrate your efforts in the Core and Process Ring. You will be surprised how easy it is to tell stories when your internal and external powers of listening are improved and when you engage your mind in indexing, reflecting, and synthesizing. Follow a few simple principles—believing in your stories, expanding/collapsing the amount of detail, finding your unique voice, and involving your listeners; you will then be well on your way to being an effective storyteller.

Modeling Competency

There are two aspects to the Modeling competency. The first aspect can be summed up in the cliché "actions speak louder than words." Our behavior has the potential to speak volumes. Our actions can create memorable experiences for others that are retold as stories. We should strive to enact our intentions instead of announcing them. Be mindful of how your actions can create stories. The Modeling competency also describes how we use language and visual aids to explain complex ideas. Analogies, similes, metaphors, and anecdotes are just a few examples of using language to generate models.

During my interview with Dreyer's Ice Cream I heard a wonderful story that is a perfect example of how stories are created by actions. This story takes place toward the beginning of the company's history. It was a day or two before Christmas Eve, and the receptionist working the phones was not busy. There had been almost no calls that day. When the president walked by her desk, the receptionist asked him if she could leave early. The president thought to himself, "I have one of three possible responses. I can tell her what she wants to hear and instruct her to forward the phones into voice mail and to go home early and have a wonderful holiday. I can tell her that every call is important and that by greeting each customer personally she helps the company succeed. Or I can tell her to make the decision herself." The president decided to let the receptionist make her own decision. To this day he is not sure what she decided, nor does he care. She was the best person to make the decision, and he trusted her to make it. This story is retold at every employee orientation. The president enacted the values of the culture he espoused, and it left an indelible mark in the minds of his employees.

We don't realize how significant our actions can be. Ad hoc water cooler conversations are riddled with stories of people's behavior. Imagine your actions in terms of what stories they might generate. There is no need to be paranoid. Not everyone will perceive our actions positively, no matter how noble our intentions might be, but we need to be purposeful in how we go about things. A good modeler lives by example.

Exercise 13a. Modeling Competency—Memorable Actions

Take a few moments and reflect on stories that involve memorable actions. Were you a beneficiary of someone's action? Are there any stories in your organization's folklore that describe memorable actions? How have any of your acts become stories for others? Have you ever purposely acted in a particular way with the intent to create a story? What were the circumstances? What were the consequences?

If we spent as much time thinking about our actions as we do about what we say, we would have a greater legacy of stories. And stories have a longer shelf life than even the most powerful words. In the next exercise you will look for opportunities to model your thoughts and leave your story mark.

Exercise 13b. Modeling Competency—Creating Stories Through Actions

Identify a key message you want to communicate. Perhaps it's a message you have tried communicating several times but it has failed to stick, or maybe it's a new idea you have been trying to advance. Consider what actions you could take to model it. One of my favorite examples comes from a client who was having difficulty with his quality control department. The CEO of the company held a luncheon and had everyone's lunch orders purposely mixed up. Sometimes these actions will be single acts that have a big dramatic effect, as in the quality control example. However, sometimes you may need to try a series of actions. Think of what actions you can take to model your message. Will anyone else be involved in the actions you need to take? Why do you think these actions will be effective?

There are times when you cannot directly reach your target audience. In these instances you need to mold the actions of others. You need to act as a coach by helping others determine what actions they can take that have the potential to create stories. Guide them to look for opportunities that are a natural part of the organization's activities. These are great places to look because when we introduce variations in otherwise stable behaviors, they are likely to be noticed. When you are coaching someone, have them consider the impact of their actions and how others might respond. Help them prepare for the possibility that their actions may not create a positive story. How will they handle any negative ramifications? Ask them to imagine how any of these can be transformed into positive ones.

Let's move to the second aspect of Modeling. Explaining an idea with words can take a fair amount of time. Each piece of the idea has to be carefully laid out, and all of the pieces have to be put in order. I am always amazed at how much time it takes me to present an idea when I lecture. The same idea can almost always be quickly grasped with a simple illustration that takes a fraction of the time compared to more didactic modes of communicating. That, of course, leaves us lecturers without much to say and our recipients with more retention. The problem lies in the effort it takes to come up with a compelling illustration.

I was once teaching a technical writing course. In one of the exercises I had the group write a technical explanation for some engineering principles that could be understood by a twelve-year-old and that used an analogy to help explain the principle. They were forced to use constructs that an average twelve-year-old would know. It proved to be tough to come up with the analogies, but when they did they were amazed at how simple the principles really were and how easily they could be explained. There is a natural fear that if you oversimplify an idea, people will miss out. That is an incorrect assumption. Once a construct is in place, it is far easier to refine it. Much of what we assume to be important turns out to be unnecessary detail that cannot nor need not be retained by most people.

We can model with words by coming up with analogies, similes, anecdotes, or metaphors to illustrate our ideas. This is a form of synthesis. We are using a known entity to explain a new one. A new entity can be explored by establishing a baseline with a known one. In essence, through words we are painting vivid pictures. The assumption is that these pictures correspond with our listeners' experiences. We are invoking their imaginations. Our word pictures serve as tantalizers, summoning rich associations. Without some form of association our ideas will fizzle before they ever come to life. This next exercise explores the key questions you need to answer in order to effectively model with words.

Exercise 13c. Modeling Competency—Answering the Key Questions

Here is a mental checklist of questions to run through when you are interested in using verbal models:

1. *What do I want to communicate?*
2. *What constructs are known to this person or group?*
3. *How does the new construct relate to what is already known and understood by them?*
4. *Are there gaps between the two constructs being related to one another?*
5. *If there is a gap, can we work within the proposed model to explicate the differences?*

Pick an occasion when you will need to explain something to an individual or a group. Walk through the questions above and come up with some potential models. Try them out and evaluate the impact. How did you close the gap between the model you used and the full construct you were trying to communicate? Did you notice any difference in the recipients' level of engagement? How did they respond?

It is not important for our model to be perfect. Inevitably it will fall short. However, once we have a fertile learning space, we can expand our model and allow the recipient to refine it to successfully complete the transfer of information. In Chapter 2 we discussed how stories are tools for thinking. When we use word pictures and facilitate a discovery process to close the gap between the model and the desired construct being transferred, we are engaged in using stories as tools for thinking.

Exercise 13d. Modeling Competency—Presentations

There is a technique used by presenters to focus their message. They are taught how to look at a slide of information and develop a single sentence that summarizes it. You can build upon this technique by looking for a "word model" that encapsulates your key sentence. It could be any of the verbal models we

have identified (analogy, metaphor, cliché, anecdote, etc.). Take a presentation
you have written and transform each slide into a key sentence. Next, see how
many of your key sentences can be converted into verbal models.

We know that the population is not comprised entirely of verbal learners. Models can be effectively used to work in multiple modalities. Someone with a well-developed Modeling competency should be able to create compelling visual representations. Even a crude drawing can bring a concept alive. I am not adept at drawing, but with simple representations and a little sympathetic humor from my audience I can reach visual learners. They have something concrete to work with while I am off doodling with words. Models can be translated across other modalities. Kinesthetic learners can be drawn into an interactive physical example. Role-plays are a perfect way to create a story that can engage kinesthetic learners. Kinesthetic learners tend to be more naturally emotionally sensitive. Use models that include emotional components to them.

Organizational Practices for the Interaction Ring

Communications can be stiff in organizations. Efficiency rules, and stories are often deemed as inappropriate. We do not make the time to work with stories. I have already argued that stories are the most efficient way of storing, retrieving, and conveying information. Since story hearing requires active participation on the part of the listener, stories are the most profoundly social form of communication.

In one of my workshops, a director of engineering participated. He was an extraordinarily bright individual, fair minded and even in his approach to all things. However, he struggled with how to invest time in the people around him. When a project called for it, he would gladly work with whoever needed his guidance, but as a general rule he preferred the solitary peace of his unperturbed work environment. Throughout the workshop I kept pushing him to see the value and long-term speed of a sinuous path between two points. In other words, I was challenging him to discover that sometimes engaging in inefficient behaviors such as mutual storytelling sows seeds for future benefits. He could see my point intellectually, but I could tell he was struggling with its application. So I gave him a homework assignment. I instructed him to come in the next day with three or more personal stories that he was to weave together into a story collage. The next morning he came in very excited. He shared with me how he had come up with three stories while he was running. Upon examination he was surprised to realize that the stories were not personal. In fact, he further realized that he had a habit of never using personal stories. Next he sat down and started thinking about some key personal stories, and before long he had a string of them. The class was amazed when he sat in front of the group and began his web of stories with an explanation of the instructions I had given him the day before and the series of events leading up to his discovery of his personal stories. That was just the tip of the iceberg. His series of stories was rich, engaging, and full of insights. When he was done, he sat back and smiled. Nodding his head, he said, "Now I understand what you mean by a sinuous path being the shortest distance between two points." He experienced the value of selecting and telling stories and realized they would not get in the way of his being more efficient. I also set him up to experience the model, and I now have the added pleasure of sharing his actions with you to reinforce my assertions.

Leaders need to promote storytelling, modeling behaviors to generate stories, and verbal models by practicing these competencies. We are not talking about the use of these competencies during only all-hands-on meetings or other large events. These competencies need to be seen all the time in every type of interaction. For less verbally oriented employees, written communications provide just as much of an opportunity to put in play the competencies of the Interaction Ring as any other. Individuals do not need to carry the burden of coming up with effective stories or models all on their own. Remember the principle of push-to-pull-to-push from our discussion of the Communications Matrix in Chapter 3? Stories can be discovered in a collaborative process. People can work with one another to turn an idea into a compelling story or model. Until it becomes second nature, story facilitators can be used to help organizations develop repeatable processes for utilizing the competencies in the Interaction Ring. These processes should be woven into a wide range of organizational activities. As a facilitator I might prompt someone to support the introduction of a new idea by telling a story or providing a model. Clear command of an idea is demonstrated by the use of either one of these.

Selecting stories is a central part of an organization's knowledge management efforts. What stories are chosen to become a part of the formal institutional memory? Contrary to what many assume, these stories are better selected by employees than by leaders. Certain stories will naturally rise to the surface. Stories about how the organization started, what the early days were like, and so forth—the stories with the greatest impact will come from the memories of individuals both inside and outside of the organization. These are hidden gems. If leaders encourage people to remember stories and carry them forward, there will be less pressure on them to broadcast the perfect story. In this sense, organizations can support the development of all the competencies in the Interaction Ring by providing employees with ample opportunities to share stories.

Summary of the Interaction Ring

The competencies in the Interaction Ring are the most visible but the least important. The Process Ring and Core are the foundation. Selecting stories depends upon the existence of a rich index of stories that can only be gained through reflection, synthesis, and all of the listening competencies in the Core. We looked at some ideas on how to determine what kind of story to select. Telling stories was shown to be less concerned with execution and more concerned with being sensitive to expanding and collapsing the amount of detail in a story, eliciting stories from others, and telling stories in an interactive manner. We concluded our tour of the Interaction Ring by looking at the different ways we can use models.

17
Summary

We have established the concept that effective organizational communication and learning depends upon stories. Stories are a way of understanding the underlying operating principles behind organizational communication and learning. In Chapter 2 we laid the groundwork by showing how stories work. We identified nine functions and saw how they produce unique effects. These functions and unique effects help us peer into the black box of effective communication. Figure 17.1 provides a visual summary of the book.

The Communication Matrix in Chapter 3 breaks organizational communication into targets and channels. The matrix is a new framework that identifies opportunities for improving organizational communication. Out of twelve possible areas we concluded that most organizations succeed in reaching only half of the areas characterized by the matrix. These represent critical strategic opportunities missed by organizations. Because of their unique effects, stories can help us reach these untapped areas (see Figure 17.2).

Organizations need to develop their own unique, customized processes and tools to implement the push-to-pull-to-push strategy explained in Chapter 3. This strategy demonstrates how we can organizationally tell stories in order to elicit other people's stories, listen to them in order to gain new insights while adjusting our strategy accordingly, and catalyze people to share them. The result is an increase of the strength and reach of our initial broadcast.

Some organizations are beginning to put in place story mechanisms to improve organizational communication and learning. I recently learned about the story initiatives begun by Krispy Kreme Doughnuts. They have created a position called "Story Master." The Story Master is responsible for eliciting stories from employees and customers. They are committed to building a story culture. Employees are the beneficiaries. The stories are not for the company's marketing department. These stories work in the personal channel and the nonspecific target of the Communication Matrix. According to Krispy Kreme Doughnuts, these stories are giving employees a greater sense of alignment between their job responsibilities, the business objectives they need to execute, and the organization's mission.

226

Figure 17.1 Visual Summary of the Book

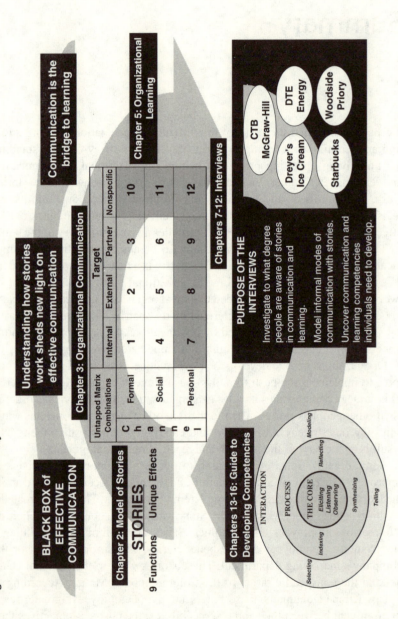

Figure 17.2   The Relationship Between Story Functions and the Communications Matrix

STORY FUNCTIONS	The Relationship Between Story Functions and the Communications Matrix	UNIQUE EFFECTS of STORIES
Empower a speaker		Entertaining
Create an environment	The functions of stories enable us to reach untapped areas 7–12 of the Communications Matrix...	Creating trust and openness between yourself and others
Bind and bond individuals		Elicit stories from others

Untapped Areas of the Communications Matrix

Communications Matrix	Target			
Channel	Internal	External	Partner	Nonspecific
Formal	1	2	3	10
Social	4	5	6	11
Personal	7	8	9	12

STORY FUNCTIONS		UNIQUE EFFECTS of STORIES
Require active listening		Listen actively in order to:
		Understand context and perspective
		Find the critical point in a system
		Uncover resistance and hidden agendas
Negotiate differences		Shift perspectives in order to:
		See each other
		Experience empathy
		Enter new frames of reference
		Hold diverse points of view
Encode information		Become aware of operating biases and values
		Creating a working metaphor to illuminate an opinion, rational, vision, or decision
Tools for Thinking	Stories are effective at reaching areas 7–12 of the matrix because of their unique effects	Establish connections between different ideas and concepts to support an opinion or decision
Weapons		Think outside the box to generate creative solutions and breakthroughs
Healing		

Next we demonstrated that communication is the cornerstone of organizational learning. Chapter 5 articulates six key assumptions about learning, its relationship to communication, and the role of stories. Examining organizational learning from the vantage point of communications gives us a new way to think about it. It is a holistic view that focuses less on structures and processes and more on people. The growing interest in the field of knowledge management is indicative of the evolving importance given to people's experiences and organizations' need for people to continuously learn.

Organizations are challenged to facilitate how people connect to one another and how they share their experiences. Learning can be aligned with dynamically changing enterprise objectives when it is managed as a communications process. With dialogue, reflection, guidance, and a modicum of organizational constraints in the form of policies, procedures, and practices, employees can determine what they need to learn in order to achieve results. This learning does not need to be captured in a formal way. It can be disseminated within the personal channel of communication in the form of stories. In turn, the stories become placeholders, which act as triggers. When necessary, these unstructured forms of learning that are stored and transmitted in stories can be formalized into more concrete containers such as documents, trainings, or procedures.

Although stories are commonly understood to be powerful, the "Nine Functions of Stories and Their Unique Effects" are a new way of looking at them. Stories are fundamental to how we communicate, learn, and think. The interviews in Part II of the book explore to what degree people are aware of stories in communication and learning. People agree on the power of stories, but not everyone is able to readily explain how to use them more effectively.

The interviews serve as good examples of how stories can be used for informal modes of communication. From them we can observe how much of our most effective communication looks like storytelling. The major themes from the interviews also help us identify several important communication and learning competencies. The most prevalent of these is Reflection.

The themes found in the interviews led us to the development of the Competency Map in Part III (see Table 17.1). The map consists of three rings with three competencies in each ring. The material in Part III emphasizes individual development over organizational interventions. We typically shy away from managerial and organizational development strategies that target individuals. On the surface such strategies appear idealistic and unlikely to produce systemic changes. However, in the case of improving organizational communication and learning through stories, focusing on individuals is the secret to success. Naturally, individuals working on their own will not create any long-lasting impact on an organization. Their personal changes will create

Table 17.1

The Relationship Between Themes from Interviews and the Competency Map

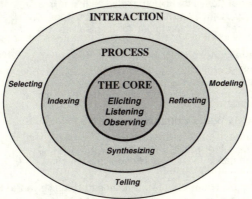

Interview themes	Competency
Bernice Moore—CTB/McGraw-Hill (Chapter 8)	
1. Stories can clarify a subject being discussed.	Modeling
2. Sharing personal stories brings people closer together, establishes connections among members of a group, and makes a group more effective.	Selecting
3. A masterful storyteller creates a space for the story, which encourages listeners to follow along.	Telling
4. Stories need to play a central role in retrospective project debriefs because they facilitate dialogue and because they can be carried forwarded as a valuable resource for later projects.	Reflecting
5. Making room for personal and organizational reflection is a key to leveraging the power of stories.	Reflecting
Robert Kraska—DTE Energy (Chapter 9)	
6. The length of a story needs to be adjusted for the context in which it is being told.	Telling
7. "After-action reviews" provide a structured opportunity for reflection and storytelling.	Elicting/ Synthsizing
8. In order for stories to work in meetings people need to trust one another, be skilled in interpersonal communications, and know how to ask the right questions.	Listening/ Observing
9. In training, people learn the most from dialogue among themselves and with the instructor.	Synthesizing
10. There is an integral relationship between stories and reflection.	Reflecting

Sherrie Cornett—Dreyer's Ice Cream (Chapter 10)

11. Stories from our personal lives can be effectively used at work.   Indexing

12. Analogies are stories that help people see things in a different way that may have more meaning for them and that gives them something to use for themselves.   Modeling

13. Stories have more impact than any other mode of communication.   Telling

14. Important messages need to be communicated in stories.   Selecting

Marty Fischer—Starbucks Coffee (Chapter 11)

15. Stories have intentionality. The teller has a reason for sharing and hopes to lead his listeners in a direction.   Selecting

16. Storytelling is a two-way street. Listening to stories gives you the context for what another person is trying to communicate.   Eliciting/Listening

17. The critical role of context in communication establishes a common ground between those who are communicating so that they are focused and directed toward the same thing.   Observing

18. Stories create a sense of comfort between people, which opens up all kinds of possibilities.   Eliciting

19. Storytelling can be as simple as saying the right word at the right time, which can produce a rich set of associations.   Modeling

Father Marus—Woodside Priory School (Chapter 12)

20. Finding stories requires introspection and reflection.   Reflecting

21. Stories help us find the message we want to share and make it relevant for our listeners.   Indexing

22. Stories allow us to communicate more directly.   Eliciting

23. Stories we tell should be a part of us.   Indexing/Selecting

24. Stories connect us to the moment.   Listening/Observing

25. Business leaders who acknowledge the importance of each person for both the role they play in business and for who they are will be the most successful.   Modeling

perturbations and may inspire others, but in the end these changes will be of limited value. Organizations must create a supportive environment to encourage and promote the cultivation of these competencies, but individuals must do the work. In combination, the results are powerful.

The key competencies lie in the first two rings of the Competency Map. The Core characterizes various aspects of listening. This relates directly to the most important function of stories—"stories require active listening"— and it also supports our assertion that it is far more important to elicit stories than to tell them. The majority of management literature on stories places emphasis on characterizing stories as vehicles of communication. In actuality, the communicative power of stories lies in their role as a tool for listening and reflecting.

The second ring of the map is called the Process Ring. Here we find a tangible way to grasp the elusive nature of reflection and synthesis. Once again we use stories to better understand methods for developing reflection. Stories also demystify the way in which our minds synthesize information in order to produce new insights and learning.

The outermost ring of the Competency Map, the Interaction Ring, contains all the visible and commonly thought-of competencies associated with stories. Despite the apparent measurable effects of telling stories, we achieve only limited results from doing so. Stories are to be exchanged. Using stories to hear each other more deeply, to reflect on our experiences, and to synthesize new learning yields the best results and provides organizations with a wealth of benefits. Stories will disappoint if we do not embrace what may appear to be a counterintuitive notion—"tell fewer stories and elicit more."

We live in a complex, rapidly changing world. In order for organizations to succeed in this competitive environment, they require a tremendous amount of differentiation and integration. Old paradigms are being challenged. Management as a system of control, communication as a completely constructed broadcast, and learning as a perfectly scripted collection of premeditated objectives are giving way to new possibilities.

Social and organizational systems are mirroring nature more and more with each passing day. Even the evolution of information technology, with its dependency on increasingly evolved networks to carry all of our information, outpaces our social adoption of the natural principles governing these changes. We rely on one another, yet we insist on our isolation. We will not be able to resist the forces of change. Organizations will have to develop more collaborative forms of self-governance.

I see a convergence. There has been a growing trend of management theories that is facilitating the changes required to be successful in this new world. (These include but are not limited to Harrison Owen's work in the late 1980s called Open Space Technology; David Cooperrider's introduction of a positive-based approach to studying systems known as Appreciative Inquiry; Peter Senge's work on organizational learning, Communities of Practice; and Henry Mintzberg's work on developing managers.)

We are on a threshold. Like any other point in evolution, organizations that understand the implications of these changes and seize them as opportunities will carve a path through the future's uncertainty and be the winners of tomorrow. Understanding the way we communicate, learn, and think through stories will prove to be a critical success factor. Stories will help us elevate one another to new heights and realize new possibilities by helping us listen more actively to one another and to ourselves.

Appendix: Folktale Illustrating Principles of Active Listening

This is a wonderful story I tell to MBA students to illustrate active listening and the relationship of empathy with stories.

Once upon time there was a mighty king by the name of Stephan. Now King Stephan had almost everything—land, wealth, and tremendous power. Sadly, Stephan was missing one thing: a wife. One day he turned to his chief advisor and said, "You have the most beautiful daughter in the land. My life is complete, but I need a companion. I will marry your daughter. Go tell her my wishes. We must arrange a stupendous wedding feast as soon as possible."

The chief advisor went home in terror. He knew his daughter was very picky about men. What if she would not marry the king? The king would have the advisor's head for sure. Cautiously, the chief advisor approached his daughter, Zalea, and began his plea.

"My dear Zalea, I have great news to share with you. The king wants to marry you. Isn't that wonderful?" Without pausing to take a breath or look into his daughter's eyes, he continued, "I'll run back to the palace to tell the king you have accepted his proposal."

"Father, wait," began Zalea. "How could I possibly marry the king? I neither know nor love him. I am flattered by his proposal, but I certainly cannot accept it."

The chief advisor's face contorted with worry. "Zalea, your poor father's head may be at stake here. You don't want to disappoint the king, do you? He is such a wonderful king and employer. Think of all the perks you will have as queen. I don't think it is a career opportunity you should pass up."

Zalea's face lit up. "You're right, Father. I know the king has a reputation as a good man, but he is young and lacks any marketable skills. Tell the king I will accept his proposal on one, and only one, condition."

The chief advisor's face relaxed. "And what might that be?"

Looking her father square in the eye, and with the autocratic tone of a queen, she said, "The king must learn a trade. When he can demonstrate to me that he has a marketable skill, then I will accept his proposal."

The chief advisor's face became sullen. He recognized the tone of voice. His daughter had made up her mind and there would be no changing it. Slowly he walked back to the palace.

Once there, the chief advisor did everything he could to avoid the king. Finally, the king tracked him down. "Where have you been? I have been looking all over the palace for you. Tell me your daughter's decision."

"Well, Your Highness," the chief advisor said, "my daughter will gladly accept your proposal. However, she had one little request. Zalea wants you to learn a trade."

"A what?" roared the king.

"A trade, Your Highness." Fearing the worst, the chief advisor closed his eyes and pressed his hands together in prayer.

"Hmm," muttered the king. "Chief advisor, I know now that your daughter is as wise as she is beautiful. I will fulfill her wish. Tomorrow I will begin to search for a trade to learn."

The chief advisor let out a huge sigh of relief and ran all the way home to tell his daughter the news.

Over the next few days, the king observed and spoke to all sorts of craftsmen. He watched the Marketing and Advertising Department haggle over product positioning and branding. He listened to overbearing sales pitches. He yawned uncontrollably as the bean counters in the Accounting Department verified his financial position, and he came close to losing his lunch as he listened to technologists in the Information Technology Department frenetically espouse their e-commerce strategies. Finally, the king found an old weaver who began to show him the intricacies of his trade.

The king worked at his loom night and day to learn this new trade. One day he called in his chief advisor to show him a splendid scarf he had woven. The scarf showed a red rose on a dark, forest green background. The king asked his chief advisor to take the scarf to Zalea as gift. When Zalea saw it, she knew the king had learned the trade of weaving. Happily, she agreed to marry him, and there was a grand and joyous celebration.

The king quickly saw that his wife was indeed very wise. He sought her advice on all of the affairs of the kingdom. One day he said to her, "Zalea, I don't know what people in our kingdom want, or how they feel. I cannot rely on my advisors. They tell me what they think I want to hear. How can I learn to be sensitive to my people's needs?"

"My dear," Zalea began, "you must walk in your people's shoes. Go to the market dressed as a common person. As you wander, listen to what people say to one another. Then I believe you will find answers to your questions."

So the king and some of his advisors disguised themselves and made their way to the market. As they strolled along, the king was amazed at what he learned. Around noon, the king turned to his advisors and said, "I'm hungry. Lets get a bite to eat."

"Marvelous!" responded his chief advisor. "Let's get out of these dingy clothes and head back to the palace for a proper meal."

"No," the king retorted. "I want to eat like the people in my kingdom. I overheard people talking about an excellent greasy spoon known for its burgers and Philly cheese steak sandwiches. Let's go eat there."

The king led the way while his advisors sheepishly followed him. They arrived at the restaurant. As they tried to enter, a trap door opened beneath them and they fell into a deep, dark pit. Moments later the trap door opened and a hideous man snarled at them as he threw burgers down for them to eat. "Now you know why I have the best burgers in the kingdom. My burgers are made from fat, plump people like you." The man slammed the trap door shut and went away laughing.

"What do we do now?" moaned one advisor.

"We are as good as dead," whimpered another.

"Listen, Your Highness," the chief advisor said, "you'd better tell that idiot who we are. That will end this nonsense."

"Quiet, all of you!" yelled the king. "If we tell this evil man who we are, we *are* as good as dead. Now leave me alone for a moment. I need to think. None of you must utter a word the next time he comes."

A good deal later the trap door opened. "Eat up, lads. I have lots of hungry customers to feed," bellowed the evil man.

"Excuse me, sir," the king chimed. "I know you can't set us free, but my life is so precious to me. I can weave the most beautiful scarves you have ever seen. The queen at the palace pays great sums of money for them. Surely you realize that we can earn you more money by weaving scarves than you will earn from the measly burgers you can make from our bodies. If you give me a loom and some yarn, I will show you how I can make you a richer man."

"I'll think about it," snorted the evil man. A few minutes later, the trap door opened and the evil man threw down a loom and some yarn for the king.

The king worked all night. He wove a beautiful scarf with a red rose on a dark, forest green background. In the morning he gave it to the evil man, saying, "Take this scarf to Queen Zalea. She will pay you a handsome price for it."

The evil man ran all the way to the palace. The palace had been in total chaos since the king and his advisors had disappeared. When Zalea saw the scarf, she immediately recognized the work of her husband. She paid the evil man four pieces of gold and gave him stock options worth a good deal more. When the evil man left, Zalea had the king's army follow him.

She herself rode at the head of the army. When they reached the evil man's restaurant, the army seized all his assets, instructed the Justice Department to break up his franchise, told the executioner to cut off his head, and freed the king and his advisors. And Zalea and the king rode off together into the sunset and lived happily ever after.

Suggested Reading

Books

Abrahams, Roger D. *African Folktales*. New York: Pantheon Books, 1983.

Allen, Julie, Gerard Fairtlough, and Barbara Heinzen. *The Power of the Tale: Using Narratives for Organisational Success*. West Sussex: John Wiley and Sons, 2002.

Armstrong, David M. *Managing by Storying Around: A New Method of Leadership*. New York: Doubleday, 1992.

Berman, Michael, and David Brown. *The Power of Metaphor*. New York: Crown House, 2001.

Boje, David. *Narrative Methods for Organizational and Communication Research*. London: Sage Publications, 2001.

Brown, John Seely, Stephen Denning, Katalina Groh, and Laurence Prusak. *Storytelling in Organizations: Why Storytelling Is Transforming 21st Century Organizations and Management*. Burlington, MA: Elsevier Butterworth-Heinemann, 2005.

Bushnaq, Inea. *Arab Folktales*. New York: Pantheon Books, 1986.

Calvino, Italo. *Italian Folktales,* trans. George Martin. New York: Harcourt, Brace and Jovanovich, 1980. (Originally published in 1956 by Giulio Einaudi Editore, S.P.A.)

Campbell, Joseph, and Bill Moyers. *The Power of Myth*. New York: Doubleday, 1988.

Canfield, Jack, and Jacqueline Miller. *Heart at Work: Stories and Strategies for Building Self-Esteem and Reawakening the Soul at Work*. New York: McGraw-Hill, 1996.

Chinen, Allan B. *In the Ever After: Fairy Tales and the Second Half of Life*. Wilmette, IL: Chiron Publications, 1989.

———. *Once Upon a Midlife: Classic Stories and Mythic Tales to Illuminate the Middle Years*. New York: Tarcher/Putnam, 1992.

Clark, Evelyn. *Around the Corporate Campfire: How Great Leaders Use Stories to Inspire Success*. Sevierville, TN: Insight Publishing, 2004.

Collins, R., and P.J. Cooper. *The Power of Story: Teaching Through Storytelling*. Boston: Allyn & Bacon.

Creighton, Helen. *A Folk Tale Journey*. Wreck Cove, Cape Breton Island: Breton Books, 1993.

Denning, Stephen. *The Springboard: How Storytelling Ignites Action in Knowledge Era Organizations*. Boston: Butterworth-Heineman, 2001.

———. *Squirrel Inc.: A Fable of Leadership Through Storytelling*. San Francisco: Jossey-Bass, 2004.

Dorson, Richard M. *Folk Legends of Japan.* Rutland, VT: Charles E. Tuttle, 1962.

Erdoes, Richard, and Alfonso Ortiz. *American Indian Myths and Legends.* New York: Pantheon Books, 1984.

Feinstein, David, and Stanley Krippner. *The Mythic Path.* New York: Tarcher/Putnam, 1997.

Fulford, Robert. *The Triumph of Narrative: Storytelling in the Age of Mass Culture.* New York: Broadway, 2001.

Gabriel, Yiannis. *Storytelling in Organizations: Facts, Fictions, and Fantasies.* London: Oxford University Press, 2000.

Gardner, Howard, *Leading Minds: An Anatomy of Leadership.* New York: Basic Books, 1996.

Gargiulo, Terrence L. *Making Stories: A Practical Guide for Organizational Leaders and Human Resource Specialists.* Westport, CT: Greenwood Press, 2002.

Garvin, David A. *Learning in Action: A Guide to Putting The Learning Organization to Work.* Boston: Harvard Business School Press, 2000.

Jensen, Bill. *Simplicity: The New Competitive Advantage in a World of More, Better, Faster.* Cambridge, MA: Perseus Books, 2000.

Lipman, Doug. *Improving Your Storytelling: Beyond the Basics for All Who Tell Stories in Work or Play.* Little Rock: August House, 1999.

Maguire, Jack. *The Power of Personal Storytelling: Spinning Tales to Connect with Others.* New York: Tarcher/Putnam, 1998.

Meade, Erica Helm. *Tell It by Heart: Women and the Healing Power of Story.* Chicago: Open Court, 1995.

Morgan, Gareth. *Imaginization: New Mindsets for Seeing, Organizing, and Managing.* Thousand Oaks, CA: Sage, 1993.

Neuhauser, Peg C. *Corporate Legends and Lore: The Power of Storytelling as a Management Tool.* New York: McGraw-Hill Trade, 1993.

Parkin, Margaret. *Tales for Change: Using Storytelling to Develop People and Management.* London: Kogan Page, 2004.

———. *Tales for Coaching: Using Stories and Metaphors with Individuals and Small Groups.* London: Kogan Page, 2001.

———. *Tales for Trainers: Using Stories and Metaphors to Facilitate Learning.* London: Kogan Page, 1998.

Sawyer, Ruth. *The Way of the Storyteller.* New York: Penguin Books, 1976.

Schank, Roger. *Knowledge and Memory: The Real Story.* Vol. VIII, *Advances in Social Cognition,* ed. Robert S. Wyer, Jr. Hillsdale: Lawrence Erlbaum Associates, 1995.

———. *Tell Me a Story: A New Look at Real and Artificial Memory.* Chicago: Northwestern Press, 1995.

———. *Virtual Learning: A Revolutionary Approach to Building a Highly Skilled Workforce.* New York: McGraw-Hill, 1997.

Simons, Annette. *The Story Factor.* Cambridge, MA: Perseus, 2001.

Stone, Richard. *The Healing Art of Storytelling: A Sacred Journey of Personal Discovery.* New York: Hyperion, 1996.

Tichy, Noel M., with Eli Cohen. *The Leadership Engine: How Winning Companies Build Leaders at Every Level.* New York: HarperCollins, 1997.

Wacker, Mary B., and Lori L. Silverman. *Stories Trainers Tell: 55 Ready-to-Use Stories to Make Training Stick.* San Francisco: Jossey-Bass/Pfeifffer, 2003.

Wolkstein, Diane. *The Magic Orange Tree and Other Haitian Folktales.* New York: Schocken Books, 1978.

Zeitlin, Steve. *Because God Loves Stories: An Anthology of Jewish Storytelling*. New York: Touchstone, 1997.

Articles

Akin, G., and E. Schultheiss. "OD through stories and metaphor." *Journal of Managerial Psychology* 5, 4 (1990).

Akin, G., J.M. Jermier, T. Domagalski, and G. Fine. "Learning about work from Joe Cool." *Journal of Management Inquiry* 9, 1 (March 2000).

Beech, N., and J. McCalman. "Sex, lies and videotropes: narrative and commitment in high technology teams." *Journal of Applied Management Studies* 6, 1 (June 1997).

Boje, D.M. "Consulting and change in the storytelling organization." *Journal of Organizational Change Management* 4, 3 (1991).

Boje, D.M., J.T. Luhman, and D.E. Baack. "Hegemonic stories and encounters between storytelling organizations." *Journal of Management Inquiry* 8, 4 (December 1999).

Boyce, M.E. "Organizational story and storytelling: A critical review." *Journal of Organizational Change Management* 9, 5 (1996).

Breuer, N.L. "The power of storytelling." *Workforce Magazine* 77, 12 (December 1998).

Buckler, S.A., and K.A. Zien. "The spirituality of innovation: Learning from stories." *Journal of Product Innovation Management* 13, 5 (September 1996).

Butler, R. "Stories and experiments in social inquiry." *Organization Studies* 18, 6 (1997).

Calman, K. "Storytelling, humour and learning in medicine." *British Journal of Health Care Management* 6, 10 (October 2000).

Cash, M. "Stories within a story: Parables from 'The New Zealand experiment.'" *The Learning Organization* 4, 4 (1997).

Cheng, C. "Experience, essentialism and essence: Changing organizations through personal work and gender stories." *Journal of Organizational Change Management* 8, 6 (1995).

Cohen, L., and M. Mallon. "My brilliant career? Using stories as a methodological tool in careers research." *International Studies of Management & Organization* 31, 3 (Autumn 2001).

Crumbley, D.L., and L.M. Smith. "Using short stories to teach critical thinking and communication skills to tax students." *Accounting Education* 9, 3 (September 2000).

Czarniawska, B. "A four times told tale: Combining narrative and scientific knowledge in organization studies." *Organization* 4, 1 (February 1997).

Danzig, A.B. "Leadership stories: What novices learn by crafting the stories of experienced school administrators." *Journal of Educational Administration* 35, 2 (1997).

Dennehy, R.F. "The executive as storyteller." *Management Review* 88, 3 (March 1999).

Durrance, B. "Stories at work." *Training & Development* 5, 12 (February 1997).

Eaton, J. "Coaching stories (narrative psychology in coaching)." *Organizations & People: Successful Development* 7, 1 (February 2000).

Fleming, D. "Narrative leadership: using the power of stories." *Strategy & Leadership* 29, 4 (July–August 2001).

Ford, J.D. "Organizational change as shifting conversations." *Journal of Organizational Change Management* 12, 6 (1999).

Gold, J. "Learning and story telling—The next stage in the journey for the learning organization." *Journal of Workplace Learning: Employee Counseling Today* 9, 4 (1997).

—————. "Telling stories to find the future." *Career Development International* 1, 4 (1996).

Gold, J., and D. Holman. "Let me tell you a story: An evaluation of the use of storytelling and argument analysis in management education." *Career Development International* 6, 7 (2001).

Greco, J. "Stories for executive development: An isotonic solution." *Journal of Organizational Change Management* 9, 5 (1996).

Hansen, C.D., and W.M. Kahnweiler. "Executive managers: Cultural expectations through stories about work." *Journal of Applied Management Studies* 6, 6 (December 1997).

Hegele, C., and A. Kieser. "Control the construction of your legend, or someone else will: An analysis of texts on Jack Welch." *Journal of Management Inquiry* 10, 4 (December 2001).

Hernández-Serrano, J., S.E. Stefanou, L.F. Hood, and B.L. Zoumas. "Using experts' experiences through stories in teaching new product development." *Journal of Product Innovation Management* 19, 1 (January 2002).

Jensen, R. "The story of the future." *Across the Board* 36, 1 (January 1999).

Johnson, G. "Strategy through a cultural lens: Learning from managers' experience." *Management Learning* 31, 4 (December 2000).

Jones, M.O. "What if stories don't tally with the culture?" *Journal of Organizational Change Management* 4, 3 (1991).

Kaye, B.L., and B. Jacobson. "True tales and tall tales: The power of organizational storytelling." *Training & Development* 53, 3 (March 1999).

Linde, C. "Narrative and social tacit knowledge." *Journal of Knowledge Management* 5, 2 (2001).

Lounsbury, M., and M.A. Glynn. "Cultural entrepreneurship: Stories, legitimacy and the acquisition of resources." *Strategic Management Journal* 22, 6–7 (June–July 2001).

Midgley, G., Y. Kadiri, and M. Vahl. "Managing stories about quality." *International Journal of Technology Management* 11, 1–2 (1996).

Murray, T. "The power of stories." *Organizations & People: Successful Development* 6, 4 (November 1999).

Nash, L.L. "Intensive care for everyone's least favorite oxymoron: Narrative in business ethics." *Business Ethics Quarterly* 10, 1 (January 2000).

Olsson, S. "Acknowledging the female archetype: Women managers' narratives of gender." *Women in Management Review* 15, 5–6 (2000).

Parkin, M. "The power of storytelling: Using stories and metaphors to enhance learning." *Training Journal* (April 2001).

Pentland, B. "Building process theory with narrative: From description to explanation." *Academy of Management Review* 24, 4 (October 1999).

Reiter, S.A. "Storytelling and ethics in financial economics." *Critical Perspectives on Accounting* 8, 8 (December 1997).

Shanahan, M., and A.N. Maira. "Creating change through strategic storytelling." *Prism* no. 4 (1998).

Shanahan, M., and S. Ober. "Encouraging enrollment: Personal stories as a vehicle for change." *Prism* no. 1 (2000).

Shaw, G., R. Brown, and P. Bromiley. "Strategic stories: How 3M is rewriting business planning." *Harvard Business Review* 76, 3 (May–June 1998).

Snowden, D.J. "The art and science of story, or 'Are you sitting uncomfortably?' Part 2: The weft and the warp of purposeful story." *Business Information Review* 17, 4 (December 2000).

————. "Story telling: An old skill in a new context." *Business Information Review* 16, 1 (March 1999).

Taylor, S.S. "Making sense of revolutionary change: Differences in members' stories." *Journal of Organizational Change Management* 12, 6 (1999).

Valkevaara, T. "Exploring the construction of professional expertise in HRD: An analysis of four HR developers' work histories and career stories." *Journal of European Industrial Training* 26, 2–4 (2002).

Van Buskirk, W., and D. McGrath. "Organizational stories as a window on affect in organizations." *Journal of Organizational Change Management* 5, 2 (1992).

Watson, T.J. "Beyond managism: Negotiated narratives and critical management education in practice." *British Journal of Management* 12, 4 (December 2001).

Wilensky, A.S., C.D. Hansen, and T.S. Rocco. "Understanding the work beliefs of nonprofit executives through organizational stories." *Human Resource Development Quarterly* 12, 3 (Autumn 2001).

Wilkins, A.L., and M.P. Thompson. "On getting the story crooked (and straight)." *Journal of Organizational Change Management* 4, 3 (1991).

Index

Achieve business objectives,
  with learning, 60–63–64
Active listening, 4, 9, 12–18, 40, 78, 163,
  233–234
Agile culture,
  Fostered by stories, 52
Answering the key questions, 221
Attending, 191
Attitudes elicited by stories, 30–50
Audience, targeting the, 24

Behavior goal, 42
Beliefs elicited by stories, 30–50
Binding and bonding individuals, 4, 9,
  11–12, 40, 78, 163, 227
Broadcasting, 28–30
  versus Frequency tuning, 28–30,
    77–161
Building bridges, 55–64
Building, 175–178
Bukantz, Jeff, 65–75
  Dreyer's Ice Cream, Case Study,
    42–54
Business objectives, 55–56, 60–64
  Achieve with learning, 60–63, 64
  Learning dynamically linked to, 58,
    164

Care/Intention, 172–175
  Fostering positive intentions, 175
  Name badges, 175
  Self-assessment, 174
Career path, 51
Case studies, 42–54, 65–75
  Dreyer's Ice Cream, 42–54

Case studies *(continued)*
  DTE Energy and Jeff Bukantz, 65–75
Change management, 65
Childhood stories and me, 206–108
Clarification and follow-up questions, 188
Climate of sharing, 191
Collective experiences and learning,
  60–61, 64, 71
  Ties together with learning, 60
Collective knowledge, 66, 161
Communicate, 164
Communicating,
  Experience through stories 63
Communication plan, 215
Communication, 3–6, 7, 24–41, 161
  and stories, 7
  channels of, 24–41, 78, 161, 162–163,
    227
    formal channels, 24, 27, 34–36, 40,
      78, 162, 163, 227
    personal channels, 24, 27–28,
      30–34, 37–39, 40, 42, 53,
      60–61, 65, 78, 161, 162,
      265, 227
    social channels, 24, 27, 36–37, 40,
      78, 162, 165, 227
  Conceptualization of (Organizational),
    25
  Cornerstone of, 55
  Face-to-face, 53
  Forms of, 24–41
    Channels of, 24–41, 78, 161, 162,
      163, 227. *See also: Formal*
      Channels; *Personal channels*;
      Social channels

Communication
  Forms of *(continued)*
    Targets of, 21–41, 77, 161, 162, 163,
      227. *See also: External targets;*
      Internal targets; Non-specific
      targets; Partner targets
  Improving, 7
  Informal, 31
  Intervention, 42, 53
  Learning cannot occur without, 56, 64
  Learning is the cornerstone of, 55
  Matrix
    Communication, 28, 29, 40, 42,
      65, 77, 227
  Model informal mode of, 79
  Nature and dynamic of, 8
  Oral versus written, 39
  Organizational, 3–6, 7, 23, 24–41,
    55–64, 77, 179
  Paradigm, 8
  Potential Opportunities, 77
  Stories in, 79
  Targets of, 21–41, 77, 161, 162, 163,
    227
    External targets, 24–26, 33–34, 40,
      78, 162, 163, 227
    Internal targets, 24–25, 30–33, 40,
      78, 162, 163, 227
    Non-specific targets, 24, 26–27,
      34–39, 40, 78, 161, 162, 263, 27
    Partner targets, 24, 26, 33–34, 40,
      78, 162, 163, 227
  Ties learning and collective experiences,
    60–61, 64
  Tools of, 25
  Untapped area of, 29 40
  Written versus oral, 39
Competencies
  Used to engage the external world, 165
Competency Map, 161–232
  Interaction Ring, 164, 221–224, 231
    Modeling Competency, 6, 218–222.
      See also: Answering the key
      questions; Creating stories
      through action; Memorable
      actions; Presentations

Competency Map
  Interaction Ring *(continued)*
    Selecting Competency, 6, 164, 166,
      168–170. *See also: Communication*
      plan; Decision Matrix for selecting
      types of stories; Other people's
      personal stories; Personal stories;
      Stories from other domains
    Telling Competency, 6, 164, 166,
      168–170. *See also: Listener*
      Involvement; Movies in Five;
      Stories in Conversation
  The Core, 164–170, 171, 195, 231
    Eliciting Competency, 5, 164, 170,
      191–195. *See also: Attending;*
      Climate of sharing; Job
      interview questions; Statement
      story; Trust; Words and feelings
    Listening Competency, 5, 164, 166,
      170, 185–190. *See also:*
      Clarification and follow-up
      questions; Editorial
      interpretation; Following
      directions; Frame of reference;
      Life story; Music; Paraphrase;
      Tape-recorded Conversation
    Observing Competency, 5, 164,
      166–170, 171–185. *See also:*
      Building; Care/Intention;
      Conversation recorder;
      Conversation Tracking; External
      Focus; Fostering positive
      intentions; Group Discussion;
      Journaling; Locking eyes; Name
      badges; New people/new
      situations; Organizational
      practices for; Power of breath;
      Process daily; Recall; Room
      awareness; Self-assessment;
      Self-awareness; Sensitivity; Sore
      spots and hot buttons; Strengths
      and Weaknesses; Survey of habits
  Process Ring, 163, 196–210, 231
    Indexing Competency, 6, 164, 170,
      196–199. *See also: Personal*
      history; Themes; Triggers

Competency Map
  Process Ring *(continued)*
    Reflecting Competency, 6, 164,166,
      168–170, 200–204. *See also:*
      Daily rewind; Historical
      visualization; Inviting; Personal
      history; Sifting; Sitting;
      Visualization
    Synthesis Competency, 6,
      164–167,168–170, 204–208.
      See also: Childhood stories and
      me; Crystal Ball of Synthesis;
      Knowledge; Learning; Mind
      map of experiences; Wisdom
Conversation recorder, 184
Conversation tracking, 183
Conversation, 56
  Recorder, 184
  Tracking, 183
Cooperrider, David, 223
Cornerstone of communication, 55
Cornett, Sherrie, 118–135
  Dreyer's Ice Cream, 42–54, 118–135
Corporate universities, 55
Creating and environment, 4, 9, 10–12,
  40,77, 163, 227
Creating stories through action,
  219–221
Creative and personal outlets, 51
Crystal Ball of Synthesis, 206
CTB/McGraw-Hill, 86–102
Culture, 52

Daily rewind, 204
Decision Matrix for selecting types of
  stories, 212–214
Development plans, Professional, 59
Difference between training and learning,
  57, 64
Differences
  Negotiate, 4, 9, 18–19, 40, 78, 163,
    227
Dreyer's Ice Cream, 42–54, 118–135
  Philosophy, 42–49
  Grooves and stories, 49–54
DTE Energy, 65–75, 103–117

Editorial interpretation, 189
Effects of stories, 3, 9
Effects, 40
Eliciting Competency, 5, 164, 170,
  191–195
  Attending, 191
  Climate of sharing, 191
  Job interview questions, 193
  Statement story, 194
  Trust, 191
  Words and feelings, 193–194
Eliciting, 3, 5, 9
  as a function of, 30–50
Empathy from participants, 51
Employee retention, 51
Employees' experiences,
  Enhancing with learning, 60–63,64
Employees, 50, 52
  as contributors, 50
  Managers need to hear stories, 50
  Motivated, 50, 52
Empower a speaker, 4, 9, 10, 40, 78, 163,
  227
Encode information, 4, 9, 19–20, 40, 77,
  163, 227
Enhance employees' experiences,
  with learning, 60–63, 64
Enhancing intelligence 51
Environment, create an, 4, 9, 10–12,
  40,77, 163, 227
Experience as story, 206
Experiences, 60–61, 63–64
  Collective and learning, 60–61, 64
  Communicated through stories, 63, 64
  Enhancing employees,' 60–63, 64
Expressions elicited by stories, 30–50
External Focus, 181–183
  Conversation Tracking, 183
  Locking eyes, 182–183
  Recall, 182
External targets of communication,
  24–26, 33–34, 40, 78, 162–163, 227

Facilitation of knowledge transfer, 51
Fischer, Marty, 136–150
  Interview: Starbuck's Coffee, 136–150

Folktale: Illustrating principle of active
    listening, 233–234
Following directions, 188–189
Forms of communication, 24–41
    Channels of, 24–41, 78, 161, 162, 163,
        227
        Formal channels, 24, 27, 34–36, 40,
            78, 162, 163, 227
        Personal channels, 24, 27–28, 30–34,
            37–39, 40, 42, 53, 60–61, 65,
            78, 161, 162, 265, 227
        Social channels, 24, 27, 36–37, 40,
            78, 162, 165, 227
    Targets of communication, 21–41, 77,
        161, 162, 163, 227
        External targets, 24–26, 33–34, 40,
            78, 162, 163, 227
        Internal targets, 24–25, 30–33, 40,
            78, 162, 163, 227
        Non-specific targets, 24, 26–27,
            34–39, 40, 78, 161, 162, 263,
            27
        Partner targets, 24, 26, 33–34, 40,
            78, 162, 163, 227
Forum for sharing,
    Stories, 50
Foster agile culture, 52
Fostering positive intentions, 175
Frame of reference, 190
Framework of stories, 3–74, 161
    Theoretical, 77
Frequency tuning, 28–30, 77–161
    Versus broadcasting, 28–30
Functions of communication, 55
Functions of stories, 4, 7, 9, 10–23,
    40, 78, 163, 225, 227, 228
    Act as medicine for healing, 4, 9,
        22–23, 40, 78, 163, 227
    Act as tools for thinking, 4, 9,
        20–21, 40–77, 163, 227
    Act as weapons, 4, 9, 21–22, 40,
        77, 163, 227
    Binding and bonding individuals,
        4, 9, 11–12, 40, 78, 163, 227
    Create an environment, 4, 9, 10–12,
        40,77, 163, 227

Functions of stories (continued)
    Empower a speaker, 4, 9, 10, 40, 78,
        163, 227
    Encode information, 4, 9, 19–20, 40,
        77, 163, 227
    Negotiate differences, 4, 9, 18–19, 40,
        78, 163, 227
    Nine Functions, 4, 7, 9, 10–23, 40, 78,
        163, 227
        Act as medicine for healing, 4, 9,
            22–23, 40, 78, 163, 227
        Act as tools for thinking, 4, 9,
            20–21, 40–77, 163, 227
        Act as weapons, 4, 9, 21–22, 40, 77,
            163, 227
        Binding and bonding individuals,
            4, 9, 11–12, 40, 78, 163,
            227
        Create an environment, 4, 9, 10–12,
            40,77, 163, 227
        Empower a speaker, 4, 9, 10, 40, 78,
            163, 227
        Encode information, 4, 9, 19–20, 40,
            77, 163, 227
        Negotiate differences, 4, 9, 18–19,
            40, 78, 163, 227
        Require active listening, 4, 9, 12–18,
            40, 78, 163, 227
    Require active listening, 4, 9, 12–18, 40,
        78, 163, 227

Goal, 42
    Behavior, 42
Grooves and stories, 43–54
    And stories, 49–54
    Philosophy, 43–49
Group Discussion, 185

Healing
    Stories act as medicine for, 4, 9, 22–23,
        40, 78, 163, 227
Hire smart, 44
Historical visualization, 203
Hoopla, 46, 53–54
How stories work, 161
Human resources, 57

Identifying forms of communication, 24–41
Forms of, 24–41
  Channels of, 24–41, 78, 161, 162, 163, 227. *See also: Formal Channels*; *Personal channels*; *Social channels*;
  Targets of, 21–41, 77, 161, 162, 163, 227. *See also: External targets*; *Internal targets*; *Non-specific targets*; *Partner targets*
Indexing Competency, 164, 170, 196–199
  Personal history, 198–199, 203–204
  Themes, 199–199
  Triggers, 198–1299
Indexing, 179
Individual,
  learning plans, 59
  respect for the, 44
  binding and bonding, 4, 9, 11–12, 40, 78, 163, 227
Informal mode of communication, 79
Information, encode, 4, 9, 19–20, 40, 77, 163, 227
Initiative, Knowledge Builder, 66–74
Intelligence, Enhancing, 51
Interaction Ring, 6, 164, 221–224, 231
  Modeling Competency, 6, 218–222
    Answering the key questions, 221
    Creating stories through action, 219–221
    Memorable actions, 219
    Presentations, 221–222
  Selecting Competency, 6, 164, 166, 168–170
    Communication plan, 215
    Decision Matrix for selecting types of stories, 212–214
    Other people's personal stories, 212–214
    Personal stories, 212–214
    Stories from other domains, 212–214
Interaction Ring *(continued)*
  Telling Competency, 6, 164, 166, 168–170

Listener Involvement, 218
Movies in Five, 216–217
Stories in Conversation, 217
Internal targets of communication, 24–25, 30–33, 40, 78, 162, 163, 227
Interpersonal traits, 179
Intervention, 42
Interviews
  CTB/McGraw-Hill, 86–102
  DTE Energy, 103–117
  Starbuck's Coffee, 136–150
  Woodside Priory School, 151–158
Inviting, 201, 202
Involvement, People 45

Job interview questions, 193
Journaling, 177–178

Knowledge Builder Initiative, 66–74
Knowledge transfer, 51
Knowledge, 51, 206
  Facilitation of knowledge transfer, 51
  Knowledge transfer, 51
Kraska, Robert, 103–117
  Interview: DTE Energy, 103–117

Learning and collective experiences, 60–61, 64
Learning cannot occur without communication, 56, 64
Learning dynamically linked to business objective, 58
Learning plans, Individual, 59
Learning, 3, 7, 161, 164, 206, 228
  Accelerate, 51
  Aligning objectives, 59
  And collative experience, 71
  Communication cannot occur without, 56, 64
  Communication ties collective experiences and, 60, 64
  Cornerstone of communication, 55
  Difference between training and, 57, 64
  Dynamically linked to business objective, 58, 164

Learning *(continued)*
Ensures organizational success, 59
Function of communication ion, 55
Learn, Learn, Learn, 46
Management, 56
Measuring, 56
Needs to enhance employees'
experiences, 60–63, 64
Organizational, 3–6, 7, 23, 55–64,
161, 228
Outsourcing, 58
Stories in, 79
Ties collective experiences and learning
together, 60
to achieve business objectives, 60–63,
64
Training and the difference from,
57, 64
Life story, 186
Listener involvement, 218
Listening Competency, 164, 166, 170,
185–190
Clarification and follow-up questions,
188
Editorial interpretation, 189
Following directions, 188–189
Frame of reference, 190
Life story, 186
Music, 186–187
Paraphrase, 187–188
Tape-recorded Conversation
189–190
Listening, 5, 40, 78, 227
Active, 4, 9, 12–18, 40, 78, 163,
233–234
Locking eyes, 182–183

Management, 43, 49, 52, 56, 65
Change, 65
is people, 43, 49
Layers, 52
Learning, 56
Managers, 50, 51
as story collectors, 51
Hiring, 50
Need to hear employees' stories, 51

Marus, Father, Interview: Woodside
Priory School, 151–158
Medicine for healing,
Stories act as, 4, 9, 22–23, 40, 78, 163,
227
Medium of healing, 4, 9, 22–23
Memorable actions, 219
Memories as story, 206
Mind map of experiences, 208
Mintzberg, Henry, 232
Mode of communication, 79
Model informal mode of communication,
79
Model of Stories, 7–23, 161
Modeling Competency, 6, 218–222
Answering the key questions, 221
Creating stories through action,
219–221
Memorable actions, 219
Presentations, 221–222
Moore, Bernice
Interview: CTB/McGraw-Hill,
86–102
Movies in Five, 216–217
Music, 186–187

Name badges, 175
New people/new situations, 184–185
Nine Functions of Stories, 4, 7, 9, 10–23,
40, 78, 163, 227
Act as medicine for healing, 4, 9,
22–23, 40, 78, 163, 227
Act as tools for thinking, 4, 9, 20–21,
40–77, 163, 227
Act as weapons, 4, 9, 21–22, 40, 77,
163, 227
Binding and bonding individuals, 4, 9,
11–12, 40, 78, 163, 227
Create an environment, 4, 9, 10–12,
40,77, 163, 227
Empower a speaker, 4, 9, 10, 40, 78,
163, 227
Encode information, 4, 9, 19–20, 40,
77, 163, 227
Negotiate differences, 4, 9, 18–19, 40,
78, 163, 227

Nine Functions of Stories *(continued)*
  Require active listening, 4, 9, 12–18, 40, 78, 163, 227
Non-specific targets of communication, 24, 26–27, 34–39, 40, 78, 161, 162, 263, 27

Objectives, 53, 59
  Aligning of and learning, 59
  Organizational 53
  Personal, 62
Observing Competency, 5, 164, 166–170, 171–185
  Care/Intention, 172–175
    Fostering positive intentions, 175
    Name badges, 175
    Self-assessment, 174
  External Focus, 181–183
    Conversation Tracking, 183
    Locking eyes, 182–183
    Recall, 182
  Process daily, 183–185
    Conversation recorder, 184
    Group Discussion, 185
    New people/new situations, 184–185
  Self-awareness, 175–178, 179
    Building, 175–178
    Journaling, 177–178
    Power of breath, 176
    Strengths and Weaknesses, 178, 179
    Survey of habits, 176
  Sensitivity, 178–181
    Room awareness, 182
    Sore spots and hot buttons, 181
Observing, 5
Oral versus written communication, 39
Organization upside down 47
Organizational communication, 3–6, 7, 23, 24–41, 55–64, 77, 179
Organizational learning, 3–6, 7, 23, 55–64, 161, 228
  Role of stories in, 161
Organizational practices, 194, 208, 222–223
Organizational skills, 179

Organizational success,
  Learning ensures, 59
Other people's personal stories, 212–214
Outsourcing learning, 58
Owen, Harrison, 231
Ownership, 43, 53

Paraphrase, 187–188
Partner targets of communication, 24, 26, 33–34, 40, 78, 162, 163, 227
Patterns, 6
People involvement, 45
Perceptions elicited by stories, 30–50
Personal history, 198–199, 203–204
Personal outlets, 50, 51
  Creative, 51
Personal stories, 212–214
Philosophy, Grooves, 43–49
Plans,
  Individual learning, 59
  Professional development, 59
Power of breath, 176
Presentations, 221–222
Principles of active listening, 233–234
Process daily, 183–185
  Conversation recorder, 184
  Group Discussion, 185
  New people/new situations, 184–185
Process Ring, 6, 163, 196–210, 231
  Indexing Competency, 6, 164, 170, 196–199
    Personal history, 198–199, 203–204
    Themes, 199–199
    Triggers, 198–1299
  Reflecting Competency, 6, 164,166, 168–170, 200–204
    Daily rewind, 204
    Historical visualization, 203
    Inviting, 201, 202
    Personal history, 203, 204
    Sifting, 201, 202–203
    Sitting, 201, 202
    Visualization, 201, 203
  Synthesis Competency, 6, 164–167, 168–170, 204–208
    Childhood stories and me, 206–108

Process Ring
  Synthesis Competency *(continued)*
    Crystal Ball of Synthesis, 206
    Knowledge, 206
    Learning, 206
    Mind map of experiences, 208
    Wisdom, 206
Professional development plans, 59
Push-to-pull-to-push, 39, 42

Ready, Fire, Aim, 48
Recall, 182
Reflecting Competency, 6, 164,166,
    168–170, 200–204
  Daily rewind, 204
  Historical visualization, 203
  Inviting, 201, 202
  Personal history, 203, 204
  Sifting, 201, 202–203
  Sitting, 201, 202
  Visualization, 201, 203
Reflection, 226
Relationship between story functions and
    the Communication Matrix, 40, 78,
    227
Respect for the individual, 44
Retention, employee, 51
Rings 6, 163, 164, 196–210, 221–224,
    231
  Interaction Ring, 6, 164, 221–224,
    231
  Process Ring, 6, 163, 196–210, 231
Room awareness, 182

Schank, Roger 49–50, 54, 167
Selecting Competency, 6, 164, 166,
    168–170
  Communication plan, 215
  Decision Matrix for selecting types of
    stories, 212–214
  Other people's personal stories,
    212–214
  Personal stories, 212–214
  Stories from other domains, 212–214
Selecting types of stories, 212–214
Self-assessment, 174

Self-awareness, 175–178, 179
  Building, 175–178
  Journaling, 177–178
  Power of breath, 176
  Strengths and Weaknesses, 178, 179
  Survey of habits, 176
Senge, Peter, 232
Sensitivity, 178–181
  Room awareness, 182
  Sore spots and hot buttons, 181
Sifting, 201, 202–203
Signal Repeater, 31
Sitting, 201, 202
Sore spots and hot buttons, 181
Speaker, Empowering the, 4, 9, 10, 40,
    78, 163, 227
Starbuck's Coffee, 136–150
Statement story, 194
Stories
  Foster agile culture, 52
  Act as medicine for healing, 4, 9,
    22–23, 40, 78, 163, 227
  Act as tools for thinking, 4, 9, 20–21,
    40–77, 163, 227
  Act as weapons, 4, 9, 21–22, 40, 77,
    163, 227
  and communication, 53–54
  Attitudes elicited by, 30–50
  Beliefs elicited by, 30–50
  Binding and bonding individuals, 4, 9,
    11–12
  Binding and bonding individuals, 4, 9,
    11–12, 40, 78, 163, 227
  Build flexible and dynamic minds, 52
  Create an environment, 4, 9, 10–12,
    40,77, 163, 227
  Creating and environment, 4, 9, 10–12,
    40,77, 163, 227
  Creating through action, 219–221
  Effects of, 3, 9
  Elicit (function), 30–50
  Empower a speaker, 4, 9, 10, 40, 78,
    163, 227
  Encode information, 4, 9, 19–20, 40,
    77, 163, 227
  Encourage people, 51

Stories *(continued)*
Experience as, 206
Experiences communicated through
stories, 63, 64
Expressions elicited by, 30–50
Forum for sharing, 50
Framework of stories, 3–74, 161
Theoretical, 77
Functions of stories, 4, 7, 9, 10–23, 40,
78, 163, 225, 227, 228
How stories work, 161
Learning in, 79
Managers as collectors of, 51
Mechanisms of, 4
Memories as, 206
Minds, flexible and dynamic built by,
52
Model of, 7–23, 161
Need to hear employees,' 51
Negotiate differences, 4, 9, 18–19, 40,
78, 163, 227
Nine Functions of Stories, 4, 7, 9,
10–23, 40, 78, 163, 227
Act as medicine for healing, 4, 9,
22–23, 40, 78, 163, 227
Act as tools for thinking, 4, 9,
20–21, 40–77, 163, 227
Act as weapons, 4, 9, 21–22, 40, 77,
163, 227
Binding and bonding individuals, 4,
9, 11–12, 40, 78, 163, 227
Create an environment, 4, 9, 10–12,
40, 77, 163, 227
Empower a speaker, 4, 9, 10, 40, 78,
163, 227
Encode information, 4, 9, 19–20, 40,
77, 163, 227
Negotiate differences, 4, 9, 18–19,
40, 78, 163, 227
Require active listening, 4, 9, 12–18,
40, 78, 163, 227
Opportunity for sharing, 50
Perceptions elicited by, 30–50
Principles of, 161
Pulling, 165
Pushing, 161, 165

Stories *(continued)*
Require active listening, 4, 9, 12–18, 40,
78, 163, 227
Role of, 30
in organizational learning, 161
Sharing,
Dynamics of, 31
Thoughts elicited by, 30–50
Tools for thinking, 4, 9, 20–21, 40–77,
163, 227
Triggering, 53
Types of, 212–214
Selecting, 212–214
Understanding, 40, 163, 227, 228
Unique effects, 40
Strengths and Weaknesses, 178, 179
Survey of habits, 176
Synergized teams, 49
Synthesis Competency, 6, 164–167,
168–170, 204–208
Childhood stories and me, 206–108
Crystal Ball of Synthesis, 206
Knowledge, 206
Learning, 206
Mind map of experiences, 208
Wisdom, 206
Synthesizing, 6

Tape-recorded Conversation, 189–190
Targeting the Audience, 24
Targets of communication, 21–41, 77,
161, 162, 163, 227
External targets, 24–26, 33–34, 40, 78,
162, 163, 227
Internal targets, 24–25, 30–33, 40, 78,
162, 163, 227
Non-specific targets, 24, 26–27, 34–39,
40, 78, 161, 162, 263, 27
Partner targets, 24, 26, 33–34, 40, 78,
162, 163, 227
Teams,
Synergized teams, 49
Training, 49
Telling Competency, 6, 164, 166,
168–170
Listener Involvement, 218

Telling Competency *(continued)*
  Movies in Five, 216–217
  Stories in Conversation, 217
  The Core, 164–170, 171, 195, 231
  Eliciting Competency, 5, 164, 170,
    191–195
    Attending, 191
    Climate of sharing, 191
    Job interview questions, 193
    Statement story, 194
    Trust, 191
    Words and feelings, 193–194
  Listening Competency, 5, 164, 166,
    170, 185–190
    Clarification and follow-up
      questions, 188
    Editorial interpretation, 189
    Following directions, 188–189
    Frame of reference, 190
    Life story, 186
    Music, 186–187
    Paraphrase, 187–188
    Tape-recorded Conversation 189–190
  Observing Competency, 5, 164,
    166–170, 171–185
    Care/Intention, 172–175. *See also:*
      Fostering positive intentions;
      Name badges; Self-assessment
    External Focus, 181–183. *See also:*
      Conversation Tracking; Locking
      eyes; Recall
    Process daily, 183–185. *See also:*
      Conversation recorder; Group
      Discussion; New people/new
      situations
    Self-awareness, 175–178, 179. *See*
      also: Building; Journaling;
      Power of breath; Strengths and
      Weaknesses; Survey of habits
    Sensitivity, 178–181. *See also:*
      Room awareness; Sore spots
      and hot buttons

The Core *(continued)*
  Organizational practices for, 194–195
  Themes, 199–199
  Thinking style, 179
  Thoughts elicited by stories, 30–50
  Tools for thinking, stories as, 4, 9, 20–21,
    40–77, 163, 227
Tools of communication, 25
Training and the difference from
  Learning, 57, 64
Training,
  and the difference from learning, 57,
    64
  Didactic, 51
  Information, 51
  Teams, 49
  Trends in, 58
Traits, Interpersonal, 179
Trends, iIn learning, 58
Triggering stories, 53
Triggers, 198–199
Trust, 191
Turnover, 50
Types of stories, 212–214
  Selecting, 212–214

Understanding, 7
  Stories, 40, 163, 227, 228
Unique effects of stories, 40
Untapped areas of the Communication
  Matrix, 29
Upside down, organization, 47

Visualization, 201, 203

Weapons, stories as 4, 9, 21–22, 40, 77,
  163, 227
Wisdom, 206
Woodside Priory School, 151–158
Words and feelings, 193–194
Work, Creative and personal outlet, 50
Written versus oral communication, 39

About the Author

Terrence Gargiulo is an international speaker, author, organizational development consultant, and group process facilitator. He holds a Master of Management in Human Services from the Florence Heller School, at Brandeis University, and is a recipient of *Inc. Magazine*'s Marketing Master Award. Among his numerous clients, past and present, are General Motors, Dreyer's Ice Cream, DTE Energy, U.S. Navy, U.S. Coast Guard, Merck, Boston University, City of Boston, City of Lowell, Arthur D. Little, Raytheon, and Coca-Cola.

Phone: 781-894-4381
Web: http://www.makingstories.net
E-mail: terrence@makingstories.net